In SatNav We Trust

A search for meaning through
the Historic Counties of England

Jack Barrow

~ Cosmic Jellyfish ~

In SatNav We Trust

by

Jack Barrow

Published by Cosmic Jellyfish, England.
Copyright © Jack Barrow 2020
ISBN: 978-1-527 2-6030-6

BISAC Classification:
TRAVEL/Essays & Travelogues - TRV010000
PHILOSOPHY/Metaphysics - PHI013000
HUMOR/General - HUM000000
Primary Geographic Location - England
BIC Classification:
Classic Travel Writing - WTLC
Popular Philosophy - HPX
Philosophy: Metaphysics & Ontology - HPJ
Humour - WH
Geographical - England - 1DBKE
Thema Classification:
Travel Writing - WTL
Popular Philosophy - QDX
Humour - WH
Geographical Qualifier - England - 1DDU

Dispatches

Thanks to
My Muse,
Manda for ongoing support and assistance,
and Hidden Design and Miguel Mocho for video production

But also to
Cindy, Dana, Ron, Lisa, Ivor,
Debbie, Ann, Heather, David, Marie,
Tim, Adam, Lee, Tish, Katy,
Mark, Rebecca, Joss, Yvonne, Corrinne,
Louise, Rebecca, Scar, Rob, Mark,
Gareth, Bev, Laurie, Lucia, Simon,
Malcolm, Martin, Amanda, Charlotte, Rob,
Frank, Jacqui, Russell, Diana, Bob,
Mia, Bruce, Mat, Mart, Philip,
Michael, Kris, Richard, Olivier, Jack,
Nicky, Raine, Karen, Susan, Robert,
Jodie, Stephen, Payam, Ali, Graham,
Lili, Roy, Sorita, James, Gavin,
Lionel, Snowy, Jennie, Tony, Sarah,
Matt, Matt, Dave, Melissa, Steven,
Danni, Sarah, Dave, Brian, Nick,
Lorraine, Andrew, Floortje, David, James,
Debra, Neil, Nick, Roxanne, Neil,
Chris, Natalie, Sue, Noam, Lisa,
Ellie, Ed, Phil, Jackie, Karl,
Carol, Isabelle, Nick, Stu, Peter,
and... of course, Kathy

Dedicated to

Graham and Eric

In SatNav We Trust

A search for meaning through the Historic Counties of England

Jack Barrow

Sometimes it's not about the big questions of meaning and value; at that crucial moment it's more often about where you can find the best sausage in a bun.

Contents

Day 1 - Oxfordshire

Wednesday May 1st

Miles on Truck: 43

May Morning in Oxford is a bit of an event. It's one of those great British occasions that few people know about. I say Britain but I suppose I should say England, as this is supposedly a book about England, although that was never the plan.

I first heard about May Morning around the turn of the millennium when I was dating a woman who lived in Oxford. She arranged tickets for one of the college May balls. I imagined a ball to be all women in sumptuous gowns and men in dress suits, with a regency ballroom opening at one end onto a veranda looking out onto manicured gardens with fountains and, perhaps, a maze—nothing too grand you understand. At the other end of the ballroom, across a sea of penguin men and willowy women, would be an orchestra, or at least a full-sized dance band with those music stands that have their name and a treble clef on the front. There would be an air of privilege and exclusivity and I would clearly be right out of place.

What we got for our tickets was a double-decker bus that took us some distance out of Oxford to a field full of marquees. I remember there being one marquee with rows of dinner tables (but I don't remember having dinner) and there was a series of fairground rides that we didn't go on and a few marquees containing discos. I say discos because I have no idea what else to call them, which is probably due to my age. If such a disco were in a building you might call it a night club (not the sort with a dance band, alas) but you can't call it that in a tent, surely; rave might be a better word (still showing my age), but ball would not be the word that immediately leaps to mind. The place was populated by smart young men in dinner jackets and women in evening dresses, some but by no means all of whom, were willowy so at least I wasn't disappointed on that front. I think, perhaps, we didn't have dinner because we didn't have a dinner ticket, but I may have been too drunk to remember. What I do remember is that I spent a significant portion of the night sitting and snogging with my girlfriend. Some student types seemed terribly impressed by our snogging, presumably because we were so old and

1

they wouldn't have thought we could possibly have it in us. I was in my thirties, it would be inappropriate to discuss her age.

To say I was disappointed would be correct. I felt I'd been sold a classy night out and, instead, I got an all-night rave (of the legal variety so not that exciting) populated by people pretending to be from between the wars but really no more stylish than a bunch of school leavers in tuxedos. I suppose there were classier events in Oxford on May Eve, but my girlfriend didn't have the contacts to access them.

So, these days I skip the ball and go to Oxford May Morning each year, unless it's raining in which case I stay in bed as is sensible. This year, having decided to tour each of the counties of England, I was faced with the decision of where to start my journey, and May Morning in Oxford seemed like it might give me something to write about.

* * *

On the morning of May 1st I cheated. In fact, I'd cheated the night before when I drove to Oxford thus shortcutting the first day of my journey. In the morning I reaped the benefit of my swindle, waking up in Oxford, or rather just outside in a friend's back garden, with only a couple of miles to get to the day's events.

The plan had been to arrive outside Magdalen College Tower to hear the choristers sing at 6am, for which you need to be up at 5am, even if you are a local. Coming from Hertfordshire would have meant surfacing at an even more ungodly hour, hence the great travelogue swindle.

A friend of mine had recently erected a yurt in his back garden and, being allergic to his house what with the cats, the yurt seemed like the best bet. For those not in the know, a yurt is a sort of portable round hut favoured by the nomads of central Asia. I say portable—that's portable in the sense that you have many horses or preferably a long wheelbase transit van and about fifteen people to help you put the yurt up. Modern nomads are very fond of transit vans, though they often favour oversized caravans rather than yurts, but I suppose the transit van, at least, is a link to that nomadic past.

After a chilly night, despite my hot water bottle, my friend and I, along with a small group of early risers, drove into Oxford, parking somewhere out of range of the traffic wardens at about 5.30am. Walking into town and across Magdalen Bridge, the street was packed with people of all kinds—revellers who might have been up all night including university types in black tie and ball gowns, various hippie types in ceremonial garb including people dressed as Jack in the Green, and all sorts of Joe Public, men, women and children, babes in arms, pushchairs and everything that you might imagine. All of life was there.

As we approached the tower, the throng was such that we had to negotiate hard to get through the crowd, weaving our way sideways through narrow gaps, always trying to keep track of our small group to avoid getting lost in the throng. However, we arrived at the base of the tower with ten minutes to spare, where the street was strangely empty, with room to organise a small football match had we wanted to do so. It's almost as though people won't push their way through crowds to hear choristers. I wonder if it's the same with rock bands; is there a small area of tranquillity at the front of every rock concert?

I'm not particularly into choral music, being more of a blues and soul-funk or alternative rock kind of guy, but it has always struck me that events such as this are about quality. I don't suppose it's possible to go anywhere in the world and hear a better example of choral music, especially of the Olde-English Christian but apparently non-Christian variety (which is a bit odd when you remember that this is a Christian choir with regular gigs in the college chapel singing at Evensong and the Eucharist). It may not be delta blues, swing jazz, Paul Simon or David Byrne, but it's probably just as genuine, and is an example of excellence that you'd be hard pushed to improve on anywhere in the world.

Each year the Magdalen College Choir sings at the top of the 144ft Magdalen Tower, starting with the *Hymnus Eucharisticus*, all terribly churchy. This is a tradition said to go back over 500 years, although I'm sure I read somewhere that it was revived in the Victorian period, but such apparent ambiguity is often the way with traditions. Following *Hymnus Eucharisticus* they follow with a prayer and a selection of madrigals and old English songs variously including *This is the Month of Maying, The Silver Swan* and *Sumer is Icumen In*.

May Day is one of those great traditions where Christian and apparently non-Christian symbolism are intertwined, such as people often like to point out when they see green man bosses in cathedrals. Of course May Day is replete with May poles, a Queen of the May and all that burgeoning spring and fertility paraphernalia, so it's no surprise that the choir sings a hymn about one of the great Christian rituals, followed by madrigals full of stories of young lads cavorting off into the wild with their maidens to be laid down on the green for a bit of how's your father. Except that this is as far from ideas of your heavenly father as you can imagine. Still, religion is often a bag of contradictions, but then again so are we all.

Where all this apparent contradiction leaves us is anyone's guess but I'm sure it's all very meaningful and, having been to May Morning on quite a few occasions now, standing at the base of the tower feels meaningful to me, regardless of which god, gods or goddesses are evoked by the occasion.

After the choir, leaving the tower with my small group of friends, we passed multiple Morris dancers, an oompah band playing James Brown and lots of people in the most astonishing costumes. We made our way to the steps of the Clarendon Building to listen to the *Hurly Burley Early-in-the-Morning Band*, an ever-changing annual line up of folk musicians—fiddle players, pipers, percussionists, hangers on and all manner of people in various states of fancy dress and otherwise. They pumped out a fine selection of jigs and reels, with people dancing in the May morning sunlight for an hour or more. Someone was handing out flags in the shape of leaves. (It was May and it's all about the return of growth and all that is spring.) A friend's small child had come by one of the flags and he proffered it towards me with an expression that said 'I'm a bit pissed off with having to hold this flag now, so I'd like you to hold it and be pissed off instead.' Taking the flag, I thought what a romantic idea it would be to have it in the photos I planned to take of my tent every evening as I toured each English county. Readers or friends on Facebook might ask about this mysterious leaf-shaped flag that is seen in each image, perhaps the locations becoming more obscure with each day. People would say, 'What is that flag?', 'How did you come by it?' Readers would be intrigued and it would be a way for me to engage with my readers. I think that idea lasted about three days. Is it in the nature of romance that it quickly wears off under pressure of practicality? Are the great romantics those that resist that tendency?

From the Clarendon building we headed off for our always excellent breakfast in Brother's Café in the Oxford Covered Market. The covered market is a 200-year-old building that has more of the appearance of an arcade of shops than a market with stalls. It's populated with butchers and fishmongers and traders of all sorts. Within the building is a network of lanes between small premises, with the occasional open space where stalls trade in flowers, fruit or fromage. The place has variously tiled lanes or alleys with a wooden or glass roof above and the whole place is slightly reminiscent of those shops in Harry Potter where he buys his special wizard paraphernalia. Some of the premises have windows onto the lanes as do normal shops; others, with no panes in the windows, are open to the air with their produce spilling over the windowsill and out into the lane. The whole place is rather marvellous.

After breakfast, with something of a send-off from my friends with comments of, 'Enjoy your holiday' (this wasn't a holiday, this was a serious trip of exploration, this was research!), it was back to the yurt to try to sleep (unsuccessfully), and some intermittent ukulele practice. The day went downhill from there, too cold in the yurt with the cool spring air and too hot in the sun. Strumming away on the uke generated an untuneful noise as the battery on the tablet drained at an alarming rate, causing my anxiety levels to soar not knowing where I would camp or how easy it would be to sort out a pitch.

This wouldn't do. I was supposed to be travelling, exploring the country, and here I was sitting in a canvas house in a back garden in Oxford, feeling a bit chilly. To be frank, I was a bit intimidated by the whole scenario. It's probably in my nature to over-prepare; in my early twenties I'd spent a year preparing to go on a backpacking holiday on the Ridgeway, probably longer than some people spend preparing to ascend Everest. Still, people die on Everest; I'm not sure if anyone ever died on the Ridgeway, even though there aren't many places to fill your water bottle. At some point I had to leave the yurt and go out into the big world. It was time to go. Consulting the Big Book of Campsites, I picked somewhere inside the county of Oxfordshire and set off into Oxford's legendary traffic.

* * *

The idea of trust in sat nav came about not long after I bought a phone that would run sat nav and I duly installed Kathy, her soft and slightly sexy posh Irish tones being my preferred sat nav voice. One day I found myself travelling into deepest Suffolk to take a drum for repair. It is said of the gentleman in question that you can buy cheaper drums, but you can't buy better drums, so the four-hour round trip, followed by the same the following weekend, puts the expedition into perspective. As a new convert to the pleasures of sat nav, I set off from Hertfordshire with the device programmed to take me to a location just off the Suffolk coast. I understood the route intellectually simply by looking at the map seeing that the most obvious route would be around the M25 and up the A12. I didn't need sat nav for this but it was programmed for the whole journey and it would be a chance to put it through its paces even if I only needed it for the last half mile. I sort of knew where it would turn me off the main road, so I wasn't expecting any surprises.

Sure enough, I travelled around the M25 and up the A12, largely oblivious to the instructions and paying more attention to the music on my phone where the app was installed. Then, suddenly, at a point a little before I expected to turn off, I was told to take the next right turn in about half a mile. I wasn't sure about this as I thought I'd be heading to the next town but I decided to go with it to see what happened. People of a generation younger than me might not expect my surprise, but I remember the introduction of the first computers into schools. Before the arrival of school computers whenever we had Computer Studies lessons we had to fill out batch sheets and received a bunch of punch cards a week later along with the results of our programs being run on the local polytechnic mainframe. All we were able to do was to write programs that drew pictures from letters on a dot matrix printer or, at best, played blackjack badly. Computers that actually did anything useful began to appear as I grew older, and each step forward, while intellectually understood as binary and logic gates, was, at the same time, a wonder.

Turning right, away from the A12, I found myself driving down a country road, left then right down narrow lanes, across a tiny single-track railway at a level crossing that looked as though it hadn't seen a train for twenty years, past high hedges, verges with long grass in the sunshine and under shady trees that arched over the road. Very soon I realised that I had absolutely no idea where I was and I was completely at the mercy of Kathy. My road atlas would certainly not show details of roads this small. I understood my phone only at the level of knowing that electricity is the movement of electrons along conductors and that on or off signals can represent ones and zeros. I knew that the programme would consider numerous routes between two points on the map though I really had no idea how it makes those decisions. My best understanding was probably of the satellites, a grasp of how triangulation of radio signals worked. The fact that this device could pinpoint my position to within a few metres was still impressive and, frankly, hard to believe. If any of these descriptions of the technology are inaccurate then it's really no surprise and further emphasises my point. There's a famous quote from Arthur C Clark that says when any technology becomes sufficiently advanced it is indistinguishable from magic. Traveling through Suffolk towards an unknown destination, I was putting my faith in this device so utterly that it felt no more rational than faith in God.

Eventually, after much twisting and turning, the target postcode turned out to be just two houses down an unpaved track, literally in the middle of nowhere. I know it was just those two houses as Kathy told me I had reached my destination when I was next to the front door. Apparently, according to the drum doctor—said to be someone of whom you can buy cheaper drums, but you can't buy better drums—if you travel past the two houses you pass through a farmyard (presumably with a different postcode) and end up in the sea. There was not a soul for miles, which was probably a good thing when you consider the guy made drums for a living.

* * *

Back on May 1st, allowing Kathy to guide me, I eventually arrived at Common Leys Farm in east Oxfordshire, just on the border with Buckinghamshire but sufficiently in Oxfordshire to count. Directed into a small field, perhaps once a paddock, I pitched up with a few caravans as neighbours.

'Are you settled in?' asked the lady from the campsite, possibly the farmer's wife, or perhaps these days a farmer in her own right if you listen to The Archers.

'Yes thanks, I think I'm okay. Do you want the money now?' I replied, not really knowing how these things work.

'No, you pay when you leave, she replied, that way you can stay as long as you want and total it up at the end.'

'Ah, that makes sense. I'm a bit new to this.' I paused for a moment as we both looked into the middle distance. 'I did wonder about the sign that says no alcohol to be consumed on the premises unless purchased here.' I kept quiet about the fact that I'd already opened the wine which was hidden in my tent.

'No that's for our restaurant.' she responded. 'You'd be surprised how cheeky some people can be.'

'I'm sure they can,' I agreed as we continued to chat slightly awkwardly. 'I was wondering how strict your rules could be if I wanted to drink my own wine, but you never know when you try something completely new.'

'Have you not camped before?' she asked.

'I've done plenty of camping but mostly at camps and festivals rather than commercial campsites,' I responded.

'No, it's fine,' she reassured me.

'I mean, I was beginning to think that I might even have to pay for a shower,' I replied, before we eventually made polite noises and I returned to my tent while she returned to her nice cosy farmhouse.

* * *

After dinner, and half a bottle of new world Shiraz, I succumbed to the continued anxiety of charging my phone and computer. Searching for a spare charging cable in the glove compartment, I stumbled across two bars of chocolate that the government had told me to put there during the snow the previous winter. Unfortunately they didn't tell me to take them out when the weather warmed up, so I found a fine layer of melted chocolate coating the charge cable, pens, supermarket till receipts and other ephemera that inhabit the bottom of the glove box. Just before bed I feasted on the remains of the chocolate that had not leaked out of the silver paper. Any chocolate left in the bottom of the glove box could be saved for a further emergency.

As the light faded, I boiled some water for my hot water bottle and took to my bed. The night was cold as the heat from the sun was only warming as long as it was shining, it was spring and the ground was still cold, as was everything once the sun went away.

Lying in my sleeping bag, I stared at the power pack I'd bought a few weeks before. As it charged my tablet computer, I could hear the battery pack fan run, becoming quieter and more intermittent, eventually, silent as the tablet charged its last ten percent. The sound of the fan, with the red, amber and green LEDs glowing in the darkness, was absorbing and I soon became anxious about the whole arrangement.

The battery pack had four indicator lights, one light went out after merely charging the phone and tablet on the first night. I also had a camera if I chose to use it and who knows what else I might need to charge. I was relying on this technology; surely a battery that can start a car would charge a small tablet computer and a phone each night with no trouble. But using a quarter of the available power on the first night seemed excessive, and it dawned on me that keeping all these devices topped up might be more difficult than I'd imagined. Lying there in the dark, illuminated by glowing LEDs that diminished as I watched, I was losing faith in the arrangement.

When I'd arrived, the campsite people had asked me if I needed an electrical hook-up, which I considered a bit odd as I had a tent rather than a caravan. I drifted off to sleep wondering about the possibilities of getting some sort of device to bring electricity into a tent.

Day 2 - Oxfordshire to Buckinghamshire

Thursday May 2nd

Miles on Truck: 73

The morning on Common Leys Farm was as clear and sunny as the day before. Stumbling around half hung-over from the previous night's wine, I listened to the end of the Radio 4 *Today Programme* only to discover that Melvyn Bragg was discussing Gnosticism on *In Our Time*. Gnosticism, a religion that developed a short while after the time of Christ, wasn't nearly what I understood it to be but I was, at least, able to understand why some people are attracted to it. It seems it teaches that each individual has potential for self-realisation rather than the teaching of many religions of the day, i.e. that all paths to salvation are mediated by their various priesthoods, which means the priests get to tell you who can be saved and when you are saved. The priests have all the power and the people have to do as they are told. Gnosticism seems a much better arrangement.

Feeling enlightened, I clutched my towel and shampoo, and strolled over to the shower looking forward to a thorough drenching in piping hot water. Stripping off, I stepped up only to discover a notice telling me how to put a pound in the coin slot in the utility room next door.

Just a little disgruntled, I dressed again and shuffled back to my tent, feeling somewhat more distant from salvation than I had when the pleasure of the shower was more imminent. I managed to find a pound coin and shuffled back to the shower once more with my towel and undressed. This time, though, I'd left my shampoo at my tent so I got dressed again and shuffled back, each time feeling as though watery salvation was becoming more distant with every step. If salvation can be likened to a hot shower, then the denial of that shower is surely akin to Purgatory.

The holy script of the shower directed me to go next door to run the tap before putting the pound in the slot. When it came, the shower was hot and powerful and the instructions ensured that it was so. I looked upon it and it was good. Actually I stood beneath it and it was good but, as a line, that doesn't work nearly as well.

Sometimes these things can seem a bit complicated when you don't understand why people set them up as they do, but people usually have a reason for everything. Teenage oiks leaving the water running for a laugh is probably good enough reason to charge a token fee for a shower. Not having used proper campsites before, I wondered if this is actually quite normal and needn't have been surprised.

Leaving Common Leys Farm I drove down to Tiddington, thinking that I could pick up a cable to connect my power supply into a caravan hook-up and banish my power anxiety demons. I saw my first red kite of the trip over the village of Ickford, seeming much redder than those I'd seen over High Wycombe when I'd been working there a few years before.

Red kites are scavengers that used to be common in the skies over England up until the Victorian period. However, their fate was sealed by a combination of being a bit dim and their inability to get out of the way of a shot gun.

Hang on though, wasn't that the story of the dodo, and those turtles from somewhere? No they died because they were tasty, that's the turtles, not the dodo; I have no idea how a dodo tastes but, then again, neither does anyone else now. I suppose that's the story of many extinctions. Of course the red kite didn't become extinct, continuing to survive in other parts of Europe, and now they've been reintroduced in the Chiltern Hills where they abound. However, they're known to be a bit lazy and unadventurous so they tend not to expand their territory if they are fed by the locals. It seems people are rather fond of putting scraps of meat out to see them descend dramatically into their gardens. With their five foot wing span you might understand why. If you've grown up, as most of us have, seeing nothing bigger than a pigeon, then a massive bird of prey descending into your garden would be a bit of excitement on a dreary day in suburbia. But please don't try this at home as it makes them fat and lazy and it discourages them from spreading into new territories.

✳ ✳ ✳

Having picked up a hook-up cable from Tiddington Caravan Centre, I headed into Thame with its broad high street and fine Victorian red brick town hall forming an island that you could circle around if you were a kid on a bicycle. The town has numerous old buildings and bags of character.

However, you can't eat character and failing to find a supermarket with a café and Wi-Fi,

I drove along an arrow-straight road towards Princes Risborough. I don't know if it was a Roman road but it certainly looked like one. You might think that it takes an invasion, or a government that's uninterested in the rights of its people, to build a straight road. I don't know if it's true but it's said that roads that meander often do so because they follow boundaries between properties thus not cutting a property in two. Perhaps it's the protection of land owners' rights and a lack of invasions that have given Britain the twisty lanes we know and love. Then again perhaps one person owned the land between Thame and Princes Risborough and wanted a straight route between the two. Perhaps there is some other explanation or perhaps, more likely, I have no idea what I'm talking about.

* * *

My first visit to Princes Risborough was back in the late eighties when I was writing advertising features for the local newspaper in Aylesbury. They asked me to write a series of features about surrounding towns and villages and Princes Risborough had been one of them. My strategy was always to head for the local library to dig up interesting local history from previous news clippings, evidence from local history books and the like.

It seemed that Princes Risborough was famous for the chalk carving on Whiteleaf Hill overlooking the nearby village of Monks Risborough. (Such carvings are common on the chalk ridge that runs to the southwest and down into Wiltshire.) This assignment took place over twenty years ago so my memory is a bit vague but I seem to remember reading that there had been a chalk carving on the hill for some time before the arrival of the monks at some point in the late mediaeval period. As I remembered, it was only from that date onward that the chalk carving became known as a chalk cross, whereas before it was something else.

My theory was that the monks moved in, thus the name Monks Risborough, and modified what was until then some sort of pre-Christian symbol. (I imagined phalluses and the like reminiscent of the Cerne Abbas Giant only without the giant if you get my drift.) Forever after it was known as Whiteleaf Cross. It struck me that the clue is that the cross features a strange triangular shape beneath the cross, quite unlike traditional Christian crosses. When a teenager draws a cock and balls on his chemistry exercise book, it often features symmetrical balls below a vertical cock, just about the same proportions as the triangle today. Were it not for the monks moving into Monks Risborough, would the chalk carving now be known as Whiteleaf Cock?

Anyway, this was my theory from my extensive half an hour of research in Princes Risborough Library in the late eighties so that's what I wrote, along with my invoice for forty quid, and that was that. I've driven through the town since but otherwise I've not visited and I've never really given the matter that much thought.

Parking in the first supermarket I could find, I was disappointed that not only did they not have free Wi-Fi but they didn't even have a café. Buying a 'meal deal' consisting of a salad in a box, a bottle of water and a packet of cheese things, I set off for somewhere to eat my wonderful lunch and spotted the very library I had visited on my trip to the town all those years before. Moving on, looking for somewhere to sit, I strolled down the road and discovered the town cross, one of those village centre structures with pillars supporting a roof with no walls. Apparently in Princes Risborough it's called the Market House. They can be found in many market towns where they have evolved from a simple cross on a plinth to become more elaborate, eventually sitting atop a roof structure on legs. The only visible bench was already occupied so I circled in looking for somewhere else to sit, circumnavigating the building, before swooping on the opposite end of the bench from the other side.

Asking the occupant if he minded me sharing I got no reply other than the briefest of silent glances, but by then I was sitting down anyway so it turned out to be a rhetorical question. Sitting there, I cursed quietly discovering that my salad in a box had leaked all over my bottle of water and packet of cheese things. My dining partner sat there eating his chips with quiet determination ignoring my grumblings under my breath. Chips, I thought, had I missed an opportunity there, looking at my leaky salad with disappointment?

For a few minutes I watched the world go by, shoppers coming and going from the shops across the street, a hairdresser sitting outside to have a cigarette, people doing their shopping, etc.

Soon my lunch was over but not before I spotted that we were sat next to a bus stop with a notice on it declaring 'Bus stop closed'. When are they ever open I wondered? Could they be open or closed? Inoperative perhaps, not in use, cancelled, abandoned due to budget cuts, who knows, but closed?

It was a printed notice so one imagines that there are closed bus stops all over the country. Perhaps I would find more in the weeks to come.

Getting up to leave, I bid my dining partner goodbye and received a slight, but somewhat uncomfortable glance. This almost confirmed my theory that he was the Forest Gump of Princes Risborough and he was entitled eat his chips in whatever fashion he should deem appropriate.

As I left I spotted a crystal shop across the road and, being a bit of a collector of flat pieces of hematite, I thought I'd pop in to see what they had.

* * *

Crystal shops are a bit of a thing for me. Some people believe that crystals have innate abilities but my interest in flat pieces of hematite is not due to their possible healing properties. My interest came about after reading that the Elder Sign, described in the works of H.P. Lovecraft, was carved on silver stone. Hematite is silver in colour, or at least shiny grey when polished. However, all of this is nonsense to varying degrees.

Since then I've discovered that Elder Signs from the Lovecraft stories are said to be carved on green soapstone, presumably because it's soapy and easy to carve. So it seems the silver stone that I've been thinking of must be some sort of mistaken memory. But as I'm never likely to need to fend off an attack by the Deep Ones, mostly because they are made up, it doesn't matter.

Anyway, the point is that I've been collecting bits of hematite for some time now and it's become a bit of a thing that I do whenever I find myself in a head-shop or similar establishment.

As regards any other properties of crystals, when hippies get hold of them and claim them for healing or whatever, well I'm a bit of a rationalist in that sense. As far as I'm concerned, crystals are nothing more than rocks dug out of the ground and, in some instances such as when unnecessary damage is done to the environment, they might be better off left where they are; although my feelings on the digging up bit are a bit ambivalent.

On the subject of crystals vibrating, or whatever is said of them, I've long suspected this is a misconception from the discovery that, when a current is passed through quartz, it vibrates at a very specific frequency and, I guess, those vibrations can be accurately counted to represent the passage of time, so many vibrations to a second, or whatever. Of course, my level of understanding of this sort of technology is about as sophisticated as my understanding of the ones and noughts in a SatNav or a computer.

However, it turns out that my understanding of hippie vibes might be a misconception built upon a misapprehension. What I've only recently learned is that the concept of vibration, as referred to by countless hippies, freaks, mystics and the like, comes from Hinduism where it can refer to the concept that the universe is manifest via the pulse (or vibration) of consciousness. Students of Tantra (or even Babylon 5 for I'm sure the two are related, though it's hard to say which came first) will recognise this as the idea that the universe is conscious in the same way that we all are. Unifying the consciousness that we experience with the consciousness of the universe might well be what is meant by all those phrases such as oneness with the universe, being one with everything (not a pizza) and even that old favourite, unification of the microcosm with the macrocosm. Personal consciousness is expressed through vibration which is manifest in us through our in-out breaths, known in Hinduism as prana. (In which case my personal vibration is slow and deep but can sometimes be a bit wheezy especially after running upstairs.) Of course, a great deal of hippie culture was influenced by gurus from India and the Far East so it's easy to understand that the concept of hippie vibration or vibes (man) might have been a cultural transfer from Hinduism and nothing to do with appropriation of the idea from digital watches.

Of course there seems to be a parallel here in my misreading of HP Lovecraft and my understanding of what hippies mean by vibrations.

Nevertheless, as much of a rationalist as I like to think I am, there are things that I just enjoy for their own sake, and pieces of polished hematite, despite the mistaken reason for starting my collection, are amongst life's little meaningful, but otherwise pointless, pleasures even if the inspiration is a bit irrational. I suppose you could say I think of myself as a rationalist who allows himself to do irrational things.

* * *

Talking about my travelling plans, the shop's proprietor and I got talking about Whiteleaf Cross. As I explained that I had once written about the chalk monument, I asked her if she had heard about the possibility that the monks had vandalised an earlier pagan symbol to which she responded that it was entirely likely. It was only as I left that it occurred to me that my article, some twenty years before, might have been sufficient to plant the seed of the idea in a local population no matter what the truth ever was.

Since that day I've done more research on Whiteleaf Cross and Monks Risborough. According to the Interweb, Monks Risborough has been so named since somewhere around the time of the Normans or at least some time around mid-morning. It seems that the cross only dates back to tea-time so my article probably counts as nothing more than misinformation. The lady in the crystal shop may have got it from me, some other source, or she may have been humouring me with a thought in the back of her mind that silently said what an idiot, take his money and hope that he goes away.

Heading off thinking that I was the enlightened researcher that I clearly wasn't, I headed for the library. Separating my lunch from my Wi-Fi needs still left me with the need for a desk at the very least.

* * *

Arriving in the library, the only table was occupied by a group of ladies for their book group, discussing the merits of various works of contemporary literature, many of which I'd heard of but none of which I'd read. With nowhere else to sit I took up a position at one of the Internet workstations nearby and set up my tablet and tiny keyboard to catch up on my notes for the first day and a half. I found, however, that I couldn't help listening in on their meeting as I fantasised about them one day being amazed to discover that a famous author had been present at the next table.

After an hour or so their meeting came to an end and they vacated their table so I began to think about moving over from the Internet workstation.

'Excuse me, are you using this workstation?' asked an assertive librarian who appeared at my side.

'Yes I know, I was only sitting here because the literary group was sitting at the other table,' I protested.

'Well these workstations are for people using the Internet,' she repeated.

'I understand that, but when I arrived they were sitting there and this was the only place to sit,' My second line of defence, being the same as my first line, was ignored.

'Well you'll have to move. These workstations are for the Internet only.'

I felt like saying, 'What part of there were no tables when I arrived don't you understand?' but I thought better of it. I also thought about saying, 'Do you realise who I am? I'm working on my book and if you are not careful you might end up in it.' However, I thought better of that too so I made my excuses and left.

***

Getting back to the Truck, I got on the phone and managed to book myself a campsite just outside Aylesbury. It was a little disappointing that Kathy's shortest route took me down main roads all the way but by that time of the day I couldn't care less about the plan. I was more interested in getting somewhere to sleep. I arrived at Oak Farm under a cloudless sky with just a slight feeling of sunburn.

I was travelling with a Khyam Igloo, a solidly robust dome tent big enough for three people (so long as you don't have too much stuff) but plenty big enough if it's just yourself. It features the legendary Khyam quick erect system, vital if you are putting the thing up and taking it down again every day. (Actually, it was the other way around but that somehow doesn't read right so I'm sure you get the picture.) After pitching the Khyam, I headed to the supermarket for a good old slap up supermarket café meal, all cholesterol and too many carbs. Of course it was only when I arrived that the penny dropped and I realised that it was years since I'd seen a supermarket café, most having been replaced by franchise coffee shops. So at 5:30, shattered after what seemed like the longest of days, I had a large breakfast, which seemed to be mostly toast or some similar equivalent, and three pots of tea, being all that was available.

For some reason I couldn't post my blog. It seemed I was blocked because my post contained 'age related, inappropriate or illegal' content. This was a camping holiday for heaven's sake and I hadn't even mentioned the Khyam quick erection!

Dejected, I headed back to my tent for another slightly sleepless night. What was planned as a trip where I would explore one thing in each county, perhaps saying something about the history of each was turning into a nightmare scenario of technology letting me down, not enough hours in the day, rushing to keep up, being permanently tired and constantly stressed out. I had thoughts of cursing all those people who had waved me off with a happy smile saying enjoy your holiday. This was clearly not a holiday and could turn out to be the hardest six weeks' work I had ever done.

Day 3 - Buckinghamshire to Bedfordshire

Friday May 3rd

Miles on Truck: 96

During the night I'd managed to charge everything from the battery pack. My pitch didn't include an electrical hook-up. My charging anxiety was growing, having no idea how long the battery pack might take to recharge. When it was new it took a day and half to charge. I had visions of having to trickle charge it whenever I had the opportunity but never managing to get the thing fully charged up. Couldn't I just charge it overnight whenever I had an electrical hook-up? All I could see ahead was the time pressures of travelling, setting off late and having to find somewhere to stay, and in between finding something to blog about and nothing but unimagined grief ahead. I wasn't thinking straight. Add to all this the thought that packing the Truck for the third time, knowing it had taken an hour each time before, I would have to unpack it that evening and repeat that process again every day for the next six weeks. I really felt like going home and curling up in bed. But I'd invested so much so far in terms of time and energy, finding six weeks in my diary when I could do this, plus people go up Everest and all that, what the hell was I thinking? I had to continue.

* * *

So here's the thing. For the last few days I've been talking, on and off, about things that might be described as rational or irrational but I suppose I should define what I mean. Collecting crystals is neither rational nor irrational, in the same way that collecting shoes is neither irrational nor irrational. (Well actually collecting shoes in the way that some people collect shoes can seem irrational, though I'm sure there are those who would express a need with some sort of explanation.) So, collecting anything, stamps, or coins or bus tickets is not irrational in itself. (But let's reserve judgement on the bus tickets.) A collector might see a certain beauty in the things collected such as stamps, which might have some artistic or design aesthetic. The thing collected has merit as an object of beauty. Collecting pieces of polished hematite could, therefore, be described as rational in that the hematite is desired for its lustre and rich colour, even though that colour is grey. However, collecting pieces of hematite, or any other crystal for that matter, because the collector believes the crystal has specific powers, such as driving off Deep Ones, is irrational. So the act of collection is not irrational in itself but the belief is, mostly because Deep Ones don't exist and are just fictional monsters created by the author HP Lovecraft.

So I'm using the term rational to define that which can be scientifically verified whereas the irrational has, or seems to have, no basis in scientific terms. Rational is that which is based on facts or reason, often referred to as evidence based. There are no facts that say a piece of hematite will drive off Deep Ones or anything else for that matter. It won't help you organise your thinking, decrease negativity, bring balance to your mind-spirit connection (whatever that is) or make your penis bigger. (Many things make that last claim and that's bollocks too.) In this case these ideas are irrational because there is no evidence for these claims.

However, if you gain a certain pleasure from holding or examining a piece of hematite, or quartz, amethyst, jade or whatever, then that pleasure may be a benefit in any number of ways. We talk of paintings as calming or energizing so why not a rock (although such benefits might be more personalised)? Music certainly has similar effects but those effects may be more easily measured. I've got a fist-sized lump of smoky quartz that we dug out of the garden. I use it to hold my front door open when I take the rubbish out. I don't believe the quartz does anything more than stop the door blowing shut. I have a certain fondness for it though, as it was dug out of my garden decades ago, so it has meaning. That meaning is personal to me. I would not describe that meaning as rational and it can't be measured, unless you connected me up to an ECG every time I take my rubbish out. I imagine, though, the experience might be changed so much by the attachment of all the brain monitors, that the results of your measurement would no longer be valid.

On the other hand, the anxiety I had about charging my devices was rational as the situation could have scuppered the whole trip. Anxiety at the logistics, the effort of the driving, finding somewhere to camp, time to write and two hours of packing and un-packing each day; all that seems rational, but those thoughts may grow to be irrational if they get out of proportion. If your collection of bus tickets gets so large that it takes over your life then it could be said to be irrational. But these issues of anxiety or peace of mind seem to lie somewhere between the rational thing that can be measured (such as a measurement of what can be achieved given a certain number of hours in a day) and the irrational thing where something in your head gets out of hand.

At that point I had to drive within a few miles of home. I came so close to popping in on the pretext that I could pick up anything I'd forgotten; charge the power pack, my phone and tablet on the mains all at the same time, have a sit on a comfy chair. I came so close to giving up completely. The fact that there's anything written on the next page is testament to the fact that I continued.

* * *

Passing through Harpenden I stopped to adjust the truck's window washers after the less than comprehensive pre-trip main dealer service had left them ineffectually pointing at the bottom of the windscreen. They had been adequately positioned before the service so I can only assume the local Vauxhall dealer had adjusted them thus to spite me. Yet main dealers wonder why people don't trust them and complain about the price.

In the petrol station, while I had a sewing pin trying to clean out the washer jet, I was approached by a woman who asked me to assist with her diesel nozzle. Her car was a brand-new Audi and it had some sort of metal guard inside the filler hole that I didn't understand so I did my best and ended up with diesely fingers after failing to help; thus I made my excuses and left.

Having adjusted the screen wash jets I grabbed a packet of wet wipes from the glove compartment only to find them covered in a delicately fine layer of chocolate. The flimsy layer of chocolate would have been an amazing achievement for a master Belgian chocolatier. The resultant combination of diesel and chocolate, however, I cannot recommend.

Selecting the shortest route, Kathy took me down lanes between Harpenden and Hitchin, all single track and lovely, often passing through woodland with dappled shade in the afternoon sun, up hill and down dale involving many gear changes and probably using far too much fuel, but hey, that's what this was supposed to be about and the lanes were delightfully clear of traffic with rush hour taking place on the main roads. I say up hill and down dale but I suppose we'll get to that in Yorkshire in a week or so.

* * *

Leaving Hertfordshire along lanes that I'd never travelled, I found myself driving into Henlow in Bedfordshire. I have a connection to Henlow from my childhood when I was in the Air Cadets. My squadron was in Hertfordshire Wing and we used to have our annual Wing Parades at RAF Henlow. I remember standing to attention for what seemed like hours, until my mind would play tricks on me thinking I wasn't standing straight so I would twist sideways. Looking down I would discover had been standing straight all along and my twisting was simply over-compensation. The mind can play interesting tricks on you, as anybody who has ever meditated or worked in a mailing office stuffing envelopes will attest.

However, Henlow in the 21st century was a shock. New houses all over the place, little boxes just different enough from each other for the developers to say that they are no longer ruining our environment by throwing up second-rate homogenised cubes. Those houses on the opposite side of the road looked suspiciously like the MoD houses that used to be part of the airfield. So where was RAF Henlow? Had they sold off the RAF station and built houses on my childhood memories?

I was pleased to see that the gate of RAF Henlow still features a Hawker Hunter on display, though these days it's probably a plastic replica as the original aircraft are far too valuable, not to mention elegant, to leave them rusting in the elements.

But hang on! I was in Hertfordshire Wing! RAF Henlow is in Bedfordshire, not that I'd known that in those days. Did they move the boundary? Did Hertfordshire not have an RAF station where we could stand to attention all day while some self-important retired Wing Commander strolled around us in his medals pretending to be more interested in how shiny our boots were as opposed to the bonus on his pension he got for skipping church on a Sunday morning? (Actually I'm sure he did it out of love for the RAF but never let the truth get in the way of a good line.) If there is something amiss with my recollections of childhood what is it? Did they lie to us? Was I not listening? Have I got somebody else's memories? Am I a replicant?

As I progressed, a black squirrel skipped across the road in front of me only adding to the sense of the surreal and the Bedfordshire/Hertfordshire sci-fi childhood experience, or something.

The campsite at Turnpike Farm, a broad flat field peppered with a few trees to break it up, was a delight and I had a friendly and helpful welcome from the owners. I had a massive choice of pitches, spoiled for choice really, and I had electricity! At last I could keep everything powered up. The battery pack still wouldn't display as full by the next morning so I had no idea how long it should take. Perhaps the lights were lying to me. Whatever the case I would take every opportunity to keep it charged and use it conservatively.

Using the tool box that contains my camping gear, I was able to set up a desk for the tablet and keyboard. By removing the two detachable boxes at either end of the lid I had a flat level surface either side of the tablet allowing me to put a camping lamp on one side and a glass of wine on the other. This trip was beginning to look as though it might actually work.

Settling into a night of blogging in my tent, I felt like a Victorian explorer, only with a computer, and LED lighting, in a nylon tent... in Bedfordshire; so really nothing like a Victorian explorer. The campsite manager had invited me to pop over for a drink but I had writing to catch up on and by the time I'd finished, their party was over. I was particularly disappointed as, by the sound of it, they had quite a bash and somewhere outside it sounded like there was a considerable bonfire. Still, I was warmer than the first two nights and I dozed off illuminated by the orange glow of my battery pack slowly recharging... ever so slowly.

Day 4 - Bedfordshire to Huntingdonshire

Saturday May 4th

Miles on Truck: 155

Saturday started with a rain shower at 7:30 but by 10:00 the sun reappeared. The battery pack was still not fully charged but it was getting there slowly. I just managed to get my gear into the Truck before the heavens opened heralding a showery day. Looking at the map of the Historic Counties I realised that I really ought to visit Huntingdonshire next. Of course, Huntingdonshire doesn't exist anymore, or at least it does but the boundary doesn't exist, having been swallowed up by Cambridgeshire. It's not that someone has scooped it up and replaced it by Cambridgeshire or that Cambridgeshire invaded, although if they had you might find a fine straight road between St Ives and Godmanchester.

Referring to campsite locations in the Bumper Book of Campsites would be of no help as they would all say Cambridgeshire, yet I needed to identify a site in the now defunct county of Huntingdonshire. I stopped in a supermarket car park in Sandy and made a few calls. Shortly, I was booked into a four-star campsite in Huntingdon. I figured that camping in Huntingdon, having been Huntingdonshire's county town, would be one way of guaranteeing I was within the old county boundary and, by this stage, I was past caring.

Asking Kathy to take me to Huntingdon, she insisted I took the A1. Having decided that I would avoid motorways, I didn't really want to take dual carriageway A roads either. I asked her to avoid the A1 but somehow she still insisted. Clearly she is a wilful woman. At every instruction to join the A1 I resisted. At one junction, guided through an underpass, I found myself at a deserted mini roundabout with no option other than to join the slip road or go back the way I'd come. There was nobody around so, in my indecision, being nagged by Kathy, I drove right around the roundabout in a large circle as I attempted to resist the pull of the A1. Just at that point a beat up old blue pickup appeared through the underpass, the back loaded up with ladders and tools and the sort of equipment that says this vehicle is driven by builders, the sort of builders who would be unsympathetic to the plight of a bloke who is attempting to drive around England avoiding main roads. As they watched, I relented and gave in to Kathy in defeat and humiliation. The builders gave me a look that portrayed a combination of bemusement and distain. I'm sure Kathy made some comment of smug satisfaction.

The A1, however, was a short-lived transgression and I was soon back on a B road passing through St Neots. I'm pretty sure St Neots is the town where I once had a date, more than a decade ago. We agreed to meet there as it was between where we both lived. We got on well and agreed to meet again but, after a couple of extra dates, we decided the miles were just too much.

Strangely, as I passed through the town I was caught in a dramatic downpour just as The Feeling came on the MP3 player with their song *Rosé*, a nicely mournful song that sort of went with the sudden change in the weather. Many villages along my route had been pretty chocolate box locations, suitable to film murder mysteries that could be sold around the world and recognised by millions; St Neots on the other hand, or this bit at least, had a particularly drab appearance. Then again, perhaps, it was the rain. (I do seem to remember St Neots being prettier all those years ago, so perhaps I'm being unfair to the place.) Anyway, the combination of the memory of that relationship, the rain, the music and the drab surroundings, seemed to produce a brief but powerful feeling of melancholy.

Very shortly, the rain and the song stopped at about the same time followed by The Marshal Tucker Band's *In My Own Way*, a shit-kicking country music song of lost love slightly lifted from the depths of delightful gloom that is Rosé. The Marshal Tucker Band were followed by some good ole R&B with Rufus Thomas' *Walking The Dog*. (Rhythm & Blues always has an emotionally lifting inclination despite the name of the genre.) As Rufus walked the dog (a euphemism I'm sure but I've never bothered to think about it) there was a break in the clouds and brighter times were defiantly on the way.

What happened to the woman from St Neots? Well, she became a very great friend and confidant, deeply trusted. We just don't discuss those early days as they are now in the past and don't really matter, although perhaps they matter from a point of view of foundation. Perhaps we don't discuss it because our friendship is just too precious. Finally The Cure came on the stereo with *Love Cats*, what could be brighter? I could feel the heat of the sun through the windows of the Truck and all the melancholy was over.

What's the point of telling you all this? I'm not sure but it was a strangely overwhelming experience and seemed relevant at the time.

* * *

Continuing north, I passed through Great Paxton and then into Offord DÁrcy followed by Offord Cluny. (Members of the army should refrain from sniggering at this point.) Between the villages of Great Paxton and Offord DÁrcy there was a stand of perhaps ten wind turbines turning majestically on a rise in the landscape. You couldn't call it a hill as ever since Bedfordshire, and the landscape around RAF Henlow, the topography had been very flat. Here, in Huntingdonshire, there were occasional undulations, with wide skies as one might imagine Montana; if, like me, you had only heard of the place but never visited. In the distance to the east there was a single wind turbine picked out white on the horizon against the deep blue, near black, of the rain clouds. The sun was shining from the west through a break in the clouds causing the windmill to stand out like a sentinel in the darkness.

Over the years I've been somewhat ambivalent about wind turbines. I understand the arguments of people who don't want them to blight the landscape but I think they can look rather elegant. Things of a mechanical or engineering nature can be beautiful, it's just that these days we don't seem to bother. The Victorians were known for decorating great feats of engineering but they were show-offs. To me, serried ranks of slender white turbines, turning majestically as they catch the sun, their blades almost but not quite rotating in synchronisation but never seeming to catch up, can be rather beautiful.

Obviously, when it comes to the placement of wind farms there is a compromise to be made between placing them so close to people that they blight their lives and placing them so far away that they blight the wilderness, but beauty is in the eye of the beholder, and that lone windmill on the horizon was beautiful (though it may have been an eyesore if you lived beneath it). The other point that never seems to be mentioned is that they don't have to be permanent (although I'm happy to be corrected on this). When you build a power station you cause a huge amount of impact, massive structures that take years to build and years to restore the landscape when they are done with. Surely a windmill, or wind farm even, requires much less engineering. Each one has a considerable foundation but nothing that can't be removed without a little effort, cables are buried, and the control boxes and other infrastructure would be small buildings or metal cabinets that can be taken away with relative ease. Surely, if we decide a wind farm is in the wrong place we can take it down and nobody need know it was ever there. Let's try this, with appropriate caution, and if we find they are a real problem then we can take them away.

Soon I drove into Godmanchester. (What's that name all about?) The town has something of the feel of a village, although on the map it looks much like it's been swallowed up by Huntingdon. Perhaps Huntingdon invaded, but the roads are still twisty so conceivably there was an amicable truce. The town seemed almost deserted, all large puddles and reflections of the sun against the sky. There were just a few people on the streets, presumably the brave or the waterproof, with everybody else sheltering inside.

Driving into Wyton Lakes Holiday Park it seemed to be the sort of place I would normally stay right away from, thinking of myself as a serious camper but, the thought of guaranteed access to electricity, showers, washing up facilities and all the comforts I had been missing, suddenly I could understand the appeal.

They asked me if I wanted to pitch away from the main road, which would have meant me being with other campers, or away from other campers but close to the road. I opted for the latter, not because I was being antisocial, quite the opposite but because I knew now that if the Truck didn't start first time in the morning it could take a while to go and it could be very smoky if it did take a few attempts, so I sacrificed the rural idyll for the sake of not spoiling anybody's morning the next day. The road was a bit noisy, being the other side of the hedge, but as Elwood said to Jake in the Blues Brothers, when asked how often the trains go by outside the window, 'So often that you don't even hear them.'

Day 5 - Huntingdonshire to Cambridgeshire

Sunday May 5th

Miles on Truck: 184

Sunday started early (for a Sunday at least) at about 8:00, but when you are on the road like this, it's amazing how quickly you lose track of the days of the week. You quickly realise how arbitrary they are. Robinson Crusoe was sick for a few days before he was joined by Friday and, being alone, he didn't know long he had been ill. Crusoe was horrified to discover, when he was rescued years later, that he had been keeping the Sabbath on the wrong day. He seemed less concerned that he had been getting Friday's name wrong when his real name was clearly Tuesday. Of course, Robinson Crusoe is made up but, apparently, so are the days of the week.

Driving aimlessly about for an hour or so I headed east, thinking this would take me into Cambridgeshire. Of course after the great Cambridge invasion of Huntingdonshire there were no signs to define the boundary, so, heading east seemed the best bet. Somehow I ended up in St Ives, passing over a viaduct across a floodplain of what turned out to be the River Great Ouse. This all seems rather strange, as it should probably have taken me about thirty seconds to get from Huntingdon to the centre of St Ives. I put this down to my aversion to main roads along with an unreliable sense of direction. From the road across the floodplain, I could really see just how flat this county was and I was clearly heading into the fens.

I drifted into the town centre and then out again without getting out of the Truck. St Ives is pretty and quiet, similar to Thame although, I'm sure, quite different in history. The similarity is that both are very 'quite nice' which should be pronounced 'qwate nace' if you get my meaning. I don't know if it's me being a townie that makes me feel this way, but when I visit these places I always feel a little out of place. However it wasn't this that made me move on from St Ives, it was a combination of wanting to do something with the day rather than head straight to another campsite, perhaps to have a Sunday lunch in a nice country pub, but also aware that this being a bank holiday weekend I might find it hard to find a pitch if I didn't book something early. The original plan, of spending a carefree six weeks not knowing where I would sleep until late in the day, had been deeply affected by the difficulties of keeping everything charged up. I did want to do some proper wild camping at some point, all carefree, roll up in some corner of a field whenever you like and live off the fat of the land and whatever battery is available, but I didn't envisage that until I got out of the South East where everywhere is so over populated.

Stopping in Fenstanton, I pulled into a car park overlooking a cricket pitch, got a strange look from a dog walker as I reversed the Truck into a position with a view across the green, and tried to get a signal on the tablet. Asking Google Maps where I could get some lunch, it recommended the pub I'd just passed so after making some notes about the morning's epic journey from Huntingdon, I headed back to the village centre. The King William IV was like any other country pub, not too crowded, with just enough patrons to give it an atmosphere, plus the landlord knew how to make a St Clements (which is not very complicated if you know the nursery rhyme). I ordered a steak and ale pie and searched for somewhere to stay and something to do.

The meal arrived hot and included lashings of gravy. By that time I'd used the app from the Caravanning and Camping Club to find somewhere to stay the night. After the app crashed for the fourth or fifth time (apps have given ordinary geeks the chance to commercialise their software skills but sometimes I wonder if that is such a great thing) I was about to give up when I spotted Karma Farm, an eco-camping site just inside Cambridgeshire and a little south of Ely. The site was far enough away from the road to be a different experience to the time I'd had at Wyton Lakes Holiday Park.

On the phone I asked about the name Karma Farm and he told me that it was an eco-campsite with all that entails. He also went on to explain that there was a group of people having a 21st birthday party but the noise would stop at 11:00. This didn't bother me, being the seasoned party animal that I consider myself to be. It all seemed rather ideal and heading southeast would give me a chance to have a look around Ely on the way.

I must have become a bit enthusiastic about the idea of staying at an eco-campsite, as I began to imagine the type of thing I'm used to at hippie camps I've been to over the years, being a bit of a hippie myself, although there are as many shades of hippie as there are of any other sub culture. I was thinking communal fire, perhaps some acoustic music, that sort of thing. Of course eco hippies are not the same as music hippies, biker hippies, alternative therapy hippies, alternative philosophy hippies, or general camping hippies. Regardless of the differences, it was probably with an inflated feeling of fellowship that I imagined a camp with everybody getting on together, socialising, sitting around the same fire, singing Ging-Gang-Goolie and all that, or whatever cliché songs hippies sing.

I left Fenstanton instructing Kathy to take me by the shortest route, the idea being that this would take me down tiny twisting lanes, all rural and lovely. Instead, being somewhat less obedient, she took me back along the route I had come, so much so that I thought I'd made a mistake and asked her to take me back to Huntingdon. However, when she finally pointed me east, she took me along roads that looked like they were built by invaders; when bends did come they took me by such surprise that the Truck was challenged not to cross the white lines into the oncoming traffic.

I crossed the river Great Ouse again and found myself on another long, straight road adjacent to the New Bedford River, a massive navigation built to divert the Great Ouse and so drain the surrounding land. Its substantial embankments rise above your head and, from the road, it seems that it almost towers above you, though the embankments are probably no more than ten feet tall. To think such a volume of water lies above you can give you the willies if you allow it to. The river is arrow straight so clearly built by some invading army.

Truth be told, it turns out the New Bedford River was built by various land owners including a couple of Earls of Bedford, a Dutch engineer and King Charles I. What's amazing is that these people lived in the 17th century so this twenty mile stretch of double earthwork up to one hundred feet apart was built with muscle power, blood, sweat and, no doubt, tears without a hint of machinery for at least the next hundred and fifty years.

From here I could see what I assumed was Ely rising like an island out of the fens with the cathedral clearly visible above the town, for Ely once was an island before the land around was drained. It was, it seems, such projects as the building of the New Bedford River that drained the land around Ely in the 17th century. Ely has long been known as the Island of the Eels from the slippery creatures that populate the fens and rivers around the city.

The day was hot although there were clouds in the sky, of the fluffy variety, such that the sun went in so infrequently that is had become a blisteringly hot day. Crossing the fens, the fields were flat and open with hardly any hedgerows and, where the farmers had grubbed up the hedges, you could literally see for miles. The crops came to within inches of the tarmac on the arrow straight, built by invaders, roads. In one location the farmer had placed a series of car tyres on the narrow grass verge, presumably to stop people pulling onto the verge and either getting stuck or encroaching onto the crops. Now forgive me if I'm wrong but isn't this what hedges were for in the first place? Songbirds and bumblebees can't live in old car tyres.

After a coffee I ended up in Ely Cathedral. I find cathedrals quite difficult to resist and Ely Cathedral, at 5:30 on a bank holiday afternoon, has very little competition. I also have a bit of a thing for meditating in cathedrals although I'm not very good at it, either in cathedrals or out of them, suffering too much with the chattering monkey, he of the insomniac parties in my head and all that; but it feels nice to try to meditate in a space like a cathedral and you do get a sense of the space even if all you do is close your eyes and feel the sheer volume of the enclosure around you. However, I always feel a little self-conscious sitting there in the nave with my eyes closed not quite looking like a normal person would if they were in prayer; nevertheless, I have always thought, if you can't meditate in a church then where can you?

From a rational perspective you might get the same sense of enclosed space from any other large open building, but there aren't that many to choose from other than churches and cathedrals. Some office buildings might have large atriums as might some industrial buildings, but I'm not sure I could bring myself to sit, eyes closed, in the atrium of the Lloyds building with all those suits and loud jackets around me, not to mention the sound of mobile phones going off and people shouting 'Buy!', 'Sell!', and 'What the hell am I doing in the Lloyds building shouting all this nonsense? I'm a commodities trader from the nineteen seventies!'

I meditate when I can and, rationally, I reckon it's probably got some benefits although they are hard to quantify, but improved concentration span is among the sort of things often cited. My particular exercise, derived from Buddhist ideas by a group of friends in the early eighties, uses breath, mantra and asana. Many people might imagine this to be a bit weird but these apparently irrational ideas have a quite rational basis. One of the problems with meditation is that it's hard to switch off the conscious mind, the chattering monkey. Chanting is said to occupy the hearing until the brain gets bored and ignores the input until the input changes, which is when the brain starts paying attention again. Visualisation is supposed to occupy the visual sense, although I've never been any good at it. Asana, or posture, is said to occupy proprioception, the sense of the position of the body, and other disciplines serve other purposes. So it's possible to see how these apparently weird practices have genuine rational intentions, even if some may be more effective than others. Of course, once these practices have been used for generations, the reasons for them are often forgotten and can be replaced by a sense of meaning of their own. In a way, the same could be said of many of the practices that are performed in places of worship. The original intention was lost and what remains is meaning that derives from a sense of tradition.

＊＊

So here's the thing, the second thing perhaps. It seems the world is divided into two camps. There are those who live a life rich with the traditions of generations. Many of those people would be described as religious but if you look below the surface you'll see that quite a few do not conform to the strict definition of religion. Then there is the second camp, the increasingly large group of people who live a life that contains little of this and tries to avoid anything that seems to have no basis in evidence. We could call these two stances irrational and rational. However, I'm conscious that the term irrational comes with a certain emotional loading; it's an insult to call someone irrational. People who are unexpectedly angry, possibly for perfectly good personal reasons, are sometimes described as being irrational. But I need to draw a difference between the rational, logical, measurement-based experience of life that comes from a strictly scientific perspective and the intuitive, feeling-based experience of life that is the other side of the coin. So perhaps I should define these terms as rational and non-rational.

＊＊

The road south from Ely was flatter than before and the vistas were now totally uninterrupted by any rise in the landscape. Kathy, being less recalcitrant now, led me off the main road and down a single-track lane to the east. Cambridgeshire must have been invaded many times as these roads were as straight as an arrow and they were evidently the norm. Occasionally there would be the odd right angle turn just to keep me on my toes but, clearly, there was a Roman-like precision to it all.

Shortly I entered the village of Isleham, Kathy faithfully directing me through the village, down a road marked as a dead end (at which point I became very slightly excited what with the possibility of taking the Truck off-road), and eventually down a tarmac lane. A sign saying 'This way to Karma Farm Eco Camping Site' indicated to go straight on and the tarmac road became a cinder track with bumps! At least I got to use the Truck's almost legendary suspension, taking care not to damage the surface by driving too fast, understanding that big trucks apparently create a constant maintenance headache.

Karma Farm was about as far from my previous night's accommodation as it was possible to get, philosophically at least. Wyton Lakes Holiday Park had been, as the name suggests, very nice, with hard standings for caravans, closely cut grass, and what you might call all white bread. Of course it's perfect if you want to take your kitchen sink and keep all of the comforts of home while you explore another part of the country, touring but not roughing it. Hell I'm guilty of that on this trip, saying I must have electricity so that I can write or blog, so I'm sure people have their reasons, but homogenised camping wouldn't suit everybody.

Karma Farm, on the other hand, is a collection of pole barns, yurts, a log cabin or two and the odd shed. The margins, and indeed some of the central areas, are left to nature so there is an abundance of nettles and general undergrowth. There is a large pond, suitably fenced off, a bird hide up a rickety ladder complete with 'Enter at your own risk' sign, and all sorts of other constructions, some ingenious, others a tad ramshackle. There were grass areas for camping and a few hook-ups for caravans. Now let's face it, if you would like Wyton Lakes Holiday Park you probably wouldn't like Karma Farm.

* * *

Charging a minimal camping fee, the farmer offered me a couple of pitches.

'Would you like to camp over there?' He pointed to a thin patch of grass.

'That looks like it's just been reseeded,' I replied. To be honest, I was surprised, him being a farmer, that he would offer me such a spot. The grass looked so delicate and thin that I thought it wouldn't survive me camping on it. Perhaps he knew better.

'Well what about here?' He indicated the rather nettly mound we were standing on next to an even more nettly pole barn.

I sort of reluctantly agreed. Being the sort of guy who doesn't like to complain about something until I'm sure I've got something worth complaining about, I accepted the location and made the best of it. I parked the Truck over the worst of the nettles and positioned the Khyam so I could get my gear into it from the truck with minimal risk of stumbling into the nettles if I went out in the dark.

I was more concerned that the nettly mound was actually on a thoroughfare where people were walking back and forth to their tents, making me anxious that people might walk into my tent and destroy it in the night. All kinds of disasters went through my head. Parking the Truck one side of the Khyam served to keep staggering sleepwalkers away in one direction; a carefully placed LED lamp served to illuminate the tent in the other direction.

It was only for one night so I'd live with it. I took it for granted that was all there was, so I got on with it.

Day 6 - Cambridgeshire to Suffolk

Monday May 6th

Miles on Truck: 229

Bank Holiday Monday arrived, my tent was intact and nobody had fallen on it. I went off to find the loos and showers which, as I suspected, turned out to be rudimentary. The showers seemed to be a converted horse box. Strictly speaking it was a converted loose box but I'm not sure many people know the difference. A loose box is one of those trailers that people pull behind Land Rovers with one or two horses' arses sticking out the back, whereas a horse box is a lorry with a ramp at the back with HORSES written in big scary letters, accommodation for a few horses inside and often a bit at the front for tack, grooming accessories and tea-making facilities. A converted horse box could be turned into quite a luxurious shower block that could be driven around the country, parked in public places and used to extort large sums of money from people in return for the luxury mobile shower experience of a lifetime. The converted loose box however had a drain in the floor and didn't appear to have any means of heating the water. It also appeared to be in use by the children as a place for playing football when the weather was unsuitable outside, so I shuddered and left. The speed of my exit may have been the reason I missed the possibility of cleverly hidden pipes where piping-hot water came out, if there were any. Of course it may be the case that the loose box was disused and that was the reason for its condition but clear signage would seem to be the solution to this issue. The toilets, however, were still in use and they were very nearly serviceable; I say nearly as the flusher didn't work unless you followed the instructions to do two quick flushes. Of course if you missed your timing or didn't get the speed of the wrist action just right then the flush didn't work and you had to wait twenty minutes for the cistern to trickle back to full before you could have another attempt.

It strikes me that if you get the sanitation right, provide a hook to hang your clothes on and a clean floor in case you have to put something down, spend a tenner on a new siphon so that the cistern flushes, and sort out some sort of reliable hot water, then people will forgive you anything else.

As I packed up, the farmer checked up on me, had I had a good night, slept well and I suspect to make sure I didn't disappear without paying. I gave him the tiny amount of money and we passed the time of day without me voicing any of my gripes. I simply felt, in the presence of such a nice bloke, that my complaints were just too petty to mention. Apparently he has lots of regular customers and his relationship with his patrons is more relevant than his facilities which, let's face it, are quite scruffy, but what do you expect for less than the cost of a decent coffee and a piece of cake? I paid my bill and drove off down the cinder track, enjoying my suspension on the bumps, looking for a signal on my tablet.

* * *

In hindsight it's clear that Karma Farm was fulfilling a need that mainstream campsites with all the nice facilities didn't really manage. Karma Farm catered for the more enthusiastic back to nature aficionado but I wonder if they are fulfilling a desire for something more. Camping itself is a meaningful experience, getting away from it all, back to nature and all that, but it struck me that in camping at Karma Farm people may be looking for a sense of meaning that can only be understood in terms of the lack of that meaning in everyday life manifest in the earthiness of the experience. I also picked up that there is a sense of community, which I only noticed because I felt a bit of an outsider. I'm sure I could have become an insider if I went back every year for a few years but that's in the nature of community, you have to work at it. With that effort the sense of community becomes meaningful; if it came easily it wouldn't count for much. In the past I've been to similar places, where I was an insider, and I didn't worry about the dodgy toilets because I was amongst friends, in the same way you might put up with something like that at home until you get around to fixing it.

* * *

Just down the track I stopped in Isleham and found a particularly nice example of a fine early Norman church with a rounded apse. After taking a few pictures I sought out a signal for my tablet but found none so I decided that Mildenhall, a few miles away, might be a better bet, what with the US Air Force base nearby. Surely the USAF wouldn't tolerate a poor signal while they were fraternising with the locals.

Very soon I arrived in Mildenhall and the very first thing I noticed was a US airman, all bearlike, with a blue hat that didn't match his green outfit, driving a massive 4x4 that put my Truck to shame. I'm sure he was a Blah-Sergeant or something, as the Americans seem fond of unheard-of titles derived from ancient historic military functions or some-such; all very meaningful to them I'm sure.

So I pulled up by the town cross with its roof on pillars similar to the one in Princes Risborough and wrote up some notes. I stayed there for an hour and a half, saw another airman with stripes on his shoulders and a hat that did match the rest of his clothes, had a sandwich from the shop, saw a farmer with a cravat from the nineteen fifties, and wrote for as long as I could stand.

Suddenly there was a shadow across my computer on my lap as somebody stepped up to my driver's door. At the same time another figure stood at my passenger door. The large figure next to me, in a military uniform and a hat that didn't match, asked me what I was doing making notes as I was sitting in a village frequented by the US military.

I responded that I was just writing my diary about my camping holiday and that it was none of his business. At which point the second figure leaned in towards the open window on my passenger side and asked what all these papers were.

'That's my camping directory for the Camping and Caravanning Club,' I responded.

'And all the rest of these notes Sir?' he added.

'That's the notes about places I've been to,' I replied somewhat meekly, wondering if I'd been reported while sitting in the neighbourhood watch zone.

'Please show us your proof of identity sir,' added the first large figure in the unmatching hat next to me.

'I'm sorry,' I replied, 'I'm a British citizen sitting in my car in an English village where I am on holiday.'

'And where are you going on holiday?' asked the second figure.

'Well at the moment Suffolk,' I replied. 'But tomorrow I'll be in Norfolk and after that somewhere else.'

'Moving around a lot are we sir?' asked the one on the passenger side, now almost leaning in through the window.

'We have reports of intercepted traffic on your computer, sir, that leads us to believe that you may be involved in actions contrary to the interests of the US government.'

'Perhaps you would like to step out of the car sir.'

As I reached for the door handle I realised that none of this was actually happening and came to my senses, but my neuroticism was clearly getting the better of me.

Actually my short visit to Mildenhall was completely uneventful. I did see two airmen but they didn't take any notice of me and I made all this up because very little happened all day but it did pass through my rather over-active imagination. (Perhaps that's why I once had a go at writing fiction.) I'm sure the USAF are all very nice people.

Wanting to avoid the issues I'd had with the Huntingdon campsite, I chose one that appeared to be as far away from main roads as I could find. Henry's Lake camp-site in Suffolk seemed to be suitably isolated but it meant going quite a long way south, beyond the A14; but it would mean a good drive through Suffolk, which was worth it as Suffolk, if you get away from the main roads, is really beautiful, all undulating with frequent views to a distant horizon, bounded by apparently unspoilt hedgerows and scattered woodlands, illustrating how close it was to being flat without being the billiard table that is the Cambridgeshire Fens.

I passed a sign for West Stow, taking me by surprise. This was a bit weird as you could probably drive around Suffolk for years and not come across the place, although it is probably well known to the locals as the location of an Anglo Saxon village reconstruction.

The significance of West Stow is purely personal as it's the location of a tiny music festival with a single stage in a smallish marquee mostly attended by locals featuring local bands. The clever name Westo Festo sort of sticks in the mind, but to me it was memorable for getting together with a girlfriend one summer. We'd met before but this was where the magic happened. Again, and I don't mean to paint a picture of tragedy here, the relationship didn't continue because we lived so far apart but we're still great friends and meet up at events a few times a year. Unlike my trip through St Neots, there was no significant musical accompaniment to this reminiscence that I recall.

Drawn by the idea of an Anglo Saxon reconstruction, I stopped off only to discover the rest of the country was having a bank holiday. It really hadn't occurred to me as the days all seemed to be the same and I was barely aware that it was a Monday at all.

Arriving at the ticket office for the reconstructed village I was discouraged by the expense of the entry. I would have stumped up the six or seven quid but I was dissuaded by the woman behind the counter after hearing that it takes a good few hours to see the whole thing. Were I an English Heritage member I could have strolled straight in without a care but, alas not.

Leaving the thronging bank holiday masses behind, I set off south for Henry's Lake. I don't know if I misplaced my trust in Kathy but I ended up on the A14, a road far too like a motorway for my liking, and soon found myself in Needham Market. The irony is that Needham Market is nowhere near Henry's Lake but it's on a friend's doorstep and I envisaged an impromptu stay in their substantial garden where they have the most excellent parties and, as a result, better camping facilities than some of the sites I've visited. Not wanting to intrude however, I made a quick phone call to Henry's Lake and, managing to get Kathy back on task, she guided me to the campsite.

Henry's Lake was a delight, especially after the vagaries of Karma Farm. A bit miles from nowhere they'd built a considerable fishing lake which seemed to be their USP, not that I wanted to fish, but it seems other people did. But the best thing about the place was, it was cheap, including electricity, flushing loos and showers that were all clean and well maintained. They'd simply installed a couple of plastic sheds and converted them by adding the appropriate plumbing. It was all rather excellent (toilets and showers go a long way to create satisfaction) with peace and quiet by the bucket load.

Day 7 - Suffolk to Norfolk

Tuesday May 7th

Miles on Truck: 277

Tuesday was yet another blisteringly hot day, so much so that there had been lots of comments on Facebook about the unusually sunny bank holiday. After the horrendously long winter, with snow right up to the weeks before I left, this was quite a transformation.

* * *

I was becoming more relaxed about the logistics, and the excellent facilities at Henry's Lake helped, with good electrics and time to charge everything up. I also had growing confidence in the charging process. I'd not had power overnight at Karma Farm but the battery pack had done its job and Henry's Lake provided enough power to top it up again. I was getting used to the routine and, although the daily packing and unpacking still took an hour from start to finish each time, I knew how long it would take each time which began to dispel my anxiety. A known quantity is always more easily understood.

It can be difficult to identify the rational and the non-rational especially when you are firmly embedded in one or the other. At what point does your collection of stamps, bus tickets or shoes become irrational? How many stamps is a rational pleasure (if that's not a contradiction in terms) and how many becomes an obsession? Worrying about the logistics of the trip is perfectly rational but falling into the blind panic that I'd come close to in Buckinghamshire, when I'd been tempted to give up, was quite irrational. The two hours of packing and unpacking, the travelling time that left no time for meaningful exploration, the need to keep all the general logistics together had led to a temptation to give up completely. The task was clearly doable with a bit of perseverance and preparation, as I was beginning to understand. To give up would have been quite irrational. However, when you are embedded in a situation, how do we tell the dividing line between the two?

* * *

I asked Kathy to guide me to Thetford, thinking that I would be able to get a good signal there, something the most peaceful campsites lack by definition. This was when I realised that I'd gone far deeper into Suffolk than I'd intended, as I ended up travelling back along the same country lanes I had on the way south; but Suffolk was as beautiful as the day before so I enjoyed the pastoral loveliness for a second time and considered myself lucky.

One thing that those flat landscapes taught me is that the Truck drives much better if it's not driven hard. At about 40mph on the slightly uneven country roads it sort of trundles along, whereas at 50mph it's altogether too manic, and of course at 40 you can see the world go by so much more easily.

Crossing the border into Norfolk I saw my first pig farm and, until I spotted the almost invisible electric fence, I was impressed that they didn't just wander off up the lane as there seemed to be nothing to keep them in. The dry bare soil extended almost to the lane with just a narrow, flat grass verge to mark the edge of their territory on the non-porcine side of the invisible fence. I'm sure that if they made a concerted effort they could have escaped but presumably regular food and shelter ensures their loyalty.

It was only as I drove along it occurred to me that they looked, to all intents and purposes, like flying pigs (presumably on their day off) as their half round shelters, (arks I believe they are called) with open fronts looked like mini aircraft hangars. Strangely, about a mile past the pig hangars I passed a radar scanner at a nearby airfield so perhaps they were flying pigs after all.

A few miles later I arrived in Thetford, turning onto Nuns Bridges Road, with three narrow humpbacked bridges and the remains of various convent buildings now incorporated into modern buildings and garden boundary walls. Did the nuns build the bridges, were the bridges special to the nuns in some way, will there be a movie *Three Bridges for Sister Sarah* or *The Bridges of Norfolk County*? I pulled into the Black Horse Pub for lunch, putting on something more respectable than the vest I was wearing, and went inside. According to a couple of the locals, Thetford is rich with church history with a ruined abbey nearby.

On hearing of my trip, one of the locals suggested a possible campsite at Happisburgh, apparently pronounced Haze-bruh or something, which made it worth going there for the name alone. However there is much more to the place than a name that sounds like a seventies children's toy manufacturer, as I was told it was slowly falling into the sea. I decided that this was far too good to miss and set off, hopefully via old Thetford Abbey on my way. I was told that there was camping available there so, after an excellent lunch with my batteries fully charged, electrically and nutritionally, I set off for the coast in continuing sunshine.

Asking Kathy for assistance, I passed through Thetford Forest, said to be Britain's largest man-made lowland forest (which probably makes it a plantation rather than a forest) and within a spit of Norwich. Passing a snow plough going the other way (presumably on its day off as the Truck said the temperature was 24 degrees) I found myself on the same route to Norwich that I'd taken a few weeks before. I'd had the Truck serviced for the trip by an excellent group of Frontera enthusiasts just outside Norwich. Their efforts had improved the fuel consumption and general running markedly. There was something like a 25% improvement, which is hard to believe but probably indicates just how bad it was. (For the technically minded, they cleaned out the inlet manifold and replaced the vacuum tubes, both of which are a common problem for Fronteras of a certain age.) The guys just seemed to like doing this sort of thing and didn't want payment, but I insisted they took a small stack of beer that I'd bought for the purpose along with a full crate of cheaper lager I had left over from a recent party.

The countryside beyond Norwich was predictably flat but much less damaged by the removal of hedgerows than I'd seen in Cambridgeshire. Views across the landscape presented panoramas over fields to hedgerows dotted with trees, revealing a sight of more distant trees and so on to the misty horizon. Norfolk appeared to be as it would have been before the advent of late 20th century intensive farming; the landscape of Norfolk was beautiful because of its flatness, not despite it.

Rolling into Happisburgh village, I discovered it to be one of those ever-eroding coastal locations that you hear of occasionally when some poor soul's house falls over a cliff. Apparently this has been happening since there have been people living there and people have been living there for a very long time indeed. Over the winter there had been a great deal on the news about unusually high rates of winter coastal erosion. It seems the extraordinarily wet summer of the previous year, along with the long winter that followed, had saturated the ground and weakened the cohesion of the cliffs.

Happisburgh boasts archaeology that indicates it as the location of the earliest known human settlement in northern Europe some 800,000 years ago. Okay, so the North Sea might not have been there back then and it may have been the location of the Thames estuary (a different landscape caused it to emerge much further north), but you get the picture that the place has a long and interesting history. Today the village sports fine examples of a striking 15th century church and the oldest working lighthouse in East Anglia, rather interestingly owned and run by the local community.

Arriving, I took a photo of the lovely church but found myself struggling to find the campsite. The signposts shepherded me to the tourist car park (and I suppose that's what I was), where I discovered a view of the historic lighthouse and a useful illustration of the village complete with handy arrows for you are here, this is the historic lighthouse, this is the historic church, this is the caravan and campsite, this is where the caravan site is falling into the sea, etc.

With the aid of the handy illustration I made my way to the caravan site hidden behind the pub, which was conveniently close, arriving at exactly 4:59. I know that was the time because I thought that I'd barely make it before they closed for the evening. Leaping out of the Truck I strolled over to the office to find it dark and deserted. The sign said open 8:30 to 5:00 but clearly they'd gone home early. Either that or they had a really fast and quite invisible car.

Wondering what to do, I checked out the campsite to see a slightly sloping large open green space stretching down to the cliff top. Clearly it was possible to walk down the field and straight over the cliff edge. There was not a soul to be seen on the campsite or amid the caravans. Walking around I eventually found a few visitors, dog walkers and locals of various types and generally confirmed my opinion that it would be okay to pitch up and sort out the details in the morning. There were electrical points dotted around the edge but I had no idea if they were switched on and I fancied camping right in the centre with all that space around me. I did consider camping on the cliff top but imagined waking up to find myself, Kathy and the two ton Truck, all three of us dead, at the bottom of the cliff in the morning so I decided to err on the side of survival.

Swinging the truck around I left it in gear on the landward side of the tent with the handbrake firmly on determined to align my tent so that I could look out at the sea in the morning. This meant that the Truck had to face up hill if the tailgate was going to open onto the back of the tent as had become my preference. Any anxiety of the Truck breaking free, rolling over me (possibly killing me in the process), down the slope and over the cliff edge, soon dispersed and I sat with a view of the sea as I prepared my evening meal and opened the wine.

Dog walkers were in the habit of strolling down past the pub across the campsite, right past my tent and along the cliff-top path that lead away to the south.

'Good evening.'

The Khyam Igloo is one of those dome tents that sleeps about three people, two metres in diameter and about half that high; strangely it seems larger on the inside than the outside. The reason for that strange extra dimensional effect may be that the doors are quite low. As I turned away from my efforts to heat a microwave chicken korma on my camping stove a pair of legs were speaking to me at the rear entrance.

'Oh hello, just a minute,' I replied as I clambered back through the tent, the front entrance blocked by a stove, chopping board, bottle of wine and all the other indispensable requirements of a six-week trip around the country.

'I saw your tent when I came back to the office,' replied the legs. I continued scrambling, eventually emerging to see an elderly, somewhat portly man attached to the legs. 'I came back to collect my paper,' he continued as he motioned with a rolled up newspaper.

'I hope you don't mind,' I responded. 'There was nobody in the office when I arrived so I thought I'd pitch up and sort out the details in the morning.'

'That's okay, if you have twelve ponds I can take the money now.'

'Of course,' I dived back through the low door to find my wallet and returned with the requisite amount.

We chatted briefly about my trip as he wrote a receipt, explaining that he was from Nottinghamshire before moving to Happisburgh. He asked at what point I'd be visiting his home county but I had to admit I had no idea, describing how I planned to not plan, if you get my drift. Shortly he strolled back up the field leaving me to continue my attempt to cook a microwave meal in an aluminium saucepan on a single ring gas stove.

* * *

'Hello there again.' The legs had returned.

'I've opened the toilets and put the lights on.' As I scrambled out again he gestured with his newspaper toward the power points and the lights around the edge of the field. 'If you want to move to one of the power points you can have electricity.'

'Oh thanks, I'm unpacked now, I think I'll stay here. I like all the space around me and the view. I think I've got all I need.' To be honest it hadn't occurred to me what I would have done had I wanted the loo to do any serious business, other than hoping that any ablutions coincided with the pub being open, but he had saved me from that dilemma.

'I'll also put the boiler on so you have hot water in the morning.' He gestured to the open-air sinks under a shelter in the corner near the entrance.

'Oh, that's brilliant. Thanks.'

'Okay then, good night.' The legs, the newspaper and the man that connected to them walked off up the field as I dived back in to stir my microwave meal.

* * *

After finishing dinner, which was surprisingly good such that I determined to find some more the same, I left for the pub. Placing strategic lights in the Khyam I was able to ensure night-time dog walkers were not inclined to collide with the tent in the night as I'd feared in Cambridgeshire. (I've seen the results of people stumbling into tents in the dark and it's not pretty.) The Hill House Inn was warm and cosy with some good ales that on just a small meal made me good and drunk by the time I'd got to the bottom of the first glass. Overhearing conversations of the patrons, there seemed to be a mix of locals and what seemed to be a group of engineers and geologists discussing coastal erosion while looking at a laptop. As I supped my second, or was it my third, pint while browsing Facebook and other web delights, I imagined what it might be like to travel the country examining local geological features, taking surveys during the day and spending the evening in the pub before retiring to a cosy bed and breakfast.

* * *

A few years later, as I was preparing to bring *In SatNav We Trust* to publication, I attended Neil Oliver's lecture in promotion of his book *The Story of The British Isles in 100 Places*. The very first place he describes is Happisburgh. His book takes a chronological tour through the history of Britain (rather than England as I did not, being unable to afford the time to cover all of Britain). He starts at Happisburgh because it's the location of a set of footprints that were discovered in a bed of compacted ancient sediment uncovered by the eroding cliff. It seems that the footprints were left an astonishing 950,000 years before by a family of adults and children as they crossed a muddy river bed, or some such landscape, perhaps even the Thames. This discovery is amazing as the coastal erosion that uncovered them destroyed the sediment within a few days. (Some eagle-eyed local must have spotted them and had the presence of mind to notify the right people.) So, for a few days a team of archaeologists worked to record the details, take photos and plaster casts before they were carried away like tears in rain. Now I wonder if the people with the laptop discussing coastal erosion were not engineers but the team of archaeologists who were working on those footprints while I was actually there. Just a few days, nearly a million years after those footprints were left, might have coincided with the one day that I visited. If that's the case and they were not erosion engineers than that's a huge coincidence. Of course, it doesn't actually mean anything but it has that *just imagine* factor and feels personally meaningful. When Neil started his lecture on that fact and the penny dropped (possibly mistakenly) I had a hell of a buzz. (His book's pretty good too, I had a chat with him after and he signed it for me.)

Day 8 - Norfolk to Rutland

Wednesday May 8th

Miles on Truck: 358

Waking on Wednesday morning, it was a very different scene. My tent, still pitched on the gentle slope of the campsite looked out to the sea with nothing to obstruct the view. Had I the desire, I could have got up and walked 200 yards forward and straight over the edge of the cliff, apparently without even a fence to protect the unwary. There might have been a fence once but, what with all the land slips recently, it was probably floating somewhere in the North Sea or being used to make that driftwood art that you can buy at craft fairs from girls called Melinda with frizzy hair. The other change from my previous week's experience was that the weather seemed to have turned. There was a slight fog out to sea, but not such that I couldn't see where the cliff edge was.

Remembering that I'd not found a supermarket the day before, I wandered down to the village centre, passing the pub where I'd had two (or was it three) pints of Broadside after the wine I'd had in my tent before going out, so I looked and felt my best as I walked into the tiny village shop. Waiting to be served, it occurred to me that this could so easily be a scene from *The Archers* village shop. There was the obligatory Post Office counter and all the odds and ends of day-to-day living, from food to floor cleaner. Such shops are rapidly disappearing with the habit of people driving further afield to supermarkets, but hopefully the Happisburgh village shop will survive because of the remote location of the village, at least until it falls into the North Sea. The fact that the conversations between the locals and the general scene struck me as reminiscent of *The Archers*, tales of broken-into sheds and lawn mowers stolen at unknown times during the winter, is a testament both to the quality of *The Archers* scriptwriting and to my need to get out more. These tiny slices of life are the bread and butter of such soaps that have (mostly) managed to resist the Eastenders style of drama where friendships are cast aside in the most unlikely fashion for the sake of a story-line involving nothing but conflict. It seems some script writers lack the imagination for anything other than to set members of the same community at each other's throats with an unrealistic amount of shouting and scheming that doesn't reflect the world we are living in but, perhaps, influences our world negatively.

Back at the tent, having consumed my coffee, bread and cheese, I gazed out to sea. I longed for some sort of boat or interesting feature—a whale or nuclear submarine would have sufficed—to pass by, but to no avail. So I decided to try the showers. Having had the shower block opened specifically for me I thought it only polite to see how they compared to those I'd tried before.

As usual, there was the now familiar coin machine but this one said 20 pence. Surely a shower must cost a pound as that seemed to be the going rate, but I could see nothing to say it required five times 20 pence so I walked across to the office to ask for guidance.

'Is it 20 pence for the shower?' I asked.

'Yes but you'll get a better shower if you put in two.'

I didn't quite understand, did this mean a longer shower or a hotter shower. 'What, 40 pence?' I was going to continue to refine my query but I didn't get a chance.

'Yes put in two and you get a better shower.'

I decided to leave it at that and see what happened. It always occurs to me that the people who set up these places don't use them, as there was nowhere to put my clothes other than hang them from a hook or drop them on the floor. (Sometimes a chair is a table, Dr Freud.) So rolling my trousers into a small ball, I put 40 pence to one side, stacked my unhangable items, including my rolled up trousers, carefully on my shoes and considered the coin slot.

Usually there is some sort of timer attached to the coin slot but I could see none. What difference would 40 pence make over 20? What difference would 20 pence make as I could see nothing connected to the coin box; not that I begrudged the 40 pence, a pound would have been fair. So I inserted the coins only to hear them drop into what seemed like an empty chamber below. Nothing clicked, nothing lit up with numbers counting down ten minutes as I had come to expect, nothing whirred into shower-producing life at all. The whole arrangement seemed to be a bluff. I bet I could have stepped into the shower having offered not a penny. I suppose the definition of a 40 pence 'better shower' was that I had the owners good will, which was fine by me; whatever the case, it turned out to be hot and lovely.

Having decided that Happisburg was, perhaps, the nicest place I had visited so far and feeling a bit more positive toward Kathy I asked her to take me to Oakham, county town of the former county of Rutland, England's smallest county.

Stopping off at the open-air sinks as I left, I discovered that the washing-up water was also piping hot, so another reason to give the place a thumbs-up, considering the man with the legs had turned it all on just for me. Setting off with my washing-up drying on my luggage cover, I spotted a sign for the seaside village of Bacton so, having once worked on a documentation project for Bacton Gas Works (where a substantial amount of England's North Sea gas comes ashore), I decided to take a detour. Driving up the coast, I passed coastal communities of bungalows and low cottages, soon coming within a few feet of the beach on the right, with the sea stretching to the horizon just as the flat landscape stretched to the left. I passed through more communities of flint houses and flint walls. Anything that wasn't painted in the last three weeks looked weather-beaten and faded.

I did consider the possibility of taking a picture of the gas works for the sake of geeky reminiscence and my Facebook account but, wary of causing a false alarm in the anti-terrorist wing of the security forces, I thought better of it, especially considering the incident at Mildenhall that never actually happened. My circumspection might actually have been a good idea as, driving past the gas works, there was indeed a police car stationed in a lay-by designated not for public use, or some such (that's the lay-by not the police car), so I wonder if the whole place is more protected than we might imagine. Or had they been reading my notes on the Cloud and knew I was coming?

Anyway, the gas works was all industrial chic and shiny pipes set behind tall fences with barbed wire, which wasn't really that interesting, so I drove straight past without waving to the nice policeman in the lay-by marked not for public use (that's the lay-by, not the policeman).

From Bacton my plan to ask Kathy to take me by the shortest route, hence provoking lots of country lane driving, worked well. For at least an hour, under a fine summer's day with the odd spot of fluffy white cumulus, I had a real fun drive, trusting Kathy to take me where she willed with no idea what was around the next corner or up the next lane.

At some point, after heading inland to the east, the landscape became a little less flat than at Happisburgh, where it had been possible to see across field after field to the misty horizon. After a while the vistas became closer, more intimate, more like those I know from Hertfordshire. I could see into the fields either side and, perhaps, the woods beyond but no further.

Wistfully, I passed south of King's Lynn, wanting to stop just because I liked the sound of the name, but feeling the need to get to Rutland. Continuing on, I constantly crossed waterways and drove alongside long straight tidal river channels, the water low, exposing gloopy mud banks sculpted into smoothed shapes that looked like something designed by H.R. Giger. Here, the north of Norfolk was proper flat again, large open fields stretching away to either horizon with just a few hedges to break up the monoculture. I could tell I was travelling west, the most exposed trees bearing that tell-tale deformity whereby they lean towards the northeast with the windward side stunted by the onslaught of persistent exposure to high winds.

* * *

Late in the afternoon, after way too many main roads, I arrived in Rutland. Had I taken the twisty lanes I'd still be there now, and I suspect those lanes never existed as much of this land would have been reclaimed from wetlands. I wonder that we call it reclaiming as it probably wasn't ours in the first place, so perhaps we should say claimed rather than reclaimed.

Rutland is traditionally famed as being the smallest of the Historic Counties. I had high hopes for Rutland because I'd heard of Rutland Water, Britain's largest reservoir and one of the largest artificial lakes in Europe. The reservoir was formed in the seventies by flooding two valleys and submerging a couple of villages. Today it is 4.2 square miles of lake used for sailing and fishing as well as extensive nature reserves. I envisaged camping on the shores of the lake overlooking the water as I cooked, nay heated, my adapted microwave meal with a beaker of red wine and nature all around me.

My first views of Rutland Water were truly impressive. It's a massive expanse, shaped a bit like a horseshoe around a peninsula. The water is about half a mile across at its narrowest with some irregular islands and inlets making it quite a bit wider in places. From end to end Rutland Water is about four miles and you could double that dimension if you were to stretch the horseshoe out into a straight line. All I needed at this stage was one of those brown signs saying campsite with a little tipi symbol.

However, my ambitions to camp in idyllic lakeside splendour were soon thwarted as I found myself driving around in circles as the end of the day inexorably approached. A pair of friendly tourists on bicycles suggested that there was a caravan site somewhere on the peninsula but they warned me that it was a Caravan Club site. Nevertheless, I headed off in search of the brown sign with self-confidence that their scepticism was unfounded. I passed through the apparently very well-to-do village of Hambleton and on down the lane to find a Caravan Club site at a farm just before I fell off the end of the peninsula.

Those of you not in the know will be unaware that there are two major Caravan organisations in Britain, the well-known Caravan Club and the less well known Caravan and Camping Club. Being a camper it was the latter that I'd joined before leaving on my trip. Now you could say that there is something you might describe as 'a relationship issue' between the two organisations summed up by the strapline that describes the Caravan and Camping Club as, 'The friendly club.' I felt sure I had heard stories of the Caravan Club over the years, so I approached the farm with a tiny amount of uneasiness, tempered with an attitude of what the heck, a faint hope, and a significant need to find somewhere to sleep for the night.

Driving up the gravel drive of the farmhouse I pulled to one side, talking care not to block the drive while making sure I didn't park on the grass. I stayed well away from the horses and took care not to rev the engine. Surveying my surroundings, I could see some caravans to the left. I didn't really want to go knocking at the farmhouse as that seemed something of an intrusion so I strolled over to the caravans instead.

There was nobody about apart from some movement in an awning across the field. I say field, it was more like a lawn, being the size of a couple of large back gardens, a converted paddock perhaps. There were three or four caravans and plenty of room for a small Truck and tent to one side. I wouldn't disturb anyone, what could it matter?

Approaching the caravan and awning, I made polite hello type noises and stuck my head into the open door.

'Good evening.' I delivered the line in as respectful and friendly a manner as I could muster. Inside the awning sat an elderly couple at a folding table, drinking tea in that sort of nice nineteen fifties way that you imagine of elderly couples in awnings.

'Good evening,' came their polite but somewhat guarded response.

'Sorry to interrupt you. I'm looking for somewhere to camp.' The couple didn't immediately respond to my opening gambit so I continued. 'I'm aware that this is a Caravan Club site and that they don't normally take tents but I need somewhere to camp so I thought it worth asking. I don't have anywhere else to go and it's only for one night.'

'You could ask at the farmhouse.' replied the man sitting with his arms folded as he looked up at me, his body language suggesting that he really didn't like the look of me. The woman sat silently without joining in the conversation. 'I have never seen a tent at a Caravan Club site.' He smiled in that sort of courteous but smug way that says, we don't really want your kind around here.

I thought of pulling out my six gun and shooting him in proper Clint Eastwood style as I was beginning to feel like I was in a western, being the unwelcome stranger who'd just rolled into town, but I thought better of it. Besides, I didn't have a six gun anyway and I would never shoot anyone over such a trivial matter, or even a serious one. The woman sat there throughout with a polite but somewhat ambiguous smile.

'Okay I'll ask at the farmhouse.' As I walked away with my tail between my legs, I felt that they were looking daggers at me from behind while saying that I looked shifty or something. Of course this might all have been in my mind and the couple might have been perfectly nice people. In the days that followed I found caravan people to be very nice on sites where I was allowed, but here I just didn't feel welcome.

To be honest, the farmhouse was so huge and imposing that I just didn't feel comfortable asking. I climbed into the Truck, turned around as carefully and quietly as I could, taking care not to scare the horses, and drove away. I passed back through the ever so posh, looking village of Hambleton and took my leave of the peninsula, sort of feeling that I didn't really belong anywhere in the area.

The nice couple on the bikes who had, admittedly, warned me not to bother with the Caravan Club site did mention that there was a campsite at a sailing club but it turned out you needed to be a sailor to camp there.

The weather had turned from bright sunshine, with a slight fluffy cloud here and there, to overcast and somewhat gloomy. There were forecasts of unpleasantness, at least for people in tents, but at this stage all I cared about was finding a bit of ground to pitch on, any ground would do.

I still had the fantasy of wild camping on the lakeside and I'd seen places from afar where there would have been pretty good views of Rutland Water so I drove on in hope. I was thinking that if I could just find a track somewhere I could drive down to the water's edge, pitch up and be gone in the morning leaving nothing more than a bit of flattened grass.

* * *

So there's something to consider here when we think about priorities. I'd arrived in Rutland with visions of an expansive lake, a campsite down by the water, beautiful vistas as I cooked my meal and relaxed before bedtime. I'd post pictures of the idyllic scene to my friends on Facebook and all would be right with the world.

Anyone who has studied a bit of social psychology, humanism, sociology or even been on one of those right-on management-training courses (not the ones where you have to build a raft out of lever arch files and highlighter pens) will have heard of Abraham Maslow and his theory of the Hierarchy of Needs. In short he suggests that there is an order of fulfilment of needs that we as humans have. He expressed this as a pyramid with the lower levels supporting those above. Without achieving the lower levels there is little point (or little opportunity) in trying to achieve the levels above. His levels of need start with physiological needs at the base and top out with what he called self-actualisation. For the sake of our purposes we can use the word spiritual needs as might be expressed in a religious or more non-rational context. (Actually I struggle with the term spiritual as I find it impossible to pin down but then that's probably in the nature of such concepts. However, for our purposes spiritual will have to do.) Clearly, seeking a beautiful lakeside campsite, with the opportunity to eat and become intoxicated on wine and beautiful vistas, while enjoying the companionship of friends on Facebook, before I'd established any survival infrastructure at all was a bit upside down. Maslow wouldn't have been impressed with my priorities.

* * *

Finding a track into a field behind a hedge that, apparently, wasn't blocked by a gate, I wondered at the possibility of pitching up for the night in a corner of a field that might, indeed, be forever England, whether it be in a Historic County or a unitary authority that describes itself as a county out of historic pride.

Turning up the track behind the hedge I was immediately out of sight of the road and, apparently, so were the people that came here to fly tip. Amongst the nettles and other weeds there was a fine collection of junk and rubble half covered by large sheet of blue plastic. The track continued past the junk into a small wood where it ended at a gate with a field beyond where I thought I could see peacocks. That was probably somebody's extensive back garden. The track into the wood was fenced on both sides so there was really nowhere to camp other than on the rubble and junk, no doubt amid a fine collection of needles and used prophylactics. I turned the Truck around amid the rubble and rubbish. This wasn't going to work out but with the daylight ebbing away I really needed to find somewhere to stop for the night.

This was all getting a bit irrational. I'd not found anywhere by the water and now I could be reduced to camping like a vagrant amid rubbish and junk, and probably trespassing to boot. Sleeping in the Truck in a layby would be better. Admitting defeat I pulled out my tablet but the damn thing was so slow that I struggled to get a signal and, when I did, the Camping and Caravan Club app just wouldn't work. Finally, in desperation, with about an hour of light left, I began the process of phoning round numbers in the Substantial Book of Campsites.

The campsite I found, on a farm as was often the case, turned out to be one I'd driven past at least once but failed to spot. The farmer's wife was very nice despite me not phoning ahead and the fact that she was very busy with people in the farm buildings, giving cheese-making lessons or whatever it is that farm people have to do to make ends meet. She clearly recognised I was desperate and would happily accept anything, leaving me to fend for myself.

In the increasing breeziness I pitched the Khyam in the lee of a tall hedge with the Truck parked strategically in front of the entrance. It would spoil my photo of the view from my tent in the morning, but shelter was more important than keeping my Facebook readers up to date with the view.

***

So my physiological needs were catered for. I had shelter and access to running water and sanitation and didn't need to worry about camping next to someone's fly-tipping or used needles and prophylactics. Of course I don't know if there were such things at the unpleasant field entrance as I didn't look that closely, but I'm trying to paint a picture here and I feel I've made the image quite graphic enough.

***

Ironically, there seems to be a paradox here. Maslow talks about self-actualisation (or for our purposes the non-rational, spiritual aims of religion which we'll come to later) as the top of the pyramid. However, many people who camp or travel in the great outdoors, everything from mountaineering and fell walking to visiting a commercial campsite with a bloke attached to a pair of legs who kindly turns on the hot water (that's the bloke not the legs turning on the hot water), describe something akin to a spiritual uplift, some sense of personal satisfaction or fulfilment, that comes from nothing more than catering for shelter and sustenance. It seems that, for many people, simply meeting these basic needs within the natural environment (as natural as we are each able to reach) comes close to that spiritual experience and people are happy to contemplate their presence sitting on the grass with a wobbly gas stove and a cuppa-soup.

***

The only downside was that the farm had lots of birds: peacocks and peahens, chickens, ducks and geese and all sorts of big waddly birds, many of which were in the habit of squawking raucously at every opportunity. Of course an opportunity was often the previous squawk of another waddly bird which then gave the next opportunity for another waddly bird and so on until they all got bored of squawking, which they never seemed to do. Of course with the fowl comes fowl poo. There was rather a lot of it. Still, I had a good groundsheet to keep the base of the Khyam clean and I worked out where I had to walk so that I could be sure of a clear path during the inevitable night manoeuvres to the toilet block.

And it was thus that I settled in for a night of cooking my adapted microwave food, tweeting (but not squawking) and chatting on Facebook, writing up my day's experiences and drinking wine.

During the evening, amid the wine and the larking about on the Interweb, plus frequent loud squawks I heard a vehicle pull up in front of the barns just behind my tent. The engine switched off to the sound of dogs barking, five or six thousand of them it seemed. From then on the barking continued, not incessantly but intermittently for the rest of the evening. (The inside of a tent is a surreal place, cut off from the sight of the outside world but utterly exposed to the sounds which can lead to an odd experience of perception including time.) The dogs seemed to be barking at each other, and amongst the barking there was a low growling, not very loud but menacing all the same.

Lying in the Khyam, unable to see what was going on outside as the wind picked up, with the occasional sound of something just beyond the flimsy wall of fabric, the squawking, barking and growling continued into the night, and I didn't sleep until the early hours. It was more disturbing than particularly serious, but the sound of the Beast of Rutland was with me for some time.

Day 9 - Rutland to Lincolnshire

Thursday May 9th

Miles on Truck: 513

Maslow's second level is safety. Although the sounds of growling animals apparently just outside my tent were obviously not going to manifest into a ravenous werewolf shredding the Khyam and devouring me, the feelings the situation evoked were sufficient to raise my anxiety levels. When Maslow talks about safety he's really talking about safety from harm, physical harm, such as war, natural disaster or violence, but he also talks about economic safety and issues such as protection from risk. Anxiety wasn't helping me here and if I was ever going to get to the bottom of the rational/non-rational debate I'd need to not be worrying about teeth and claws, no matter how imaginary.

* * *

After a night with the Beast of Rutland, I tried to have a lie-in but by 8:30 the peacock, calling right outside, had other ideas. The wind was up, my milk had gone off because I'd forgotten to buy UHT, and I just wanted to get out of Rutland. I packed up as quickly as I could, paid my bill, made my excuses and left. Strangely, as I spoke to the farmer in the morning I mentioned the sound of the growling and jokingly made reference to the Beast of Rutland but he didn't bat an eyelid; almost as though there might actually be such a thing and he was prepared to entertain the possibility that it was in his barn. The other striking thing was that, during the conversation about the barking and the general noisiness, he didn't seem to be at all bothered that it may have disturbed me and remarked that it was merely a case of the dogs sorting it out amongst themselves. I didn't leave a tip.

Heading into Lincolnshire I made my way to Sleaford, a pleasant small market town, in the hope of finding a supermarket that might have a coffee shop with Wi-Fi. The town had a nice quiet feel with plenty of evidence of apparently local stone (whatever that is if they can dig it out of the surrounding flat landscape), a nice jumble of period buildings jostling for space in the narrow streets of the town centre. I found a supermarket and obtained my milk and other provisions but alas no coffee shop, so no Wi-Fi. By now it was lunchtime, and despite the sunshine the radio was predicting strong winds and heavy rain. So far Lincolnshire had proved to be flat, at least as flat as I'd seen in East Anglia, so my priority was to find a campsite that might give me a bit of cover. A week into the journey I had finally managed to understand the icons in the campsite book, so I understood the mysteries of the sheltered campsite icon. Taking Maslow's advice, first and foremost I needed to be warm and dry; local attractions would come a bit further up the pyramid.

The one feature I could spot was a line of low hills that turned out to be the Lincolnshire Wolds. Nestled on the leeward side of the hills, to the northeast, was a spot on the map called Louth. I'd never heard of Louth but with such a splendid, romantic, nay picturesque name how could I resist it? I dreamt of chocolate box-images of the English countryside, pastoral scenes, timeless agrarian ideals, perfect for camping heaven. That would be Louth, surely it would be if there was any justice in the world. Checking the Giant Book of Campsites list, I identified a site listed as being in Louth that also featured the sheltered icon.

Phoning ahead, a very nice lady said they could find me a sheltered spot with all my needs satisfied. With the bottom of Maslow's pyramid resolved, the rest of the day was my own and I could concentrate of the upper levels of the pyramid, express my creativity; just so long as I could find a coffee shop with suitably convenient parking.

At about mid-afternoon I found myself descending from the Lincolnshire Wolds, a line of undulating hills that rise out of the landscape featuring rolling fields, wooded spots, nice old hedgerows and occasional cottages and farms. The Wolds are, actually, truly beautiful and I had high hopes that the farm I'd booked into would be nestling into these hills as, surely, no other location on the Lincolnshire plain could qualify for sheltered site status.

The descent from the hills was steep and dramatic; before me lay the flat plain of Lincolnshire stretching into the distance. Passing onto the level, the Truck trundled across the featureless landscape uninterrupted by hill or hedgerow. If the fens of Cambridgeshire and Norfolk had been guilty of grubbing up the hedgerows, then this was a featureless wasteland of monoculture up to the roadside with barely a pimple to break it up. Granted, Lincolnshire is not completely without hedges but the impression of the place is of an endless flat plain stretching into the infinity of boredom. Of course the landscape can't be blamed for its existence, and neither can the people be blamed for the landscape in which they live, but I find it hard to believe that Lincolnshire has always looked as featureless as this, and the pressure to squeeze the maximum possible out of the land must surely play a part.

Trusting Kathy, I was guided across the landscape (you could never travel through a landscape so flat and featureless as you just seemed to be that little bit above it no matter what), over straight main roads and junctions and eventually into a farm entrance.

Now bear in mind that I chose this site because it had the icon for sheltered site in the Huge Book of Campsites. The campsite was listed as being in Louth and Louth was shown right next to the line of hills, therefore I'd hoped for a bit of cover. Of course campsites are often away from the towns they attach to but this was almost half way to Grimsby. So imagine my surprise when I trundled onto the farm in the middle of this prairie with nothing for miles around; nothing, not a sausage… not a chipolata, a bratwurst, or a chorizo, not even a coarse-cut Lincolnshire pork and sage sausage complete with its characteristic open chunky texture. If there had been anything chunky to hide behind I would have been delighted but honestly, you could measure the ground with a spirit level to the horizon. Sheltered?

Announcing my arrival I paid my fee to be directed to a space the other side of a large metal barn of the big shed variety. Clearly this farm was on the scale of the modern agribusiness. The sheltered spot, as advertised, consisted of a couple of rows of trees that may have been there for some time but hardly constituted shelter. (I learned over the following weeks that hedges are a much better wind break but farmers in these regions seem to dislike hedges.) I suppose, in Lincolnshire terms, there isn't much shelter to speak of but if that's the case don't claim to provide shelter if you live in Lincolnshire. Norfolk was flat but even my cliff-top spot overlooking the North Sea offered more in terms of shelter had I chosen to camp nearer the hedge.

Feeling a bit conned, I made polite noises to the farmer and decided to head off to nearby Louth to find food, wine and a Wi-Fi connection. There was sod all mobile signal at the farm, so much for the telephone company claiming better coverage than the competition. Okay, so ten percent coverage of remote locations is better than five the percent coverage that they might compare themselves to, but in my experience, and I now feel qualified to say, Vodaphone's coverage is piss-poor a few miles away from any town.

I decided not to pitch my tent before I went scouting, concerned that it might blow away if I left it unattended. Feeling generally dissatisfied with the campsite, more dissatisfied with Lincolnshire, and still more dissatisfied with the weather (possibly because of the general state of Lincolnshire), I thought I might stumble across a brown sign for another campsite. It was still early and paying twice in one night would be a small price to pay for a comfortable relaxed evening with the foundations of my humanistic needs catered for; I wasn't feeling that where I was currently located.

* * *

Driving off to Louth, hoping never to return to the windy, unsheltered, farm, I looked for brown signs along the way but found none. Louth does indeed nestle on the edge of the Wolds but by the time I parked in the town the rain had decidedly set in, and no amount of shelter from the hills was going to make any difference. I drifted through the streets with my head down and my hood up, looking for a supermarket café, but found nothing. The whole place had an air of depression that was probably more to do with the weather than anything else. However the town sported a good few pubs and I soon found my way into the wonderfully inappropriately named Turk's Head where I found good coffee and a good Wi-Fi signal in their conservatory restaurant. The pub must have once been a maze of buildings that had grown organically into its space, as the corridors to the toilets were all twisty and narrow with strange angles, to the point that you had to reverse a considerable distance if you encountered anyone coming the other way. I imagined that, from above, the pub occupies every square inch of floor-space between its neighbours and must display a very interesting collection of roof patterns, with intersecting angles and strange arrangements of gutters only visible to pigeons which, undoubtedly, don't appreciate such architectural curiosities.

After a coffee, I paid my bill and headed back to the Truck with my head and hood further down than before. The day had not been going well, the weather wasn't going to improve, I'd not found an alternative campsite and I wasn't looking forward to cooking inadequate food in my tent in a howling gale. I did have the thought that I might find a pizza parlour or some such. The Turk's Head wasn't able to provide food on a wet Thursday afternoon and I'd not seen anything suitable as I wandered around the town.

Walking along the pavement, looking at the pavement… looking at nothing but the pavement, I spotted a metal strip running from the adjacent building to the curb. The metal strip, apparently polished by frequent foot-fall, was engraved with the following phrase, 'magnetism - the line that runs from pole to pole beneath our feet'. Lifting my hood I looked around and on the wall I found a plaque bearing the words, 'This plaque was unveiled by the mayor of Louth to commemorate the centenary of the Greenwich Meridian on the 26th June 1984. Coun. A.S. Ward, Town Mayor. L. Riddick Esq. Town Clerk.'

Delighted by the discovery, I decided that Louth wasn't such a bad place after all and resolved that, in its honour, I would hereafter refer to the line that delineates east from west as the Louth Meridian for, clearly, this was the reason fate had brought me here. Had it not been raining so horribly I would not have been looking down and would never have made the discovery, so it was obviously all part of the grand plan and serendipity had done its job!

Finding a supermarket, I bought a bottle of wine for the evening, thinking if nothing else I could get quietly pissed as I listened to the wind and rain. Then I had a brainwave.

Kathy has a point of interest feature that includes airports, railway stations, law courts, restaurants, and the like. (At least I could find a courthouse and sue the farmer for misrepresenting his campsite.) She indicated a pizza restaurant somewhere out of town in the direction of the windy farm. The location looked remote but country pubs often are so, trusting her, I set off in the driving rain and ever more gloomy skies. It was late afternoon in early May but it looked like it was already beginning to get dark.

She led me back into the Wolds, up and down roads unfamiliar to me, along main roads, down country lanes, past a massive track-laying tractor bigger than a bulldozer that threatened to squash me, and eventually down a quiet little lane in the middle of nowhere. Keeping the faith that we now trust in SatNav, whereas we used to trust in God, I followed Kathy's directions faithfully on, only for the deceitful Irish bitch to declare that I had reached my destination! She left me on a muddy grass verge at the bottom of a slope with hedges and bushes either side. Clearly there had never been a pizza restaurant at this location. Clearly there had never been anything at this location. Clearly she was having a laugh. Of course, being new to this whole smart phone apps thing, it didn't occur to me that I could have asked my tablet to find me a restaurant in Louth (I have no idea what my tablet is called but by the end of the trip it was probably You Bastard!) but by this time I was probably not thinking straight. Needs for shelter, food and safety were looking doubtful and I definitely wasn't feeling loved. Camping food it would be again.

Arriving back at the unsheltered farm I pulled back behind the barn to discover a new arrival. A massive camper van had reversed into the spot backing onto the barn just where I was going to camp. Then it struck me that this massive vehicle would make the perfect wind break and if I put the Truck a tent's length away I could pitch between the two vehicles and the farm might thus turn out to be the sheltered spot it was promoted to be.

Setting the Truck parallel to the camper, on the windward side away from the front door so as not to impose, I started to lay out my groundsheet only to be interrupted by one of the occupants. He suggested that I might want to park on the leeward side and reverse into a position to form an L shape between the two vehicles, the camper offering the greatest shelter from the howling gale. Not wanting to be a nuisance I said that I didn't want to block their entrance, but he replied that they wouldn't be coming out anyway and persuaded me that it would be okay.

With the combination of the camper on one side, the Truck and the barn on the other side, with the tent in the lee of the whole arrangement, the windy Lincolnshire farm turned out to be the sheltered spot that I had hoped it would be. I had indeed spent the whole day getting from one campsite to another but, in the process, serendipity had shown me the Louth Meridian and facilitated my humanistic needs of shelter and warmth, and now I was feeling a tiny little bit of love.

Day 10 - Lincolnshire to Yorkshire

Friday May 10th

Miles on Truck: 629

The night of May 9th was windy, but not as bad as it might have been had it not been for my neighbours in their massive camper. Did I mention that they had a massive camper? It really was massive. Worrying that they might remove my windbreak before I was ready to leave, and knowing that the one place in Yorkshire I particularly wanted to visit was Whitby, which was a long way off, I decided to get as early a start as possible. By 10:00 I was on the road and I travelled a network of country roads and smaller lanes towards the Humber Bridge.

Leaving at 10:00 doesn't really sound very early but from the first day I'd decided to wake up naturally, not using an alarm clock, and I always seemed to wake at around 8:00. It always took an hour to get the door open, make a couple of doorstep cheese rolls and a coffee for breakfast, and take a photo of the view from my tent. Facebook and Twitter had to be updated on the view, and I posted a tweet of my destination. 'Today I will mostly be in Yorkshire.' (All credit to Jesse from the Fast Show.) By the time I'd done all this and used whatever facilities were available on the campsite (some days there were more than others so you had to take your facilities where you could get them) it was invariably gone 9:00 and I'd be ready to pack up camp. So having the Truck loaded and Kathy ready to guide me by 10:00 was not unusual.

The day was still blowy, but not like the previous day and even in the wind it wasn't cold. The roads were dry so it was a pleasant drive through small villages and hamlets, and the flat Lincolnshire plain gave way to a more pleasant rolling landscape as I approached the Humber Estuary.

I had never before crossed the Humber Bridge which, when it was built during my teens, had been a major British engineering achievement. At the time it was the largest single-span suspension bridge in the world and I remember there were all sorts of astonishing facts about it, such as the two towers are so far apart that they point in different directions due to the curvature of the earth, or that if you stacked a hundred double decker buses on twenty football pitches they would be the size of Wales… or something.

Suddenly I arrived at the Humber Bridge somewhat unexpectedly. For some reason, total lack of education perhaps, I expected to pass through Grimsby on the south side of the bridge but it seems Grimsby is some 15 miles away and not even on the estuary. I'd always thought Hull and Grimsby, being the two fishing ports, faced each other across the Humber Estuary, still you can grow up believing total nonsense such as this, or that HP Lovecraft said you needed silver stone to make an Elder Sign. Kathy led me to a massive roundabout and directly onto the road that took me to the bridge. This was a bit disappointing as I had hoped to get some pictures of the bridge as I passed but there was simply nowhere to stop. So at bang on 11:00, an hour after I'd left the campsite in Lincolnshire, I crossed the Humber into Yorkshire.

Crossing the Humber Bridge, a question struck me. Why isn't the bridge named something more interesting or romantic like the Golden Gate Bridge? Obviously we couldn't call it the Golden Gate Bridge because that name's already taken, and the Humber Bridge isn't gold, but then again neither is the Golden Gate Bridge but that's because it's named after the Golden Gate strait which many people outside of America (including me) might not have known. Surely we could have come up with something like the Silver Span Bridge or something that reflects the blue ribbon of the river, except that the river seemed sort of brown the day I crossed, which would mean calling it the Brown River Span or something. So perhaps we are better off calling it the Humber Bridge after all.

Interestingly I've since heard a story of a child looking down at the water and asking, 'Mummy, is that chocolate-flavoured water?' apparently reminiscent of the river of chocolate in Charlie and the Chocolate Factory. This tells me two things: that the river wasn't only brown on the day I saw it, and that we could rename the Humber Bridge the Chocolate Crossing.

So from here on it's the Louth Meridian and the Chocolate Crossing; don't forget that, I'll be running a test later!

On the north side I discovered some clever clogs had the idea to build a sizable car park with views of the bridge and I spent a reasonably happy hour taking photos and exploring the area in a way that would not have been allowed at all had I not been travelling alone, but that is probably the point of travelling.

After exploring the bridge and its environs, my anxiety for moving on, finding more to explore and finding somewhere to sleep, got the better of me and I set off for Whitby. Yorkshire is a big county and almost all of it was ahead of me. I found myself wondering what they call this bit of the county this week as they seem to be constantly changing the name. However, in terms of the Historic Counties of England we'll just think of it as Yorkshire, and I imagine a great many cricket fans will be happy with that.

I drove north out of Hull, which isn't really Hull as Hull is the name of a local river and the city that we all think of as Hull is actually Kingston upon Hull, but I drove out of it anyway and on into Beverley. I found myself travelling across more flat landscapes very similar to Lincolnshire which isn't really surprising as North Lincolnshire and East Yorkshire north of the Humber Estuary both makeup the floodplain of the Humber. However, there was a significant difference between the north and south sides of the estuary.

On the north side they don't seem to have dug up the hedgerows as they have in many parts of Lincolnshire and further south into the fens. I don't know if this is a result of local government decisions but I do know, had I to decide which I would prefer to live in, which would make the nicer home. It was still possible to see to the horizon across a billiard table landscape. However, instead of an uninterrupted vista of endless fields, featureless across an expanse of nothingness, the Yorkshire landscape was one of fields dotted with hedges and trees which sometimes blocked the view and sometimes afforded a glimpse across the next field and perhaps the next. The effect was to tempt the eye towards the horizon, though not offering that horizon too willingly. As a result, that horizon was a joy to behold instead of being a misery akin to the boredom of limbo. People need stimulation and Yorkshire offered it whereas Lincolnshire didn't and all I had done was cross a bridge. If the two horizons were women, then Yorkshire would have been a seductress, tempting and teasing, hiding features to be glimpsed behind trees and hedgerows, whereas the Lincolnshire horizon would have been a cheap whore saying here it is, have it if you care because I really don't.

Don't get me wrong, not all of Lincolnshire was like this but it seemed that large swathes of the county had fallen to industrialised agribusiness, as had bits of Cambridgeshire and some of Norfolk. Parts of Lincolnshire were not bad, the Wolds were even beautiful but other parts of the county really looked as though it had been plundered and despoiled. On the other hand (or, to be literal, on the other bank), the Yorkshire landscape north of the Humber showed that this really needn't have been the case.

For a few more miles I passed across the pretty, flat landscape of the North Humber floodplain or would that be the Humber North floodplain? Well, whatever it was I passed across it and ten or fifteen miles further I started to climb. To begin with the landscape turned into rolling hills, similar to much of the English landscape that is neither flat nor particularly lumpy. However, after a brief trip into Scarborough for diesel and a coffee, where I'd have liked to stop but I simply didn't have time, I pushed on north. Clearly I could have stopped for a week in any of these locations and I was beginning to see the attraction of caravanning holidays, though as a Top Gear viewer I understand how that is a heresy, but the idea of having a mobile base does rather open up possibilities. But I was doing this at a day per county, and it was going to take six weeks as it was, so I simply couldn't sample the joys of Scarborough, Flamborough Head or Robin Hood's Bay as that would have meant me spending the whole six weeks in Yorkshire, but perhaps one of you will have to write that book yourself.

Now it was really beginning to look like Yorkshire. Kathy took me up into hills with dry stone walls and vistas across fields of pasture with grazing animals and away from the ubiquitous cereal crops and oilseed rape of the lowlands. Before long the pasture gave way to moorland with rolling hills and high plateaus of what I assumed were gorse and heather, though to be honest I'd not know either of those if they were to walk up to me and offer me money. But it looked like the sort of Yorkshire Moors that you see in pictures because that's exactly where I was.

Clearly Yorkshire has never been invaded as the roads are so delightfully wiggly that the Romans would have been driven to distraction. If the Romans ever conquered Scarborough and then decided to march on Whitby they either did it without the benefit of civil engineering or the engineers were so pissed on Yorkshire ale that they were ashamed to admit to the roads and left in disgrace. These days you'd think that Yorkshire could never be invaded, at least not by anyone towing a caravan.

After wiggling with the traffic along the wonderfully twisty moorland roads, and failing to find any good places to stop to take photos, I arrived in Whitby late in the afternoon. This was a bit of a pilgrimage for me as good friends, Graham and his wife, spent some years in Whitby around the turn of the eighties. I'd heard a lot about the town and seen it in pictures but seeing it in the flesh I can understand the attraction.

Heading straight for Whitby Abbey I sat in the car park and phoned Graham in Blackpool to ask his advice on visiting the town. Making a loose arrangement to pop into Blackpool in a week or so, I got off the phone and started my exploration. I'd understood that the abbey was open to the public free of charge, however, it turned out that it's an English Heritage site so it now costs six quid to get in.

I sort of didn't mind the charge as English Heritage seem to make a good job of presenting such places with sympathetic enclosures that don't impact on the eye, providing clean toilets (always a recommendation as you get older), but I do worry that everything of value in our culture costs money to visit. As I left there was a bloke poking his head over the wall presumably because he was either too poor, too tight or just too late in the day to make it worth paying the entry fee. (I'd had the same experience at the English Heritage Anglo Saxon village at West Stow.) In the end I was in the abbey for about an hour having seen just about all there was to see, which worked out at about ten pence a minute.

It strikes me that there's something wrong if we package all of our national treasures so that the casual observer cannot have their interest piqued by a ruin or a monument. Then we complain that people have no attention span and are only interested in gassy beer, X Factor and newspapers that offer only gossip and vindictiveness. Give people a diet of gruel and charge them too much for flavour and they won't bother with it; as a result we end up living amongst barbarians. There was a time when these sites were open to the public, no fences, no boundaries, no toilets; so not everything about the past was good, such as diphtheria and infant mortality. Granted the care of these sites has to be funded but we are stopping people finding ways of stumbling across them when they are ready. How about we really make it English Heritage and give every English person a free ticket once per year to a single site? (Do the same for Scotland and Wales etc., because I can hear people splitting hairs as I write this.) Do it on their birthday for all I care, just give the English (or the British or whatever) access to 'England's Story' as they describe it in the guide book.

I say the guide book because the nice woman at the kiosk sold me a membership that I could use on the rest of my trip, but at the time I felt as though I'd gone over to the dark side, joining the ranks of those that can afford to visit these attractions. If, by the end of this book, I've become an English Heritage enthusiast, please shoot me.

After Whitby Abbey, which was beautifully preserved and presented, and splendidly bleak, I dropped down into Whitby proper which was a delight, all picturesque and lovely with intersections of angled rooftops ever smaller into the distance. The houses are perched on a steep-sided bay with streets in terraces up the valley sides. Wandering around the harbour I found one of those giant graphical cartoon maps with a huge seagull sitting atop. The seagull, alarmed at my purposeful approach, took flight and I was able to find the places I'd been and also identify Cliff Street where my old mate Graham had lived thirty or more years before. With nothing better to do until my parking voucher expired, having seen as many seagulls, fishing boats and lobster pots as I could manage, I decided to explore that side of the town. Looking for Cliff Street, then, seemed as good a reason as any to explore the interesting twisty back streets. This sort of sounds a bit pointless when you think of it as just a house, but some thirty years ago, when I was a more impressionable youth, Graham had told me that his was the very house where Bram Stoker wrote Dracula.

Asking directions, I wandered up a narrow passageway to where I guessed Cliff Street ought to be and found myself in an alley, not really a street at all. The street (or alley) was suddenly confirmed as a street as a car came along, forcing me to duck into a doorway to let it by. Walking to the end I found number 55 which I thought Graham had mentioned, so this might have been his house, the very house where Bram Stoker wrote Dracula. Somehow I'd not imagined it this way, though that is never the case with other people's descriptions. For a start the front of the house faces onto the narrow street and away from the sea whereas the back of the house looks out across the cliff-top. (For a while I thought the houses were the other way around and imagined I was looking at the back doors rather than the front.) I suppose that just goes to show how homogenised modern houses are. Later Graham retold the story differently and said that his house was next to the house where Bram Stoker stayed. Sure enough, next door to number 55 was a larger house, all turrets and spires, gothic revival in style, so one might imagine that Bram Stoker had lived there. The location would certainly have provided great inspiration for his story about a Carpathian castle with turrets and circular rooms where doors locked mysteriously and vampires crawled out of windows in the night.

Graham has always been a bit of a trickster, and claiming that he lived in Bram Stoker's old house is just the sort of thing he would be likely to make up, especially for the entertainment of a callow youth as I was in the early eighties. So I went looking for a house that looked like Bram Stoker's inspiration, saw some turrets and assumed I'd found it. Significant experiences often happen to us in that way and that doesn't necessarily mean we've discovered the truth. However, a search of the web suggests that Bram Stoker lived in a house on Royal Crescent, a much grander location similar to other Georgian Royal Crescents in British towns such as Bath's famous Royal Crescent. Whitby's Royal Crescent though, is lacking a house with inspirational features such as the one I spotted at the top of Cliff Street.

The mystery deepens further when you consider that the house that I'd spotted, with all the turrets, is on a road called Khyber Pass (worthy of note for its own sake and one imagines that Sid James once lived there), but Khyber Pass adjoins a short stretch of road called East Crescent in front of the turreted house. Khyber Pass and East Crescent encircle a green so they are really one road. Furthermore the house with the turrets looks out across the bay, affording a view not only across the entrance of the harbour and all its goings on, but also directly towards the skeletal remains of Whitby Abbey on the opposite cliff top. Directly beneath the view of the abbey is a small beach known as Tate Hill Sands where Bram Stoker refers to Dracula's ship, Demeter, coming ashore, '…into the southeast corner of the pier jutting under East Cliff, known locally as Tate Hill Pier.' Stoker could have gazed from one of those turrets down to Tate Hill Pier and described the location in some detail without ever stepping outside.

The view from Royal Crescent, however, affords no such inspiration and merely looks out onto the bleak North Sea, some lawns and gardens. Even furthermore, Bram Stoker amended the address he lists in the book to Number 7, The Crescent, Whitby so East Crescent or Royal Crescent could fit.

The third option is Number 7 East Crescent, a respectable-looking guest house that makes no such claims that I'm aware of, yet looks out at the turreted house *and* to the abbey ruins beyond. Did Stoker sit in this unassuming house inspired by the combination of the gothic revival house and dream of turreted Carpathian castles, concocting a way to combine all of the features in this view?

With no reference to Royal Crescent in the book, I find myself wondering, with all this evidence of views and locations, where references to Royal Crescent ever came from.

Despite all this crescent confusion, Royal Crescent is the location of a holiday apartment that modern-day fans of the gothic novel can rent, complete with period furniture, a nice oxblood Chesterfield sofa, writing desk and telescope. The address of the holiday apartment is not even Number 7, though it looks very nice and I'd fancy a weekend there. Clearly everyone is trying to get in on the act, Graham included.

* * *

Parking expiry anxiety soon kicked in and I headed back down to the harbour. Armed with more wine, bread and cheese, but mostly wine, I set off for the campsite I'd phoned earlier. The lady of the house, or should I say the farm, showed me to a miserable, scruffy spot perched at the top of a grassy bank where my options for a view were either a hedge in one direction or what appeared to be piles of rubble in the other. (The rubble might have been chalk or lime for spreading on fields but whatever it was, it was in big rubbly piles.) The hedge appeared to be deliberately placed to block any view of the landscape as it sloped off towards Whitby in the distance with the abbey just visible if you squinted really hard; beyond that was the sea. All the good views were at the bottom of the bank. What's worse the top of the bank was much more exposed (for the wind from the night before had not completely died away), much less idyllic.

'Do I have to look at that?' I asked of the farmer's wife as I indicated the rubble (or chalk or lime or whatever it was).

'It's a working farm, this is what we have,' she responded matter-of-factly with a sort of like it or lump it manner.

Pretty much every farm I'd visited had been a working farm, some might be houses sold off with a bit of land but the clues of barns and bits of rusty farm machinery usually gave away which were the real farms.

'What about down there?' I gestured to the massive field at the bottom of the bank away from all the rubble or chalk or whatever it was.

'That field has been hired by a group of caravaners,' she countered. 'They've rented it for their own use.'

The field looked like quite a few acres, even to my untrained eye, not really knowing how big an acre was. Half a dozen caravans were clustered at the very top of the field next to the bank. A good seventy percent of the field was unused. With little option of anywhere else to go, having already paid, I accepted her response and silently vowed never to return. It does strike me that you might want to make a bit of effort for your customers. Granted, space might be an issue and proximity to the electric point might have meant that this was all that was available but I sort of felt they'd shoehorned these extra pitches in without much thought to the experience of the visitor. It would be interesting for a few farmers to visit some competitor's campsites just so they can see what other farms are doing, because many provided an excellent experience.

As I started to work out which way to face my tent it was still gusting enough to make me want a bit more shelter and I eyed the field below the bank with envy. There were acres of space with a dozen or so caravans at the bottom of the bank nearby the electric points. Then I did a brave thing.

There was a nice spot below the bank, in the corner a few yards away from the caravans with a car between the space and the caravan. There was easily enough space for the Truck and my tiny tent on the end of the row. With cover from the bank, the caravans and the vehicles, I'd be quite sheltered so I strolled down and preparing my best polite voice I knocked on the door of the first caravan.

A couple opened the door with a smile, him tall and grey, her small and grey, probably retired, as many caravaners are. I craned my neck to look up at them in their elevated position inside the caravan.

'Hello, sorry to bother you. I've just arrived to camp and I've been placed at the top of the bank.' I motioned towards the slope behind the caravans. 'It's a bit windy up there and the only view I'm going to get is of the big piles of white rubble.' The couple listened politely; I began to think this was going better than the previous time I'd spoken to caravaners in Rutland. 'I asked if I could camp down here out of the wind, where I wouldn't have to look at the rubble all evening, but she told me that I couldn't because you've hired the whole field.' They continued to listen politely and even smiled in a refreshingly non-smug way, despite looking down at me, as I continued thinking this really was going well. 'I did wonder if she plonked me up there as it's got access to the electrics but, to be honest, I could live without electrics if I could camp down here,' I paused, 'if you don't mind?' I included my best little boy lost look, now helped by my lower position. 'I'd not be in the way and won't spoil your view.' I probably came across as a slightly pathetic lonely solo camper.

'We wouldn't mind at all but you should probably ask our club secretary,' replied the couple. 'Just knock at the next caravan along.'

I sort of wondered, if they were a club why weren't they all in each other's caravans getting drunk and sharing stories of *great caravanning adventures I have known*, as people with a special interest are apt to do when they get together, trying to top the last story with, *'I remember the time when...'* but perhaps it wasn't that sort of club.

So off I went to the next caravan and knocked on the door and explained about the top of the bank and the horrible rubble and the hedge and the proximity to the electrics all over again, and the man gave me an equally warm reception and I wondered what all the fuss was about with the farmer ('s wife). He said I should just go ahead and have a great time with my tent in the corner of their field sheltered by the bank and the vehicles and such like.

So a few minutes later I'd driven the Truck down the steep slope, feeling as though I was going off road for the first time on the trip, although you could probably have made the descent in a shopping trolley with little fuss.

Soon I was setting up, arranging my bedding and setting up my cooking facilities.

'Hello.' Looking outside there was the petite retired lady from the first caravan. 'Would you like a cup of tea?'

'Oh that would be fantastic,' I responded, feeling that this was all going rather better than I'd expected.

'Sugar?'

'No, just white would be perfect.' I replied, somewhat taken aback by the gesture.

'Are you touring?'

'Yes, I've been going since the first of May. I'm touring every county in England.'

'Oh, that sounds very interesting. So you are doing the whole country?'

'I'm doing the Historic Counties so that includes places that don't exist anymore such as Rutland and Westmorland. I didn't want to do the modern counties because I didn't want to end up camping in big cities such as Greater Manchester.'

'And how long is that going to take?'

'Well I'm doing one county a day so 39 days; about six weeks.'

'Then you'll have to keep moving,' she observed. 'You must spend all your time on the road and not have time so see anywhere.'

'Yes it is a bit like that,' I responded rather ruefully. 'The trouble is it would take three months if I spent a day in each county with a separate day for travelling.'

'And you're doing it on your own?'

I thought about my response. I'd been told that it's best not to say I was writing a book because it can affect how people react. Some will be interested and others will just plain not believe you.

'Yes, it's just easier to do something like this alone, besides I didn't know anyone else who could find six weeks in a single stretch.'

'Well good luck. So white, no sugar?' she turned away, I suspected happy to get away from the slightly weird bloke with the tent.

It had occurred to me that the whole one county a day thing was really a bit like a MacGuffin, like the device in films around which a story revolves. The Maltese Falcon needn't have been exactly that, it could have been a million dollar note, or a briefcase containing some unexplained valuable. The point is that it's a device to provoke situations such as the kindness of cups of tea, or unexpected smugness such as 'you can't camp here, you're not a member of our club' or sitting next to Forest Gump. On a trip like this, the MacGuffin needn't have been one county a day, it could have been riding a bicycle or travelling around with a fridge. Effectively the trip itself is the MacGuffin, but the county a day just adds a level of difficulty that puts you in unexpected situations. These experiences, both good and bad, are what make life meaningful, they are the stories we tell in the pub or across the table at Christmas and they go to make an interesting tale.

I continued to set up for the next few minutes and my benefactor reappeared.

'Here you are. We thought you'd like these too.' She handed me a mug of tea and not one but two Kit Kats.

'Oh really, that's wonderful but you really shouldn't have.' I replied, feeling rather inadequate.

'Nonsense, we're happy to help.'

'Well it's wonderful of you, thank you.'

'My husband asked about your electrical hook-up.'

'Oh yes?'

'He was wondering if you had the normal caravan type cable.'

'Yes,' I replied, 'the one with the three round pins.'

'Oh well we have an extension cable that might enable you to reach the socket.'

'That would be fantastic.' I was overwhelmed by this extension of kindness and generosity, feeling utterly inadequate.

'Just pop in when you are ready and see if it will reach.'

She waved goodbye and left me to my own devices.

After drinking the tea, I returned the mug and collected the extension cable which stretched from my tent to the socket with plenty to spare.

***

Interactions with people, strangers or otherwise, are important. Maslow's next level of need is emotional fulfilment. In his scale he talks about love and belonging. You can't really make space for that in your life unless you have food and shelter sorted and safety from danger or anxiety for such risks. These relationship bonds might come in the form of a marriage partner, familial relationships, close friends or even bonds to communities such as special interest groups, teams or shared hobbies. It may not feel the same to have a bunch of mates down the model railway club as it does to have a deep relationship with a life partner but, ultimately, those connections with other, shared interests and plans, offer an acceptance that is a basic human need.

***

With a growing sense of belonging amid my fellow campers, I spent the evening in the tent, drinking the wine I'd bought in the Whitby supermarket, eating Kit Kats, playing on Facebook and wondering just how sociable strangers are on campsites. I guessed that people are quite friendly and are happy to offer assistance if you ask, but there's a personal space boundary at their door so, while I might have fantasised about sharing the bottle of rum I'd got in the Truck with some new friends, in the massive camper in Lincolnshire, or the people partying at Karma Farm, that was never going to happen. However, it probably does show that the expectations of the farmer ('s wife) who said I had to camp next to the rubble (or chalk or lime or whatever it was) were not as she might have expected. People are often more generous than we might imagine.

Had a random Kit Kat and a loan of an extension lead made me feel a part of their community and given me the sense of belonging that Maslow described?

Day 11 - Yorkshire to County Durham

Saturday May 11th

Miles on Truck: 742

After a peaceful night with the wind dropping to nothing as I eked out the Kit Kat supplies, it picked up to blow again just in time for breakfast. After an almost lukewarm shower, for 40 pence but including a handy bench to put my clothes on, I packed up and left. Taking great care to coil up the extension lead tidily, such that in the unlikely event that I met the same people again they wouldn't mind lending it a second time (more likely for the benefit of some other traveller), I handed it back and we had a chat about my destination. They seemed interested that I was heading for Durham and wished me well.

County Durham is one of the more interesting of the Historic Counties of England. (Have you noticed how this book is chock-full of historical detail of the counties of England?) A somewhat complicated series of historical circumstances meant that the county of Durham didn't accept the Sheriff of Northumberland and, by the 14th Century, it had effectively become a state within a state. In effect the county seems to have been accepted by the English Crown as a private shire under the authority of the Bishop of Durham known as the County Palatine of Durham. So I set off to see if I could find out more.

Driving north from Whitby I found myself on the coast road as I was reflecting on the conversation from the night before, on the whole county a day thing. It was becoming an issue that I wasn't getting time to explore at least something in each county and I was wishing I'd planned the trip some other way, perhaps taken longer or done it in smaller chunks so to be able to linger, stop to take pictures, explore as the fancy took me. However the logistics of life, work, being away from home, meant that I couldn't have done that. To do two days in each county, one travelling one exploring, would mean a three-month trip and that was impossible. Of course the original lottery win scenario would be different but would that make a good story? On the other hand, I had been struck by the contrast in the places I was visiting, the places I camped, some good, some bad, some apparently bad but turning out good on reflection. The other thought that struck me was that a few days ago I'd been in Suffolk, I was heading to Durham and then on to Northumberland and in a few weeks I would be in Devon and Cornwall, seeing the south coast, all on the same trip. That seemed extraordinary, and the pace of it, apparently fast but still taking weeks to complete with only a vague idea of how and when things would unfold, was an important part of the experience.

At Sandsend, just outside Whitby, the coast pushed out into the North Sea creating a dramatic rugged headland with cliffs stretching out across the water. This was one of those social media photo-ops that I'd decided I should take advantage of more frequently. A number of other people on the beach seemed to have the same idea.

Crossing the road to get the best position with the beach stretching ahead, the tide halfway in (or out) and the craggy cliffs in the distance, I found myself a few steps away from an elderly couple also taking a picture; but they seemed to be taking a shot of a building site on the landward side of the road. Rather frivolously, and not thinking to read the situation at all, I spoke to them.

'Are you not more interested in the amazing view than the building site?' I asked.

'We love the view but our house is behind these new buildings. We've just lost our view.'

Suddenly I felt bad about asking them such a flippant question as they pointed out a row of houses on the street just beyond the coast road with the building site in between. 'Oh really, didn't you get some sort of planning permission appeal?'

'We appealed to Scarborough but they just ignored our protests.'

'Why, that's terrible,' I replied, feeling lost for words as I stood on the windswept strip between the road and the beach.

'Before they started building these houses there was a boatyard here.' They indicated the building site. 'The council said that it was a brownfield site so it was designated for housing.'

'Oh, that doesn't seem very fair,' I replied, trying to be sympathetic but wondering about the boatyard, imagining some grimy industrial eyesore. Feeling a bit disenchanted by their story, I made my excuses, took my photo, and returned to the Truck to continue towards Durham.

Later I checked Google Street View and sure enough there was a boat-yard on the piece of land between their houses and the beach. But it was more like a small green of tussocky grass with a single lonely boat on it. There seemed to be an old weather-bleached fence surrounding it and noth-ing more. When I first heard their story I sort of took it with a pinch of salt, thinking of old industrial dilapidation where boats were once built but now just a collection of broken windows and grimy brickwork. That's what I think of as a boat-yard, or perhaps a disused one. Surely they wouldn't give planning permission to build on an existing thriving business. But this isn't what Google showed (and continues to show as Google now includes his-torical photos on Street View). This boatyard was a greenfield site where you could probably have grazed a horse if your horse didn't mind getting wet and tasting salt with every mouthful of tussocky grass. It was certainly not what you would imagine a brownfield site to be. I'm guessing that by boatyard it meant it was a place where people stored their dinghies and the like, so not really industrial and really quite unbrown. It seemed to me that someone had been stretching definitions. A brief search on the net for the location re-vealed a story of planning applications, a rejection by the local parish council, decisions being overturned by the bureaucrats fifteen miles away, appeals, residents being led to believe that there was a process and that process not really turning out the way it was described when a man from the planning authority arrived to declare that the decision had been made. Anyway, Goog-le still shows the original site so perhaps Scarborough Borough Council will be judged on the photographic evidence whereas they were probably hoping that people wouldn't remember what was there before.

Of course, we have to employ people to make these decisions on our behalf, but when the local parish council is overruled by people who don't live in the area it seems that little bit unjust. While researching this I found artists' illustrations of the new flats and houses to be built on the old boat-yard, some three stories high, much larger than the houses behind. And they have the damned cheek to call the development 'The Boatyard' and label them cottages! I'm in no doubt that the developers don't live in the area and that the people who do couldn't afford to buy the properties themselves. What was once Sandsend Boatyard would have been a local feature, almost a heritage site. Perhaps it was underused but marinas are popping up for the benefit of the wealthy all around the coast so why nor retain this facility? There are certainly more marinas now than I can remember as a child. Building some luxury flats on another nearby site, perhaps with a special arrangement for new residents to have use of the boatyard, could have brought new money into the area, supported a local business, perhaps helped support the local economy and preserve the lives of the people who currently live there without destroying a feature that looks as though it goes back decades. I know it was only a bit of grass but is this a total lack of imagination or just people looking out for their friends in business?

Ahem!

* * *

Leaving Whitby and its planning travesties behind, with a somewhat sour taste in my mouth, Kathy directed me up a steep twisty hill and I soon found myself back on the North York Moors. The high winds and rain felt worse because of the exposed conditions but as I crossed the moors I was amazed to discover a reservoir complete with sailing boats and what must have been a sailing club. Even on this foul day people were out on the water, but I suppose that's just an illustration of the fact that what I thought of as bad weather would be great for the sailing fraternity. A good wind would have been a positive benefit and the rain would make little difference to a wet-suited outdoors type occasionally dipping into the lake water.

* * *

Suddenly I was descending a steep slope along doubled-back hairpins and dropped into Guisborough with my first sight of massed local stone. Whitby had been a mix of Victorian red brick, painted stucco and local stone. Guisborough, or at least what I saw of it seemed, to be much more predominately local stone (although no amount of research would seem to reveal what the local stones was), with that blackened grimy look that is so characteristic of towns in the North of England. No doubt Whitby Abbey would have been built from the same material but this was the first time that I noticed it all around me.

Being a Saturday (not that I had any idea of what day it was), I soon found myself stuck in traffic. Not understanding the local geography I really had no idea where I was. I didn't really know where Guisborough was and where, if anywhere, it was joined onto. Passing through an all too brief stretch of countryside I found myself in what seemed like a sizable town with lots of traffic but, having missed any road signs, I really was trusting in Kathy

to deliver me to my destination. All I really wanted to do was get to Durham City and find something to write about. Edging forward a few feet at a time I got a surprising view on the horizon ahead.

Just above the buildings, poking over the rooftops, I could see a bright blue steel structure. At first I thought it was one of those shipbuilding cranes or a dockyard crane such, is often visible from miles away, but then the penny dropped. Apparently Kathy had brought me to Middlesbrough and I was looking at the famous Transporter Bridge.

Anyone who has seen Billy Elliot or the 2002 series of Auf Wiedersehen Pet will recognise the Tees Transporter Bridge. The bridge has the appearance of two cranes, actually cantilevers, reaching across the water to each other, joined over the centre of the river. In the TV series the story had been that a dastardly business man (no doubt called Dick and one imagines also a property developer keen on building on old boatyards) wanted to dismantle the bridge and sell it in the Far East. The series showed the bridge being dismantled and eventually rebuilt in Arizona instead of the Far East. At the end of the series it was announced that the whole thing had been done with special effects and the bridge was actually still in Middlesbrough.

Sitting in the Truck in traffic, I wasn't really in a position to find out the truth of all this and it had been ten years since I'd seen the programme. These lovely old Heath Robinson type contraptions are from a bygone age and the fact that I could see it still standing on the horizon was a reward in itself. I resolved to try to get a closer look. Even if it was out of action, at least I could get into a position to take a decent photograph for my Faceboo and Instagram friends.

Having glimpsed the bridge over the rooftops, I tried to pick my w through the streets, ignoring Kathy and her intentions to get me to Durh as soon as possible. I thought if I could just find my way to the river o open space I'd get a good photo and move on to Durham. Kathy trie guide me towards a river crossing but I ignored her instructions and t away from the main road towards what looked like an industrial, rou the direction of the bridge. I did consider asking her to take me to the but I didn't know how I'd ask her simply because I didn't know wh bridge actually was. (I might have had better luck asking James Brc Shortly I found myself traveling through an industrial wasteland o down factories and warehouses, the bridge off to the right, across patch of land with access blocked by massive boulders, presumal

undesirables moving in. A bit further along I had to negotiate a double mattress abandoned in the middle of the road. Eventually I drove amongst factories, some abandoned, others occupied and just as I considered stopping for directions, having not seen the bridge for some time, suddenly there it was before me with an empty car park in front.

Despite its age, or perhaps because of it, the transporter bridge is impressive. The whole thing is over 800 feet in length and rises 160 feet above the river. Painted in vibrant blue, it looked in surprisingly good condition for a disused contraption. I strolled about taking pictures of the two crane-like jibs, each apparently balanced on steel legs crisscrossed with struts getting narrower toward the top. Wanting to get a good picture, I walked towards the thing, half expecting to be told to sod off. Disused industrial structures, no matter how curious, are often the sort of place you find officious security guards. So I took my photo, elated that I had got this close and that nobody had shooed me away.

Then a curious thing happened; three or four cars issued forth from somewhere. At first I didn't understand what I was seeing and I wondered where the cars had come from. Was there a closer car park or perhaps a factory next to it that had stopped for lunch?

I'd got the impression that the only reason the TV story had been written was because the bridge was no longer used and therefore could, quite conceivably, be taken down and sold. Then I had a sudden realisation of the blindingly obvious. Surely the bridge wasn't still operational? It's amazing how one preconceived idea can affect your whole perception of something.

Climbing back into the Truck I drove the hundred yards or so out of the car park and up to the queuing point. Sure enough there were all the signs of a working bridge: opening times, capacity, and even a tariff of £1.30 per car. I could cross on this historic bridge for £1.30? I would have happily paid twice that. After a few minutes, during which I had plenty of time to have a proper look, the operator appeared and waved me forward. I was the only vehicle queuing; I was going to have the bridge to myself.

Driving onto the gondola (painted yellow in contrast to the bridge itself presumably to be visible to river traffic) I chatted to the operator. He told me that the bridge was far from disused and was actively being invested in by Middlesbrough Council, who offer guided tours up onto the top of the bridge. The one thing I forgot to do was look up.

Clearly the future of the Tees Transporter Bridge is bright. There is a plan to build a lift to allow disabled visitors to go aloft. The website has a price for abseiling and suggests that bungee jumps can be arranged. The Tees Transporter had its centenary a few years ago and is currently the only operating example in Britain. It's a Grade II listed structure and has been awarded the Institution of Mechanical Engineers' Heritage Plaque for engineering excellence to recognise the efforts to keep the bridge operational. All this and this wonderfully mad piece of engineering was actually en-route to Durham!

Of course it's not mad at all, it's an elegant engineering solution to the problem of crossing a river without blocking the river to traffic. The crane structures are tall enough to allow any vessel to pass beneath, while the gondola rests in a bay one side or the other. When there is nothing on the river the gondola is free to carry people and vehicles across.

All too shortly I was on the other side and I felt I'd really not had a good look. I exited the other side of the bridge and was on my way. Unfortunately this was when I discovered the visitor centre was on the south side and I hadn't thought to stop in. Still, I was building up a list of places to visit again, Happisburg, Whitby, the Transporter Bridge and others. Any future fridge magnet opportunities would have to wait.

Oh, and, if you visit, don't forget to look up as I did.

Moving into the countryside again, I passed along winding country roads, past more majestic windmills as the sun came out, giving the world that shiny reflective appearance it always has when the sun emerges after a heavy shower.

Before long I was in Durham and all I needed to do was find a place to park, a place to explore the town. This was easier said than done and, after being shooed out of a park-and-ride where I was hoping to sit and look at my maps (the attendant was very nice about it but he shooed me all the same), eventually I opted for a campsite a few minutes out of town and headed out not really having seen much of Durham at all.

The campsite was almost empty with just a few tents and caravans dotted about on terraces sloping up the side of a valley; it was a bit windy though.

'Can I have a spot with a hook-up please?'

'What do you want to plug into it?' The campsite owner looked at me questioningly.

'My mains supply box,' I replied.

'Are you sure you've got the right connection?' He looked at me more questioningly.

This was getting irritating. 'Yes, I've been using it for the last ten days in every campsite from here to Oxfordshire.'

'Are you sure?' he repeated, presumably thinking I was an idiot or a liar.

'Yes I'm sure,' I responded. 'A three pin thing with round connectors.'

'Let me see.'

At this point I was tempted to go elsewhere but, frankly, finding a place to sleep had been such a challenge at times it was a sense of relief to arrive, and I didn't want to go through that a second time in one day.

We walked down to where the Truck was parked, I opened the rear passenger door, reached into the foot well, flipped open the increasingly deformed cardboard box and pulled out the end of the cable with its three round pins, just the same as on every caravan in the country, possibly the world.

'Oh okay,' was his response. 'I'll show you to where you can camp.'

The site was practically empty but he still wanted to tell me where to camp. Other owners would often wave me in a general direction or even suggest I just help myself to a spot.

'I'm a little concerned to stay out of the wind.'

He walked me along the terraces, each wide enough for a substantial caravan with hedges between them. 'How about here?' he suggested.

'It's a bit exposed,' I replied. Despite the Khyam Igloo being a really solid tent, I was always nervous about leaving it unattended. In twenty years of camping I don't think I've ever had a tent peg come out, loose perhaps but that's it. But I've always had a sense of relief when returning to a tent after being away from it on a windy day. I know it's an irrational fear but tent anxiety is a real experience and I try to avoid it whenever possible. 'Can't I camp there?' I gestured towards a small cluster of tents along the terrace where there was a sizable hedge to shelter behind.

'You can camp here, but no closer than this.' He suggested a spot slightly closer to the shelter but right next to the bins and completely exposed to the strong winds blowing up the valley. 'The people in those tents are away for the day but they won't want you right next to them. Here's the point for your electricity and here's your card for your reading.' He handed me a strip of card printed with segments to write in numbers. 'Write down the numbers now and again in the morning and I'll calculate how much you owe for electricity.'

In every other site I'd been to, they had a flat fee for electricity; sometimes there were two rates, one for tents, one for caravans. Until I arrived this bloke didn't even believe it was possible to have electricity in a tent. Reluctantly I accepted his instructions and he went away.

I looked at the spot.

I looked at the nearby bins.

I looked at the other tents with their nice sheltering bushes.

I looked at my spot again.

Sod it, I'll ignore his instructions, silly sod. I'll put the Khyam next to the other tents close to the shelter, I can stretch my cable as far as it will go. I can make sympathetic noises to the neighbours. I'd be off in the morning anyway and I planned to go out for dinner so they wouldn't see much of me. The owner probably wouldn't notice anyway.

* * *

Twenty minutes later the Khyam was up (it only takes a couple of minutes but a bit longer to peg out if you use all the guy ropes and I wasn't taking any chances) and installing my blanket and sleeping mat.

'I told you not to camp there!' He was back.

'Well that spot was really windy.' I replied. 'Besides I didn't want to be right next to the bins. It might spoil my photo for my followers.' He seemed to ignore this.

'It's windy because we're at the end of the valley. You can't camp there. You'll have to move.'

'Really?' I struck my best sulky teenager pose. 'Haven't you got anywhere else out of the wind, a hedge I can shelter behind?' Who builds a campsite on a hilltop in a wind funnel anyway, I thought to myself?

'You can camp on the bottom terrace, but you'll close to the road though and the sound of the traffic might be a bit loud.'

'I'm not worried about a bit of noise. I'm only going to be here one night.'

'Let me show you the spot and you can decide.'

Twenty minutes later I'd bundled the Khyam over the tailgate of the Truck and driven down to the bottom terrace. It was indeed noisier as the cars changed down a gear to get up the hill but that I could live with, and just like in Huntingdonshire, after a while, you didn't notice it.

* * *

The city of Durham was a delight and I spent the evening wandering around the city centre, talking pictures of the cathedral, the castle and the wonderfully twisty streets. The whole city centre is confined by a paperclip-shaped bend in the river on a steep headland that gives the place a wonderful three dimensional quality. The old city is riddled with narrow winding streets and alleys, up and down steep inclines with cobbles and more of that characteristic North of England stone. Some of the alleys are barely wide enough for one person, which you might imagine would be a mugger's paradise, but I don't think I felt unsafe for one minute. I'm not saying you should wander the alleys of Durham alone after dark, for it was light when I was exploring, but the place seemed to have enough people about to make it okay.

Shortly I found somewhere to eat. Having driven (Trucked) out from the campsite, I decided to push the boat out and have a meal in a restaurant. After finding most places inexplicably booked up on a Saturday night (how could that happen?) I ended up in a nice Italian place for a couple of hours. I don't think I've ever seen people alone in restaurants before, although it's the sort of thing you see on TV occasionally. After a while my inhibitions, or my boredom, got the better of me, and I pulled out a book. Sitting by the window there was some entertainment to be had looking out but I felt quite self-conscious watching the other patrons. That's a couple on a date, that group are having a birthday party, that's a works do of some sort. However, I didn't want to be seen to be staring, so, reading a book—although it increased my self-consciousness, was the lesser of two evils.

The starter came and the book was put aside. However, I had a blog post to write and I didn't want to do it later. Could I get my tablet out and start typing in a restaurant? That seemed a step too far. As I ate my sliced mushrooms in garlic and white wine butter on crusty bread I allowed myself to ponder this. I'd got over the self-consciousness of reading a book in a restaurant and I'd not suddenly found myself in an American sitcom. Nobody was taking any notice of me. Nobody knew I was there.

Sod it! As soon as the mushrooms were gone, without even waiting for the plate to be cleared I got my tablet out and began to type my blog. People came and went and nobody cared. This was great, I felt so cosmopolitan.

Clearly, I'd been cut off from society and was beginning to lose touch with all social conventions, or had begun not to care.

Shortly my lasagne arrived and it was wonderful. I'm sure it would have been wonderful anyway after nearly two weeks of camping food, although in a field anything tastes delicious. However, this was wonderful and I felt like a proper traveller. Why was I not doing more of this? Surely I could afford it.

Eventually my meal was finished. I turned down the dessert and opted for another drink. I was driving so I couldn't drink alcohol, but it was nice to be inside for a couple of hours, at a table, with cutlery that wasn't plastic and not have to wash up. I still had a blog to finish.

'Could I have the bill please?' I finalised my blog post as the waiter went for the bill.

Returning with the bill, the waiter handed it over and I gave him my card, as has happened in every such transaction millions of times across the world. 'Excuse me sir, do you mind if I ask a question?'

'Of course, by all means.' I wondered what was coming. I'd crossed a line by working in his restaurant. I'd made a huge faux-pas. (What's the Italian for faux-pas?) There really are social conventions about this sort of thing. Some things that are allowed in America are not allowed in England. You can't sell your neighbour life insurance in England but in the US people do that sort of thing all the time, or so I've heard. All this went through my mind at the speed of light. Well, at the speed of thought actually which might be a bit slower, especially after a large pasta meal.

'Are you a writer Sir?'

His question stunned me for a moment. It might have been the pasta, it certainly wasn't the wine because I hadn't had any, but I was taken aback. 'Yes, actually I am,' I responded as matter-of-factly as I could manage.

Nothing more was said apart from the usual thankyous as I typed in my PIN and prepared to leave. I did get what seemed like a bit more of a nod and a wave from the staff as I left ten minutes later.

* * *

Maslow's next layer of the pyramid is esteem. Sources in the literature describe this as status, respect, recognition from others, etc. But equally important, more important really, is internal esteem, self-respect, an understanding of oneself, of one's capabilities and limitations. Understanding ourselves and coming to terms with who we are, finding value, or perhaps meaning, in what we are capable of, discovering our strengths and weaknesses, that's where we find our self-esteem.

* * *

I left the restaurant feeling like I'd arrived. It was just a random comment from the waiter and, really, I could have been a student working on an essay. Okay, I'm too old to be a student, a mature student perhaps, conceivably an Open University student. (Twenty years ago I was an Open University student.) If I were a full-time student what was I doing eating in a restaurant, alone, on a Saturday night? I should have been out living it up, partying.

Anyway, it was a weird moment and it gave me a lift on what was becoming a journey of self-discovery.

* * *

Eventually I headed back to the Truck and made my way back to the campsite, using the headlights for the first time in ten days. On my return the reliable Khyam Igloo was still there, despite the wind gusting considerably up the valley from the city. Had the hedge done the job; would it have been okay anyway? I suspect it would have been fine even if it had been blowing a force ten gale.

Day 12 - County Durham to Northumberland

Sunday May 12th

Miles on Truck: 824

I arose to a calmer day with less wind but considerable traffic noise, which you might not expect for a Sunday morning. The cars were really gunning it up the hill below me so they were bloody noisy. Still, you don't know the good from the bad of a campsite until you've spent a night there. Had I been further away from the road I would have been more exposed to the wind, but who puts a campsite on a hill?

Packing up under a blue sky full of fluffy clouds scudding past in the blustery wind, I had the Truck loaded and went to pay my electricity bill. Now this just goes to show that it's possible to get some people wrong. The site owner had seemed a bit uncompromising when I'd arrived, and I'd certainly been annoyed at the suggestion that he didn't trust me to know whether I had the right connection for the electrical hook-up. However, if you consider the other issues from his perspective, then he might have made a bit more sense. The people in the next tent would certainly have been pissed off to discover I'd camped right next to them when the rest of the site was practically empty. Granted, I didn't want to camp right next to the bins and I was concerned about the wind but they probably wouldn't have seen that. However, when I went to pay my electricity bill, he took one look at the half a digit the counter had moved before handing the ticket back to me saying I had nothing to pay. Suddenly I saw him in a different light. I suppose if people roll up with massive caravans, run TVs and microwaves, charge their batteries and possibly even run electric heaters, you might understand what he was on about. A fiver a night wouldn't cover such heavy users but most sites averaged it out and, as a light user, I was always at a disadvantage. In effect he was doing me a favour, but perhaps it took a night's sleep after a very nice meal to see that and, no doubt, he couldn't help the shape of the landscape.

* * *

Having no idea about the boundary between County Durham and Northumberland, and in a moment of old TV ad nostalgia, I spotted Consett on the map and couldn't help remembering the old Phileas Fogg adverts.

Asking Kathy for directions, I drove back through Durham and headed north. Of course I didn't need to go to Consett, but heading that way would take me west of the major built-up areas of Newcastle and hopefully help me avoid the motorways. I sort of imagined that the town might now contain a derelict crisps factory with the production moved to somewhere cheaper, the branding owned by a company in Switzerland, the marketing rights owned in The Netherlands and the profits filtered through a Cayman Islands holding company existing in name only, this being no more real than my understanding of the off-side rule in football.

Soon I found myself sitting in a layby between Durham and Consett, drinking coffee in the sunshine, looking at maps and listening to the sounds of clay pigeon shooting in the valley below me. (It was Sunday morning but I wasn't really aware of the fact.) At least I could hear the shots and see the smoke but I couldn't see who was shooting so I assumed it was clay pigeon shooters, either that or the union of campsite owners had put the word out on me and there was a price on my head.

Consett turned out to be one of those local stone sort of towns that, despite me beginning to get used to them, still strike me as having a characteristic appearance that might be representative of the North. (Truth be told, the stone-built look probably isn't particularly characteristic of the North as stone built towns might well be found anywhere. They are probably just not characteristic of the South East.) Consett had a mixture of parallel streets on a grid pattern, all orderly and carefully positioned and more of those wonderful twisty up and down streets with double-back junctions dictated by the landscape that I'd so enjoyed in Durham.

Not really knowing what I was doing in Consett, much as had been the case in Middlesbrough and even Louth before that, suddenly serendipity lent a hand and I spotted a sign for the Derwent Reservoir. I recognised the name from some long-forgotten childhood memory of the flooding Derwent village after WWII. Of course I wasn't alive at the time so my memory might be from history lessons describing the Derwent River in Derbyshire, considered by many to be the starting place of the industrial revolution. However, what I wasn't aware of, not having a consistently good mobile signal so as to check serendipity's references, was that there are two Derwent Reservoirs, one in Derbyshire and this one in Northumberland, not to mention Derwent Water in the Lake District. Add to that the fact that there are four rivers named Derwent in Northumberland, Derbyshire, Cumbria and Yorkshire, then the whole memory of flooded villages becomes somewhat less reliable. Considering all this, one wonders how tourists ever manage to find anything in this country. Of course the point is that 'derwent,' apparently, is an old English word for a location that was heavily forested with oak, so perhaps the surprising thing is that there are not more such places. Whatever the case, and ignorant of all of this at the time, I thought it worth a look.

Immediately on turning down the indicated road, while still in Consett I spotted a sign saying 'Welcome to Northumberland, England's Border Country'. So, feeling that my mission for the day was going well, I struck out along a long road so straight it must have been built by invaders, into the wooded countryside, up and down steep hills. Eventually I crested the moors just after passing through the wonderfully named Snods Edge.

Derwent Reservoir itself was less than exciting but that was probably due to the weather. It had become greyer, the blue sky had vanished and the waters looked leaden under the clouds. To be honest it was all a bit miserable. I mooched around, took a few photos and decided that I needed to go somewhere else. Torn between Alnwick Castle and Bamburgh Castle, both an hour and a half away, I decided on Bamburgh purely because of the apparent scale of the place.

Setting off, Kathy took me along a route that suddenly revealed a sign for Hadrian's Wall, which led to a bit of a bust-up between the two of us. I wanted to see the wall again, having been really impressed with Steel Rigg last time I'd been in Northumberland, but she had other ideas. Ignoring her instructions I went my own way. As I pushed north, in the direction where I imagined Hadrian's Wall to be, the weather deteriorated, spitting with rain. I failed to find the wall and in return, as the rain continued to threaten, when I once again followed Kathy's instructions she took me up the A1. There was a terrifying incident when she attempted to kill me by sending me south, then suddenly demanding a U turn to go north. I put this down to revenge. In the past, I've had instances where she'd told me to turn right across the oncoming traffic, as you sometimes find on fast A roads. However, she occasionally has a habit of doing this when there's actually a bridge and you need to be in the inside lane instead of the outside. These days I no longer trust her at all on dual carriageways, but I hadn't considered the possibility of reprisals if I ignored her for too long.

* * *

Maslow's final level of the pyramid is, perhaps, the hardest to explain; he calls it self-actualisation. People who satisfy this level of need are able to achieve their potential to the best of their ability. They aren't all great sportsmen and women or the greatest artists or mathematicians, but they are people who understand themselves, their potential and are expressing their capabilities as best they can. It's difficult to say that such people are in top jobs because that is not be necessary for self-actualisation. It's more likely that they have identified their skills and talents and found an outlet for them. A musician who has never made it as a professional recording artist might just as easily be a member of a band while having a day job that doesn't interfere with the expression of that talent. Some manuals of personal development, though, will suggest that we can all be anything we want to. However, clearly, we can't all be concert pianists or solve Fermat's last theorem. Someone with a skill for working with their hands might end up as a builder or plumber and really enjoy their job. To self-actualise we don't have to be high fliers, we just have to become who we could be and not try to be something else. Part of the definition of this state is acceptance of one's potential, which might include weaknesses and lack of capabilities as in the old saying, 'know thyself'. However, such people are likely to be on a journey of self-discovery and improvement, be that continual education or development of talents, skills and capabilities. These people live in the moment rather than forever yearning to be somewhere else, which might lead to dissatisfaction with where they are.

* * *

Having survived Kathy's attempts to kill me, I eventually arrived at Bamburgh, late in the afternoon in spitting rain. The castle is an impressive sight from more than a few miles away, built on a massive outcrop of rock right on the coast. It must be one of the most impressive castles in England on a truly epic scale. The castle goes back a very long time to the first fortifications in Anglo Saxon times, with evidence of settlements back into prehistory. It is said to be built on the site of the ancient capital of one of the first kingdoms in Britain in the 5th century after the Angles arrived, or perhaps invaded (though I don't know anything of their road-building policies), from Germany. History does not seem to record whether their roads were straight or twisty, although I suppose they might not have built roads at all favouring a track through the easiest terrain. Considering my journey up the east coast, it was particularly satisfying that serendipity led me to Bamburgh as I've heard it said that the name of the historic county of Northumberland comes from the kingdom that was north of the Humber, North Humberland, which stretched as far north as the foothills of the Scottish Highlands.

Of the fortifications that can be seen today, the main keep was built by the Normans in the 12th century while bits of it, to my untrained eye, look as though they may be as late as the Napoleonic period. The legendary 14th century knight Sir Harry Hotspur was commander here and the place is generally very impressive all round. I would have liked to have a proper look but having arrived at 4:00 it was simply too late to go in.

Feeling a little dejected at the lateness of the day I sheltered in a pub to search for a campsite, enjoying a cup of tea and free Wi-Fi. The weather had turned foul and this was no time to be outside.

An hour later, by the time I got to the Warren Caravan and Camping Park it was closed. However, dialling the phone number on the window of the locked-up office, I spoke to someone who told me to pitch up wherever I wanted. There were no proscriptive instructions here.

As the weather cleared it turned out to be a delightful spot, overlooking the sea, sheltered by a tree-covered bank but low enough to see the sun setting over the bay in the distance. I was more than a bit surprised to discover that I could see the sunset at all as, being on the east coast, I imagined the sun would set behind me. But it seemed, purely by chance, I'd found an apparently deserted campsite on the south side of a bay that faced northwest.

With the sun setting further north as the summer developed, I could watch the sun go down from the shelter of the Khyam. So, after a day of dodging the weather, grimly trying to avoid main roads and failing to find Hadrian's Wall, I spent a happy evening messing about on the web and watching the sun set over the North Sea coast, which was the last thing I expected thinking I was facing east... which I wasn't.

* * *

Beyond self-actualisation, beyond finding our place in the world and expressing it, is the concept of the peak experience. Now remember this is only a model. There are many criticisms of Maslow's five-level pyramid; some criticisms define different numbers of levels, other responses suggest it only fits western cultures or whatever, others suggest the sequence may be wrong or that the levels blend into each other. But the point is, it's not real, it's just a useful tool. Freud's model of the conscious and unconscious was a model based on ideas describing the technology of the day, which was steam and hydraulics, so behaviours or memories were described as being suppressed and then popping up later as though pressure has built up forcing them to emerge elsewhere. Some theorists will describe the mind, today, in an information processing model because that is one of the technologies of our day. Actually, the information processing model is a bit old hat now as we have neuroscience and we understand that the brain is non-linear. (Will there soon be a model of the brain or of personality that describes us in terms of apps or mobile technology?) Whatever the case the brain is not a hydraulic system or a computer but those are useful ways of understanding the brain or the mind when we have nothing else to go on other than apparently unconnected behaviours. None of this is true, it's all just a way of looking at things, but the same is said of religion or other systems. It's all a bit metaphorical.

So beyond, or perhaps within, self-actualisation is Maslow's idea of the peak experience. Of course, he didn't invent this idea, it has been expressed as part of religious thought for thousands of years. Call it transcendence, enlightenment, samadhi, whatever; it's nothing new. This experience, oneness with the universe, all that jazz, is something that is accessible to all of us no matter how fulfilled we are at which level. But those who are self-actualised are in a better position for those experiences to come to them. These moments might be characterised by a sense of intensity while being immersed in the moment, perhaps with heightened awareness but undistracted by peripheral distractions.

People can stumble across such experiences in their life but very rarely. That moment, when you are lying in a bath, at the perfect temperature, in complete peace as an experience washes over you like no bath you've ever had before, such a situation might be likened to a transcendent moment. Of course, a guru who has spent a lifetime of discipline meditating under a tree, living the life of ascetic dedication, might suggest that a hot bath is not transcendence, and who am I to say? Although I've had some long hot baths in my time. However, hippies building floatation tanks in the sixties were probably thinking along the same lines.

The point is, I can make all sorts of analogies about abandoning plans to camp by the lakeside in Rutland and just finding a basic campsite, and suggest that's a bit like the base level of the pyramid where I should have been thinking about shelter instead of aesthetics. I can suggest that finding a sense of belonging with the caravaners in Whitby was a bit like the sense of belonging at the third level of the pyramid. However, to claim a peak experience or transcendence at any point on this journey would be just a little bit arrogant.

However, sitting on the Northumberland coast, with the weather having unexpectedly calmed after a day of shitty wind and rain, a disappointing visit to a miserable grey Derwent Reservoir, failing to find Hadrian's Wall, a recalcitrant Kathy trying to kill me on the A1, getting to Bamburgh Castle only to find it just about to close... then watching the sun set over the bay, just a few miles from the ancient religious sanctuary of Lindisfarne... well, it was hardly the unification of the microcosm with the macrocosm, but it was very nice, so I decided to put the kettle on.

Day 13 - Northumberland to Cumberland

Monday May 13th

Miles on Truck: 953

It had been a delightfully calm evening, with the setting sun across the northwest-facing coast of Budle Bay, with Holy Island just around the headland (not that I knew it at the time because of continuously dodgy internet connections). However, there had been high winds and some rain in the night and the water had been driven between my groundsheet and the inner tent of the Khyam. (Back when I was camped in Cambridgeshire I'd made an attempt to trim the groundsheet because it was sticking out but I'd obviously not taken enough off.) Unfortunately the footprint of the Khyam groundsheet exactly matches the outline of the flysheet, which is a bit rubbish as the slightest breeze means the flysheet is pushed in revealing the groundsheet below, which means that any drips run onto the groundsheet and under the inner tent to soak through from below. It seemed my previous attempts to cut down the groundsheet needed to be repeated so, while I waited for my laundry to finish, I crawled on the floor in the laundry room, out of the wind, with the groundsheet and a pair of scissors cutting another four inch strip from each side. The effort took up almost the whole floor and, had anybody walked in, it might have seemed a bit odd. However, I thought of myself as a serious tourer, due to be out under canvas (or at least slightly permeable nylon) for nearly forty nights, and in such a situation you sometimes have to make modifications to your kit. I think secretly I was slightly disappointed that I wasn't disturbed as I relished the idea of being seen as a bit hardcore.

By 11:00 I was on the road heading for Carlisle. The direct, though more twisty, route down through Northumberland National Park and on through the Kielder Forest, was only thirty minutes slower than the longer but faster route down the A1 and across the top of England on the A69. Thirty minutes on a two hour drive wasn't that bad so I thought I'd give it a go, but not until after a cup of coffee on the A1.

Kathy directed me down tiny roads at all of four-miles-a-fortnight. Pushing on down narrow lanes, often doubling back, twisting around blind corners, I was barely able to get into fourth gear, let alone anything faster. The Truck really loves this sort of driving; keeping in third gear with the revs high, the diesel is wonderfully responsive and deliciously guttural, really sounding like a proper truck, but I was going nowhere, slowly, and I had at least fifty miles of this landscape ahead. I know she'd told me the difference in journey time would be just thirty minutes but I began to have a serious crisis of faith in her estimates. The roads might open up a bit further on but, looking at the maps, it really didn't look like there would be anything other than twisty double-backs. I simply didn't believe I could trust Kathy to get me to Cumberland at a sensible time. I couldn't take the chance of not finding anywhere to camp so, in my scepticism, I asked her to take me by the fastest route. Turning back towards the A1 I felt I was betraying my intentions for the whole trip. My plan to stay off trunk routes was facing compromise, but I was more concerned about getting to Cumberland in time to enjoy the place, rather than arriving in time for bed.

The road west was fast and clear but the weather suddenly closed in with a torrential down-pour that caused me to doubt the wisdom of the trip altogether. The rain hit the road in that way that it does when there's just too much of it to flow away. The shafts of rain hitting the ground caused little (actually not so little) explosions in the standing water where it briefly created a crater before the water flowed back again. (Meteorologists or geographers, or whoever, probably have a word for this phenomena and I'd like to know what it is.) I continued west, my thoughts alternating between visions of aquaplaning and the survivability of my tent in these conditions. At the worst of the squall I even considered booking into a B&B and whether that would be permissible or a cop out. I decided that I'd leave the decision to the weather report, with a severe weather warning for rain being my bail-out criteria.

By the time I arrived in Carlisle, still some twenty or thirty miles from the lakes of Cumberland, it was mid-afternoon and too late in the day for useful exploration. Pulling into a pub car park I checked the map and pushed on to Keswick. I don't know why I picked Keswick apart from the fact that it looked like it was central to where I thought the historic county of Cumberland used to be. Checking out the Met Office website it turned out they had indeed issued a severe weather warning. The list of places not to be camping for the night covered the East Midlands, East of England, London and the South East, North West England (where I'd been the night before),

South West England, Wales, West Midlands, Yorkshire and the Humber. So if I went to Scotland I'd be okay? Had they forgotten to mention the Lake District or was it included in one of the places already mentioned? At 3:20 I headed into the now historic county of Cumberland with no idea where I was going to stay.

✱ ✱ ✱

It struck me as I was driving into Cumberland that, had I not done this trip I would probably never have approached from this direction. Refusing Kathy's invitations to drive down the M6 I descended into the county from the north, along a road that I deliberately didn't write down because I don't want to turn into a B379 bore. The point being, however, that my usual approach to the area from home would be from the south, so seeing the fells from this direction is something that might never happen otherwise.

Riding my serendipity into Cumberland, I viewed the most impressive landscape of the journey so far. Central England from Oxford across to the flats of East Anglia had been a low rolling pastoral landscape becoming flatter as I progressed east. The East of England gave me fens, now mostly drained for agribusiness. The North Humber floodplain was a brief, beautiful vista of fields and scattered hedgerows dotted with trees into the distance before climbing into the Yorkshire Moors, magnificent and wuthering. Durham displayed a constantly changing vista of hills and crags becoming rolling open landscapes into Northumberland. I'd missed the Cheviot Hills and the northwest of Northumberland due to something of a breakdown in my relationship with Kathy but, in return, she'd brought me into the historic county of Cumberland to drive in awe directly towards Skiddaw standing majestically above the landscape.

✱ ✱ ✱

However, impressive as Skiddaw was, with what I can only guess was Grasmoor in the distance, I was as impressed by the presence of two well-placed laybys, one on each side of the road in just the spot where a tourist might want to stop to get a snap of the view. This was just the sort of spot where, for the past two weeks, I'd often bemoaned the lack of anywhere to stop to admire the view or take a picture. Two or three times a day I'd skid to a halt in a field entrance, on a grass verge or, god forbid, a bus stop. I'd leap out of the Truck, hastily take a picture which would be badly composed, often from the wrong location, often not level and generally dissatisfying to someone who feels he can do better. I'd leap back in the Truck and carry on, perhaps pulling out into difficult traffic, thinking that I really shouldn't have stopped in the first place.

When you think about it there are more cameras about today than there are grains of sand on the beach and all the stars in the universe... or something. So you might imagine that with England as beautiful as it is, along with all the other reasons for taking photos, somebody in the local authority must have had a realisation. And by virtue of that decision I'd been given a moment of magic, not really one of Maslow's peak experiences but I'd experienced a peak at least.

Approaching Keswick there was still snow visible on the higher slopes. From the lowlands it looked like one or two tiny drifts in sheltered dells, perhaps where the sun rarely shone, but given the distance these tiny drifts must have been substantial. The weather was currently very changeable with severe weather warnings for rain when a week before I'd been in shorts. However, only in April, in the South we'd said goodbye to the last snows of a long winter.

Eventually I used the Enormous Book of Campsites and found a campsite conveniently close to Keswick and right on the edge of the town. Actually it was on the edge of Derwent Water (there's that name again) so I set off hoping for the ideal camping spot. Of course the ideal camping spot is rather dependent on a number of things, the weather conditions being one of them.

Kathy guided me into the campsite entrance down a long drive, where part way along I was faced with a sign that, even at my sedate pace, I didn't have the chance to read, something about new arrivals. Had I had a real human sitting beside me, instead of Kathy, I might have stood a chance but on my own that was a bit more difficult. Perhaps I should have stopped in the middle of the road?

Ahead of me were two automated barriers each across one of two lanes. They were sort of staggered, so one was a car's length ahead of the other. In front of the left hand lane (where I was) there was a white line about a car's length short of the barrier with a sign saying new arrivals should stop at the line; so I stopped at the line rather full of expectation and slowly-increasing confusion.

I waited at the white line thinking something might happen, the barrier might rise, there might be an unnoticed security guard nearby that might rush to my assistance, someone might come out to me or perhaps Eamonn Andrews would run out in a spangly suit with big lapels and declare that I am indeed Schrodinger's Millionaire and I really had won the lottery while I'd been on the road.

However, none of these things happened as I dutifully sat there and waited. I did notice that at the barrier, perhaps 15 feet ahead (I don't know how long a car is) there was one of those panel things on a post that might have buttons and I wondered if there might be an intercom, so I edged forward. Arriving at the panel thing, atop the post, it did indeed have buttons, but no intercom, so I sat there confused for a while wondering what I should do. Should I reverse back to the white line? Should I reverse all the way back to that sign I'd not read because I was busy driving the car? What the hell was this, a campsite or some military site with security guards and machine gun emplacements?

Then I spied a sign with some instructions ahead of me so I squinted at it as best I could, but the last line was helpfully placed at the exact level to be completely obscured by the barrier. I did the only thing I could, I got out of the Truck to have a better look. Meanwhile an elderly lady passed by, seeming a bit perturbed by the fact that I was stuck but looking as though she didn't want to get involved. Had she had a previous run in with the camp guards, I wondered, with all their military equipment, uniforms and the like?

As I stood there a man came out of the office, perhaps fifty yards ahead and waved me back. 'Get behind the white line,' he called to me, so I dutifully reversed.

After all the confusion, it was explained that the two lanes were for newcomers and existing guests, and that the barrier had been misbehaving lately. Surely, though, this strange arrangement of incomprehensible white lines and signs that you couldn't read wasn't put in place after a recent technical glitch with a dodgy button on the barrier. And what was all that having to reverse back for, when I was the only person there? Let's remember that by the time I arrived in Keswick I'd been to twelve different campsites in the last twelve days and not a single one of them has had any kind of barrier, automatic or otherwise, let alone an electric fence, machine guns or security guards. The most expensive site I'd been to, the night before, allowed me to drive straight on-site after they had all gone home and let me pay for my laundry the next morning. They didn't even want fingerprints or DNA samples.

A few minutes later I was in the compound, strip searched, x-rayed, scanned, profiled, and interrogated. (Okay, so I might have made a bit of that up.) I paid my money (a very reasonable price as it turned out), and I was guided to the lakeside.

The lakeside was delightful; well, it would have been delightful if the sun had been shining. However the wind was blowing, the ground was like a marsh and the closest I could get the Truck to my pitch was a good 200 yards away. Granted the site owners were up against it with the weather, the whole site was peppered with puddles large and small. My choices were marshy ground close to the lake with stunning views across the water or dryer ground with less of a view but a lot further away from the Truck. The biggest problem was the wind blowing across the lake and, had I taken advantage of the view, it would have been gusting straight in the entrance of the tent. To be fair to the campsite, the guy who showed me to my pitch did offer me the use of the backpacker's room, a special room where hikers could go to defrost if they were suffering from exposure but this just seemed to add to my despondency over the situation.

So for the first time on the trip I gave in.

Before reaching the point of no return, before unloading the Truck, I consulted the Mammoth Book of Campsites again and after a shorter search than before I phoned the Castlerigg Farm Campsite to discover that they had space for me. Asking about the wind, they said their site was okay so I set off.

Now anybody who knows the name Castlerigg will most likely associate it with the famous Castlerigg Stone Circle. (Unfortunately I'm not one of those people so I missed the stone circle in the same way that I missed Lindisfarne, but I'm planning to go back.) One of the things they say about Castlerigg Stone Circle is that it stands on a hill in a natural amphitheatre between the surrounding fells. (I'm definitely going back.)

So I left a windy campsite at the bottom of a valley in extreme windy weather seeking somewhere more suitable and I headed for a hilltop campsite. This made no sense to me but I wanted somewhere drier and in my mind a hilltop might have been drier.

* * *

Castlerigg Farm Campsite, while extremely windy, was very nice, with a little shop where I bought a washing-up brush and some batteries, generally good facilities all round. The site is typical of those farms that have diversified from sheep farming, an activity which will struggle to make someone a living in the modern world.

There's a Local Westmorland sheep farmer, James Rebanks, who in his excellent book, *A Shepherd's Life*, describes how farmers now have to have 'one foot in the modern world and one foot in their living past'. To me this seems resonant with the general idea of a search for meaning. I suppose a hill farmer could give up on the sheep altogether and put the land over to other enterprises, but his story tells of deep connections to the land and the sheep, Herdwicks, bred not just over generations but centuries, perhaps even since the arrival of the Vikings. He talks about practices, skills and knowledge passed down from father to son. But he is quoted as saying that sheep farming is as much a form of culture as Picasso or punk and I think he has a point. Personally his culture, or that of any trade that goes back to *a living past* be it that of farmers, fishmongers or funambulists, strikes me as carrying more meaning into his modern life than the rather homogenised culture the rest of us enjoy. What's more meaningful, the cycle of the annual return of X-Factor manipulated to generate a Christmas number one or the cycle of preparation to get your herd through the winter as your ancestors have done for hundreds of years? And don't get me wrong, this isn't some fluffy imitation of ancestor worship, this is hard experience, knowledge that the cleft in the ridge across the fell is the place that the sheep will have taken shelter when there has been an unexpected snowfall. This culture is rational, in that it embeds practical knowledge of the land and its practices, but it also generates a sense of connection that goes deeper, experienced on an emotional level. James Rebanks talks about a connection to something that runs back into the depths of time and it seems it's an emotional experience that trusting in SatNav just doesn't give us.

* * *

Having bought my provisions at the shop, I was soon set up next to a couple of guys, collectively using our cars and a dry stone wall to arrange a substantial wind break. Half way through setting up the tent I decided discretion to be the better part of valour and faced the entrance towards the wall. I'd been in the habit of tweeting a picture of the view from my tent in the morning. Tuesday morning's picture wouldn't be much of a view but at least a close up of a dry stone wall would be representative of one of the clichés of Cumberland.

I settled in for an evening of general internet frivolousness, which was going on fine, two glasses of wine down and more to go if I felt like it, when a message arrived from a friend who had been keeping an eye on my post. Her message passed on the general news from home, all was well, the washing machine still worked, etc., when she added, '…and your new bank card has arrived.' This last statement came as something of a shock as I sat in the semi-dark illuminated by a few LED lights in a tent on a very windy hilltop some 250 miles from home.

Some weeks before I had realised that my bank card would expire at the end of May when I would be on the road. Considering that most of us get a new card issued every three years or so this was extremely bad luck. Not having access to life-giving cash machines would bring an untimely end to the journey so I phoned up the bank and they promised to send the card out a month early; thus my faith in bureaucracy was restored. Later, two days before I was due to ‚leave I realized that the card still hadn't arrived. Another call to the bank resulted in an apology for not having done what they promised and a plan was hatched to send the card to somewhere I could collect it on the way. I knew I'd be stopping to visit Graham in Blackpool so the local branch seemed just the job. Now, two glasses of wine into a fresh bottle of red, on a windy hilltop in Cumberland, I heard that the card was in Hertfordshire and detouring to collect it would add 500 miles to the trip and severely mess up the theme. So far I'd managed to avoid passing through the same county twice and I'd not touched a single motorway (although Kathy had sometimes been troublesome and tempted me more than once). Fortunately my friend in the South offered a solution and arranged to post the card, special delivery, to the Blackpool branch in time for me to get there.

Assured that all would be resolved, no thanks to the bank but by the arrangements I'd made, I poured another glass of red in the cosy gloom of my tent and lay down to listen to the wind in the hope that I'd still be there when I awoke.

Day 14 - Cumberland to Westmorland

Tuesday May 14th

Miles on Truck: 1113

As it turned out, the Khyam Igloo did an excellent job of keeping the wind and the rain out overnight. It had certainly been windier than the night I'd spent in Lincolnshire, huddled in the lee of the massive camper van. This time I'd huddled in the lee of a dry stone wall, which was the view that greeted me in the morning, bright and sunny, though still a bit breezy.

I had a quick breakfast and made my escape. Somehow I was still only away by 11:30 but why rush off from somewhere in the hope of meeting interesting people when you've got interesting people around you? It turned out that times like these were about being there, in the moment, on a windy hilltop in the mountains talking to a couple of interesting guys that I'd never see again and just making a connection no matter how brief. There was also the bank debacle to deal with, but it seemed I'd have to sort out what they were unable to.

Westmorland is one of those Historic Counties that have disappeared altogether. In Huntingdonshire and Rutland things had been simple. Huntingdonshire had been invaded by Cambridgeshire but in that case I simply needed to head for the old county town of Huntingdon to be sure I was within the bounds of the old county. Rutland was easy too. Having been invaded by Leicestershire, it had fought a valiant rear-guard action and recaptured its name in the somewhat ironic 'Rutland County Council District Council', due to the fact that Rutland is now a district that once was a county and has ambitions to be a county again. Whatever the case, heading for Rutland Water guaranteed I was in the right place. Westmorland, however, would not be as easy as it had vanished completely after being invaded by Cumberland which then disguised itself as Cumbria in the hope that the United Nations might not notice.

My best bet, I thought, would be to head the mile or two back into Keswick to find out what exactly constitutes Westmorland (with the agenda of coffee and a sandwich) and discover Westmorland's historic boundaries. However, arriving in Keswick, I had second thoughts. Could asking for a copy of a map of Westmorland from within Cumberland, the conquering county, re-open old wounds? The day was ticking by and I thought better of it, deciding to head for Westmorland itself, where my enquiries might generate a more sympathetic response. I might be in danger of fomenting revolution amongst the oppressed peoples of a county no longer in existence but there was no alternative if I was going to find out where to camp.

On the way I discovered that, if Cumberland had indeed invaded Westmorland the locals must have put up a good fight, because they seem to have retained their wiggly little roads and there had been no Roman straightening on the county's ancient routes such as I'd seen in other parts of the country.

Shortly I arrived in Ambleside, all narrow streets and fine stone buildings with truly wonderful views of streams descending between jumbles of grey granite. Stopping to take a photo, I soon attracted a series of fellow shutterbugs capturing the same view that a moment before nobody seemed interested in; sort of social validation tourism.

I started my search for the historic county and, finding a bookshop, a nice shop assistant with a slim figure, brunette tresses and striking brown eyes did her best to assist me but in the end directed me to the information centre up the road. My fantasies of an unexpected romantic encounter with bookshop girl didn't materialise and I dutifully wandered off bemoaning my lack of suitable small talk to keep the conversation going. Small talk is often derided but it's the oil that lubricates social life and it's probably responsible for the majority of new friendships and so much more.

The information centre was no better than the bookshop. Instead I was directed to the library, back past the first bookshop, where I'm sure many romantic literary tragedies occur, and eventually I was directed to the County Library in Kendal.

After a pleasant drive in the sunshine, across what I can only guess was Westmorland, Kathy led me a merry dance up and down the narrow streets of Kendal to a location in sight of a supermarket, but frustratingly on the wrong side of a wall with no access to the car park.

Manoeuvring the Truck with an eight-point turn in the narrow lane, I escaped, much to Kathy's protestations. My defiant route necessitated an extensive detour around a lengthy one-way system and eventually into Booths Supermarket car park, just yards from where I had been, but the other side of the wall.

I'd only encountered Booths Supermarkets in the North and the place has an air of well-off conservatism, and it seems that the company has never been tempted to expand into the South. Apparently it once won a food retailing award, beating Selfridges into second place.

Leaving the Truck in the care of one of the world's renowned food retailers I found my way out to the high street and to the truly impressive Carnegie Library. The Scottish-born philanthropist Andrew Carnegie built over 2500 libraries across the world as well as the legendary Carnegie Hall in New York. Kendal's is a very fine example, built in the neoclassical style with large windows and a striking two-tone, local stone finish. These libraries, built with the intention of enabling people to educate themselves to a better life, are typically accessed up a flight of steps symbolising the aspirant's elevation by learning. Kendal's is representative in this very way. The other common characteristic of Carnegie Libraries is a prominently placed lamp post directly outside: and Kendal enjoys two, very fine, gloss black, cast iron examples, perhaps fifteen feet high, one on each side of the steps. The lamp post symbolised the enlightenment that was to be found therein.

Inside, the building was just as impressive as outside, light and airy and not at all dingy as libraries are often claimed to be. I made my way upstairs to find the local history department and asked the first person I could find who looked remotely like a librarian.

Wearing a badge saying Honorary Secretary, an elderly lady sat next to a table displaying some documents and photos that I didn't really look at.

I assumed she must be important so I directed my enquiry to her. 'Hello, I'm looking for information about the historic boundaries of Westmorland. I'm told you have a local studies department.'

She looked a little surprised, 'Oh, try along the corridor.' She gestured to her right, past the table displaying the photos and pamphlets. She didn't seem very confident but I didn't think anything of it.

Walking along the corridor, I passed an elderly couple, sitting in comfortable armchairs reading, and I had that flash of jealousy of people who have the time to sit in libraries all day and read the books. A few steps further on I met a nice group of people working at desks who seemed to have the sort of jobs that I'd like to have, presumably doing research and dealing with books or some such. Evidently, what with the architecture, the visitors and the employees combined, Kendal Carnegie Library seems to have much to be jealous of. But what do all these local studies librarians do anyway?

I explained that I needed to visit Westmorland, and that it doesn't really exist anymore and, surprisingly, they didn't look at me as though I was mad. They probably thought it, but were too polite to say.

I was soon led to the maps and various resources that I needed to do my research and left to get on with it. Bear in mind the fact the Carnegie Libraries are designed for self-help, so nobody was going to tell me where the old boundaries were. The librarians were able to reel off a list of the towns that were part of the historic county but in terms of familiarity they might as well have been on Mars. I thought I might be able to find an old map of the historic county but that would have been too easy.

Suddenly I had a thought. I could use my tablet to check if any of these towns have campsites and I could use the library Wi-Fi, rather than the mobile signal that I'd come to think of as inherently unreliable. So I asked one of the local studies librarians. 'Oh just ask the lady outside that you spoke to before,' came the response. So I walked back along the corridor, past the elderly couple reading quietly, and approached the Honorary Secretary. She seemed important; she must know.

Unfortunately the Honorary Secretary was deep in conversation with a visitor so I waited my turn.

'You see, your pamphlet describes that yard as Fothergills' Yard,' said the visitor.

'Yes,' responded the Honorary Secretary, nodding politely.

'You see I remember that, in 1957, the shop along the alley was owned by old Braithwaite.'

'Oh I see,' responded the Honorary Secretary.

'And the fishmonger, he was married to the undertaker's daughter, he bought the house next door and I used to visit on a Thursday afternoon.'

'Oh yes,' responded the Honorary Secretary.

'Or was that Wednesday afternoon?'

The Honorary Secretary listened politely.

'No... no, it was Thursday afternoon, because the undertaker, remember his daughter married the fishmonger...'

The Honorary Secretary continued to listen politely and appeared not to have noticed me as I stood patiently waiting to ask about the Wi-Fi.

'Well, actually the undertaker's daughter married the baker but that was later.' He dropped his voice to a conspiratorial tone. 'She was a bit of a one you know.'

'Oh I see,' responded the Honorary Secretary.

'Of course this was the nineteen fifties so things were different then.'

The Honorary Secretary listened politely.

'Anyway, so before they painted the front doors, and I knew the man that sold them the paint, they had to repaint the sign for the yard and it was definitely Fotherhams' Yard and not Fothergills' Yard. So your pamphlet definitely contains an error.'

This went on for what seemed like another two and a half weeks... but, eventually, the Honorary Secretary, who had no defence against the barrage of historical detail and pointless nonsense, looked up and eventually noticed me.

'Can I help you?' asked the Honorary Secretary, rather overcome with all the attention.

'Do you know the password for the Wi-Fi?' I asked hopefully.

'Oh, Wi-Fi? Well, I'm not sure.' She paused. 'Do we have that here? I really don't know.' She stopped asking rhetorical questions but it seemed she had a series of others lined up that she didn't vocalise such as 'What is Wi-Fi anyway?' 'Have they invented something new then?' 'I wonder what time the shops shut?' 'What day is it anyway?'

Eventually she responded, 'Perhaps you had better ask one of the librarians downstairs,' and she directed me back towards where I had started when I arrived.

* * *

Down on the ground floor, amid the books in the main room-awash with natural light from the massive windows, I found another librarian. I knew she was a librarian because she had books, lots of them. Surely she would be the sort of person who would help with the Wi-Fi. She was also very pretty in a middle-aged, grey-haired, librarian sort of way, with a petite figure and boyish hips, but we've probably had enough of that today. It must be something to do with bookish women.

'Excuse me, I'm trying to find out the password for the Wi-Fi.'

The librarian looked at me with arms full of books.

'I was told that you would know the password.'

'Oh really?' She looked at me as though to say that she didn't but would be happy to help.

'I asked the lady upstairs, she had a badge saying Honorary Secretary, she suggested you might know.'

For a moment she looked at me puzzled when, slowly, an expression of realisation came across her face followed by a wry smile that made her all the more attractive.

'Oh her, she won't be able to help you; she's nothing to do with the library.' As she spoke there was a slight tone of disdain in her voice.

Maddeningly, the pretty, grey-haired, elfin librarian led me back up the stairs, straight past the Honorary Secretary to the people in the Local Studies Department not fifteen feet from where I had first asked for the Wi-Fi password. After some discussion about what their Wi-Fi was called, as there were many in range, including the Police Station nearby, which might have been interesting, I was facilitated with the details and I proceeded with my research.

Eventually, with some suggestions about which towns fall within the old boundaries, but still no maps and nothing solid to refer to, such as a photocopy of an out-of-print map, I abandoned the Carnegie Library, found a bookshop and bought an actual modern paper map. Clearly you can trust in SatNav, but sometimes the old ways are the best.

* * *

Shortly, after buying bread and cheese at Booths Supermarket to validate my parking, only to discover I'd not spent enough, I laid the map out on the bonnet of the Truck, found a symbol for a camp and caravan site in a location that I was assured was once in the old county of Westmorland and headed out of Kendal. I was away and heading for my chosen destination, the wonderfully named Westmorland location of Troutbeck.

* * *

After some getting lost, getting directions, discovering that what I thought was north was south, or was that the other way around, and retracing my steps, I ended up at a very posh caravan park. Now you might imagine that, thinking north was south (or that south was north) was because I was holding my low-tech map upside down. In fact the map was the right way up but I had the world upside down.

Troutbeck, just north of Windermere town, was beautiful, especially as I had to drive up and down tiny lanes at impossible angles, around tight switchbacks with dry stone walls all over and precipitous valley sides all about. The sun was shining and there was not a hint of wind. It was amazing considering that I'd almost been blown off the hilltop at Castlerigg the night before and much of England was still under a severe weather warning. It all looked like a pastoral paradise. Unfortunately being on the side of a steeply sided valley with a road along either slope, and a river down the middle, it was easy to imagine I was on the other side. I say it was easy only because that's exactly what I did imagine. It may have been quite hard to imagine that but I made a pretty good stab at it. So thinking north was south and that south was north I spent a pleasant half hour torturing the Truck up and down the tiny lanes, standing on the brakes as I descended and performing miraculous hill starts on the way back up. Sometimes the slopes were so steep that I could see nothing ahead of me because down was behind me, if you get my drift, and I could see less either side, what with the high hedges and stone walls, so that all I could see was the sky over the bonnet and nothing more.

When I got there, the caravan park wasn't your common-or-garden white touring caravan variety or even your static holiday home variety. These were all natural wood finished constructions more like chalets, each with a veranda, all done up with high gloss varnish and perfectly manicured grass. It was retirement heaven, if you were into that sort of thing. I would have happily stayed the night there, trying not to make the place look scruffy with my tent and truck of the rusty variety but unfortunately they wouldn't have me.

I explained that I needed to camp in Westmorland, and that it doesn't really exist anymore and, surprisingly, they didn't look at me as though I was mad; they probably thought it though. My low-tech Ordnance Survey map said it was a caravan and camping site with the little blue picture thing but it turned out the map was wrong and they didn't take tents. Either that or the map was correct, but they didn't like the look of me and the noisy truck of the rusty variety and they just wouldn't have me.

However they were very nice and helpful so I trundled off in the direction they recommended where they knew some sites that might help and that were definitely in Westmorland.

Eventually after more navigating with the low-tech Ordnance Survey map, I eventually found myself at the equally nice Windermere Caravan Park, a very well appointed establishment that wouldn't let me drive the

Truck on the grass but, apart from that, was lovely all the same. I had spent the whole day getting from one campsite to another but I'd been up hill and down dale, researched in a genuine Carnegie Library and seen the odd lake, so I didn't really care. I was just relieved to be set up again, and it was a beautiful evening in Westmorland so, as had become my habit, I opened a bottle of wine and got quietly drunk.

Day 15 - Westmorland to Lancashire

Wednesday May 15th

Miles on Truck: 1174

Overnight the bad weather returned with a vengeance. Clearly the lack of a severe weather warning in the North West, perhaps signifying that I was in the eye of the storm, didn't mean I was immune to what the wider nation was suffering. There had been a considerable snowfall in parts of the Midlands and Scotland, but I awoke warm and comfy due to my wonderful fleece liner, despite the sound of rain on the Khyam tent. The wind had been howling outside but, strangely, the tent had hardly been moving. I've come to learn, over the years, that the sound of the wind in the trees when you can hear it but not see it from inside, often sounds much worse than it is. Of course the trees are giving you cover and taking a lot of energy out of the wind. The same physics explains why Mars has such high winds, because there is little atmosphere and no vegetation to deplete the energy from the weather systems, or something. I'm not sure if I heard that Mars bit on a science programme or dreamt it.

So after some hiding in my tent and doing things that allowed me to avoid going outside, packing the sleeping bag and the rest of my gear, I eventually had to wash up, visit the showers and do all those other regular chores. No amount of delay was going to allow the tent to dry as I'd managed on previous wet mornings so there was only one thing for it. Stuffing the sopping wet tent in the back of the Truck, trying to put any kit (such as sleeping bags or clothes) that had to be kept dry on the back seat I ended up with dampness in the luggage bay and hoped for the best. Anything left in the damp area was either waterproof or didn't matter.

After packing up in the pouring rain I left the campsite and headed south. After a week of high moorlands and craggy mountains in the distance, I found myself driving through, gentler landscape of low hills and rolling pasture giving way to the eventual flatness of the Lancashire Fylde. Dry stone walls became less frequent to be replaced by fences and hedgerows. As I travelled south, the Pennines became a distant hint off to the east. I'd travelled up one side of the Pennines and down the other. I seemed to have been drawn to the coast but when not all counties offer a sea view, you have to take it where you can.

Driving down into Lancashire, the rain continued and I was soon passing through Carnforth and Lancaster with more heavy granite buildings, some blackened with pollution and the occasional street of the ubiquitous thirties semi as can be seen in any part of the country.

The Fylde is another area of land reclaimed from the sea and, as such, it has something of the quality of Norfolk and Lincolnshire. Having said that, it hasn't yet suffered the indignation of having its hedgerows grubbed up as in the East, although it does have the far horizons and bent-over trees growing away from the wind.

Approaching Blackpool, there was a noticeable transformation in the weather, leaving the rain behind, blue sky south of me and grey clouds to the north, the line between the two directly above me at exactly the moment the rain stopped on the windscreen. Passing into the town the thirties semis faded into Victorian red brick terraces and I pulled up outside Graham's house in South Shore at about 2:00.

With the Truck parked in the street, containing much that was important to me, I stepped inside and we sat down to a coffee with an old episode of Time Team on the TV. Meanwhile the tent dried out in the garden, the bright sunshine and blustery day turning out to be the perfect drying day for tents and laundry alike.

After the coffee we left Tony, Phil and Mick in Carenza's trench and headed off in the Truck for the local branch of a recently nationalised bank.

∗ ∗ ∗

Standing in the queue I was approached by an efficient-looking young assistant dressed in a suit all smart and business-like. 'Can I help you?'

I was impressed to be asked before even reaching the counter. -Yes, I've come to collect my new bank card.'

Very efficiently she took me off to the interview room with a little table and a computer terminal where I explained the situation. 'I arranged for the card to be sent to the Blackpool branch as I'm not going to be home until after the old card expires. Unfortunately something went wrong and the card arrived at my house a few days ago.' She sat patiently with something of an impenetrable expression as I continued. 'So I had a friend forward it to me here as was the original plan. It should have arrived by recorded delivery either today or yesterday.'

'We have had no special deliveries but I can check for you.' Leaving me sitting in the little room, the smart assistant in the smart suit went off to investigate as I began to imagine what I would do if the card was still in the post. However, she soon returned with the letter forwarded by my friend addressed to me care of the bank.

From the envelope she pulled that familiar package of letters that you normally get through the post with the card stuck to the letter, along with numerous leaflets, terms and conditions that you'll never read, exhortations to buy life insurance, codes of practice, promises to be environmentally friendly and special offers on things like patio heaters. (If you've had this particular mailing you'll know.)

This was going well. 'You'll need to sign for the new card.' She handed me a document to sign.

This was going extremely well, I thought. I was feeling like a proper traveller, you know, the English gentleman explorers who trekked across the globe in the 19th century having money wired to themselves as they progressed. Okay, I was in Blackpool instead of Bolivia and I was wearing shorts and trainers instead of plus fours and brogues, but I was fantasising about the parallels. Soon I'd be on my way making my progress around the Historic Counties of England. Had I told her about my trip, should I, would she be interested?

She handed me the new card and I handed over my old one, which still had a couple of weeks to run. 'I suggest you check the card is okay.' She handed me a card reader to test it as she typed something into the terminal.

As I entered my PIN she looked at the terminal, expressionless. 'That's strange. The card is showing up as cancelled.'

Feelings of panic and worse entered my thoughts' What would I do if I didn't have a card? I could survive until the end of the month on the old one. I could, perhaps, draw enough cash in advance if I planned things, but how much? Could I carry enough cash to pay for fuel, averaging at a tank about every four days? Did I dare to carry that much cash not knowing where I was going to be, what sort of scrapes I might get into? Should I consider carrying cash on me or would the Truck be a safer place to store it?

The efficient assistant tapped at the keyboard… 'According to the computer there is another card. It seems to have been sent to your branch.' I sat back in my seat and sort of slumped. 'I'll phone the branch.'

After a considerable delay while she listened to the phone ring, she gave up. My local branch simply wasn't answering.

'Are they short of staff down there?' I asked. 'I can't imagine them not answering the phone at all.'

'It doesn't necessarily mean they are short of staff,' she responded. I was fairly convinced that this was a policy response.

I was thinking that if they are short of staff then, surely, it's not their fault, it's the fault of the people that have caused them to be short of staff. Any organisation that is unable to respond to phone calls, even internal calls, is surely understaffed.

I leant forward and held my head in my hands.

'I'll try sending them an email. Let's see if that will get their attention,' she added helpfully. 'I'm not sure they will see it though. They probably don't check it constantly.'

I straightened up briefly. 'Well I'd like to complain.' I demanded rather unhelpfully before returning to my posture holding my head. My attempt at being assertive didn't really go with my defeated body language.

'I'll phone the complaints department,' she responded matter-of-factly.

I continued to sit, leaning forward in an almost foetal position, in a feeble attempt to communicate my state of affairs, but I figured she'd grasped the disastrous nature of the situation. Should I sit up like a sensible person? I wasn't making a very good job of impersonating an intrepid Victorian explorer. No amount of plus fours and brogues would have made a difference with the way I was behaving.

After a few minutes on hold to the complaints department, while she looked at the screen, she pulled the phone away from her ear. 'I'm just wondering about this statement on the screen. It says the card has been sent *'to branch.'* I wonder if it means this branch.' I lifted my head out of my hands and listened hopefully. She continued to explain. 'There isn't really enough space on the screen to say which branch it was sent to.' I perked up briefly. 'I'm just going to put the phone on speaker. If you get through to complaints let them know the situation and tell them that I've just gone to check if there is any other post. I'll only be a minute.'

For a minute or two I sat in the tiny interview room, in the anonymous bank branch in Blackpool, listening to the sound of a phone ringing in a call centre somewhere in another part of the country (possibly another part of the world), I knew not where. Nobody in the complaints department answered as they were probably all taking complaints from people complaining about not being able to get through to complaints.

I stopped being foetal as there wasn't anyone to watch.

After a few minutes of listening to the phone ring, the assistant returned with something of a spring in her step. 'I think we might be in luck.' She handed the card over to me. 'You should probably check it.'

I put the card in the reader, entered my PIN and it came up trumps.

'Okay, now it might be an idea to draw some cash just to make sure,' she added. 'As soon as you use the new card, the old card will stop working.'

'Okay I'll go out and get some cash just to be sure'

I stepped outside and, lo, there was cash. I drew a nice big fat chunk of twenty pound notes, just because I could. A moment later I was back in the branch so pleased that I could have kissed her, but that would almost definitely have been inappropriate. A moment later I was back in the Truck and the trip was back on plan.

* * *

In the final analysis, it was probably a case of everybody doing their best. Being a nationalised bank after the financial crisis of 2008, it's possible to see how the staff are in an impossible situation. The bank is under pressure to return to profit and therefore needs to be financially stable (so holding more financial reserves); at the same time they are told to lend more to re-float the economy (so keeping money in circulation and depleting their reserves), as well as being ready to be sold off again at a rate that returns the public money that was used to rescue it. Their staff numbers have clearly been cut to the bone and you can imagine that the counter staff aren't the guilty parties in all this. I got the impression that the Blackpool branch had no back-office staff, and it seemed my local branch were the same. They had to manage to open the post, answer the phones and respond to emails at the same time as serving customers. Well I say that, but clearly, they weren't answering the phones or opening the post and one imagines there are thousands of emails going unread. The IT systems are incapable of dealing with the unusual situation where multiple cards have been sent out. (Not to mention an awkward sod such as me had taken it upon himself to have a card sent to a branch to be picked up.) IT systems rarely deal with unusual situations very well, which is why we will always need hard-working humans in organisations. Bureaucrats and the media would do well to understand that, but being magnanimous doesn't sell newspapers.

My best guess is that the people sending the card to my home discovered that a separate instruction had ordered a card to be sent to Blackpool so they cancelled the card sent to Hertfordshire lest it fall into the hands of ne'er-do-wells, however the card was already in the post by then. The replacement card was sent to Blackpool, as they were asked, but nobody in the rest of the organisation had been told what was going on. (Are you following this, there'll be an exam later.) Fortunately the assistant in Blackpool had the insight to ask if the branch referred to was her own branch because the computer system didn't have the capacity to define it any further. Had I not had the card sent on from home we might have found the right card sooner. In the end I was relieved that the situation didn't wreck my trip and further relieved that I didn't have to write something scathing to the complaints department.

* * *

A few hours later, I'd found a campsite that seemed to be converted from someone's garden in a patchwork of hard-standings for caravans divided by high hedges and rows of trees, a sheltered lawn space for tents. It was all rather pleasant really.

The owner charged me twenty quid for a pitch with electricity, so suddenly I felt very positive towards the guy in Durham who'd given me the electricity for nothing. However expensive the back garden was, it was a contrast to a site I'd tried down the road, a mass of cinders with a tiny green space in the middle, an island of green strips no more than ten feet across amid a sea of dark blue-grey cinders; just a bit aesthetically horrible really.

* * *

A short taxi ride later, including a stop at an off-licence to buy whisky, I was back at Graham's house. (For the benefit of Americans, an off-licence is a liquor store.)

We talked of shoes and ships and sealing-wax, of cabbages and kings, metaphysics and the like, and whether pigs have wings. We spoke of the old days and matters non-rational, the nature of the universe, its workings and our connection to it until the whisky was gone and it was time to return by taxi to my tent, ready to continue my journey the next day. Some of the things we discussed were as likely as pigs might fly but that was the fun of the discussion. We were lifted by this dancing on the edge of rationality and found it meaningful even if we might admit to not believing every part of what was said were we questioned hard on the subject in a more sober moment. At times there can be a certain suspension of disbelief which can be useful, artful even, in its own way. I mentioned Bram Stoker and the house with the turrets and he suggested that was the one but what his evidence was I never ascertained.

Truth be told, just before I left, there was an incident where we got into a bit of an argument. It was a stupid thing for two old mates, me filled with enthusiasm and wanting to show my old mate something on the Internet (I can't even remember the details now), him wanting to get comfortable with a drink and a smoke in hand before the story commenced. The result was he insisted on ten minutes of fuss and faff that only served to take the wind out of my sails and control the frame of me telling my story, whatever it was. I allowed it to irritate me to the point of annoyance and a few minutes later the taxi returned. I was soon back in my tent wishing the final incident had never taken place.

Day 16 - Lancashire to Cheshire

Thursday May 16th

Miles on Truck: 1238

Waking up in the back garden campsite in Blackpool, the place had an altogether better feel than when I'd arrived. I'd not been sure about the place the night before as, when I phoned to book in, I thought the owner might have been friends with the owner of the site I'd abandoned along the road. Might he pass on my misgivings? Having said that, what would be the worst that could happen? Would the campsite mafia track me down via my blog posts, pursuing me around the country, attempting to deduce my next destination and lying in wait for me as I book in at some future site? Later I got a sense of agreement from him about the other site and their rather enthusiastic use of cinder resurfacing. I wonder if we are, one day, going to discover that cinders used as a surface material for tracks and driveways are carcinogenic in the same way that the carbon in burned carbohydrate is said to be distinctly unhealthy in large enough quantities. Kids have an intuitive aversion to anything that seems a bit untoward, spiders, haircuts, that burnt cornflake at the bottom of the packet. Should we trust to the instincts of children when we consider risks in life? Does this mean we need to be suspicious of broccoli?

Although the campsite was, effectively, a large back garden, a piece of land attached to the back of the house, converted into lots for caravans by judicious use of hedges, it had quite a nice feel in the morning. Any sound of traffic was quite distant and sounds of twittering birds were ever-present. It was the site's facilities that clinched it though; as usual it's not surprising how plenty of hot water, general cleanliness and good washing-up facilities can become so significant and you can excuse so much else. Even tiny details such as the posh squirty perfumed handwash in the loos becomes significant when you don't get it elsewhere. It's just a shame they couldn't have put in a new syphon in the toilet cistern, meaning that you have to pump the bloody thing to get it to flush, just like at the hippie campsite in Cambridgeshire. The twenty quid fee was the highest I'd paid so far but I thought, what the hell, it was a good place despite all that and in the mornings I was always grateful for having got through another night. With the randomness of the whole trip I was getting used to taking the rough with the smooth, and a malfunctioning syphon was not really that rough.

Thinking of Cheshire, one of the other campers suggested I might like to look at the Anderton Boat Lift, which seemed like a splendid idea, but a spell of research over a coffee told me that it was too close to Manchester for comfort, what with my preference to stay away from big cities. Instead I decided I needed somewhere else. The English Heritage book listed Beeston Castle; I liked the look of the picture so I headed there.

Leaving the flat of the Fylde behind, driving south, the landscape slowly changed from the hills that I'd seen over the previous week to more rolling pasture. There didn't seem to be many crops in evidence though, with the emphasis apparently still on grazing as on the high moorlands of the Pennines or up in Cumberland and Westmorland. I battled my way through Wigan, cursing Kathy and her unwillingness to give me any options other than motorways. I'd hoped that by avoiding motorways I'd find nice country routes but it seems she had other ideas and directed me along the trunk routes of old. This meant driving through the centre of towns. Add to that the fact that the area between Manchester and Liverpool is dotted with various industrial towns, sprawling to a degree that there's not much space between them and you don't get any countryside to speak of.

It was turning into a scorching hot day, a complete contrast to the last few days of intermittent rain, total downpours, powerful winds and reports of snow elsewhere. In the Truck it was hotter still unless I kept moving with the windows open; amid the conurbations of Wigan and Warrington that seemed an unlikely pleasure.

Suddenly, around Warrington, the landscape changed. Kathy brought me on a straightish route south from Preston to the western-most crossing of the River Mersey at Warrington, thus taking me southwest towards Beeston Castle, about which I knew nothing. South of the Mersey the fields were larger, with crops rather than grazing, oilseed rape and something green that I couldn't identify. Of course, to the average reader, something green sounds like grass, but even with my meagre level of woodcraft and agricultural knowledge I can tell grass when I see it. I'd not noticed the rape in flower before, and at this time of year I always wonder if it's just flowered overnight or had I been particularly unobservant in the preceding days.

After a stint along the Tarporley Road, looking suspiciously like a Roman road though I could find no definite evidence, I arrived at Beeston Castle at about 3:30. Civilised visitors would have risen at 6:00, been out of the house by 7:00 and arrived at the castle for a full day's exploration by 8:00 gaining the maximum benefit from their entrance fee. However I'm not a civilised visitor. Instead, taking advantage of my new English Heritage membership purchased at Whitby I gained entry for free.

Beeston Castle is extraordinary in a number of ways. On arrival I realised I had been there before. I went with a girlfriend a few years ago. When we arrived it was too late to go in (probably at much the same time of day and for the same reason), or it was just starting to rain or something, so we didn't bother and went elsewhere. However it was worth being turned away because we then discovered Peckforton Castle nearby.

Peckforton Castle is a spectacular pastiche built by a Victorian business magnate, John Tollemance, a wealthy Victorian Cheshire landowner and minor noble who clearly thought his status and money deserved a castle, so he built himself one… a proper one. Peckforton Castle, now operating as a hotel and wedding venue, looks authentic to the uneducated eye but if you look close and think about it you can see it's a modern pastiche. There are windows on the outside, which medieval engineers simply wouldn't have, and the sheer perfection of the stone cutting gives it away. Still, despite all this, to any fan of medieval history, Lord of the Rings or Game of Thrones, the place is a wonder because it's, perhaps, as close as you might get to an experience of a complete castle and it's possible to stay there.

Apparently Beeston Castle, a genuine medieval castle dating from the early 13th century, was also owned by the same guy but he wouldn't have been able to live in it because it's basically a pile of rocks on top of a pile of rock. The gatehouse of Beeston Castle was built by Tollemance, or at least paid for by him.

Beeston Castle is a massive enclosure on a high rocky outcrop that sticks out on the end of the Peckforton Hills. The two castles are so close together that one imagines Tollemance intended that he could gaze out from one modern castle at the ruins of the other. This portrayal of him as a self-important landowner is perhaps unfair as he is said to have been quite enlightened and generous for his day, building many cottages and farmhouses each with enough land to keep a few animals and thus allow tenants to be self-sufficient.

The natural rock crag of Beeston Castle is remarkable. On the south side the slope is gradual, though still enough to wear you out as you walk to the top. However, on the other three sides it's a sheer drop 350 feet to the Cheshire Plain below. The views are spectacular and, if you get too close to the railing on the edge, just a little scary. Apparently you can see many, many counties from there but I have no idea how people justify these claims. Do they light fires in the distance and declare that they can see the smoke? The place is known as the 'Castle on the Rock' for obvious reasons and while it's a ruin, so doesn't compete with Bamburgh Castle in that way, it more than makes up for that with its location. It's said that Richard II hid his treasure here while trying to stay out of trouble from those that wanted to depose him in 1399. Richard had trusted allies in Cheshire, at one point holding a parliament surrounded by 200 Cheshire archers to back him up against his rivals, but it seems he didn't trust the good people of Cheshire quite enough to ask them to look after his treasure. It is said many have searched for it but none have found it.

And just in case you are in any doubt as to the dramatic nature of Beeston Castle, the Google Earth photo shows a considerable shadow to the north, which says something as aerial photographs almost always give an impression of a flat landscape. Today the castle is a ruin, thanks to Oliver Cromwell but if you are passing through, even late in the day, I'd say it's well worth a visit.

Leaving the castle, after buying a guidebook and a pencil sharpener in the shape of a medieval catapult, with no leads for campsites other than a two-week-out-of-date answerphone message, I decided to drive in a random direction and hope for the best. I'd not tried the search-for-a-brown-campsite-sign-strategy yet but I decided to give it a go. What's the worst that could happen, I'd end up camping in a field entrance or sleeping in the Truck. Clearly I'd put the experience of Rutland behind me and was renewed with confidence of surviving on my own resources.

After stopping to get some spectacular pictures of Beeston Castle on its crag in the late afternoon sun, I found myself driving down a tiny lane into Tiverton, which I thought was in Devon but apparently it's also in Cheshire. Obeying the instructions to drive carefully through the village, I did as was told. They also instructed me to not break their humpback bridge which seemed like a good idea lest I end up in the Shropshire Union Canal.

The bridge was an adventure in itself, being 45 degrees off the horizontal as you approach it around a corner. At one point I couldn't see over the bonnet, taking it on faith that I was facing the right way. Get it wrong and you really would end up in the canal as the bridge showed considerable signs of wear and tear along the parapet not to mention missing bricks and yellow tape all over; long vehicles beware. Crossing the bridge I spotted the Shady Oak pub, a good name if ever I saw one and I've never heard of another, so I thought I'd pop in to see if they knew of a campsite in the area.

Pulling into the pub car park, ahead of me, at the top of the car park, through some gates, being a touring camper of some two weeks experience, my seasoned eye spied what I immediately recognised as a series of caravan hard-standings. Granted there weren't any caravans to confirm my observation but that construction on the left looked like a toilet block and behind me there was definitely a pub.

This is the wonderful serendipity of touring without a plan. Just when you think it's all going horribly wrong and you fear you will never get out of Wigan, with a day of battling through the nightmare of the Manchester/Liverpool urban sprawl, I found a stunning castle and a pretty pub campsite overlooking a humptyback bridge across a canal. I ate a wonderful pub meal of breaded place and chips with pints of real ale, looking out across the canal to the medieval splendour of Beeston Castle sitting atop its magnificent crag bathed in May sunshine. I could hardly have wished for more.

Day 17 - Cheshire to Staffordshire

Friday May 17th

Miles on Truck: 1315

After an evening in the pub at Tiverton I awoke to the sound of birds twittering and ducks quackering as they explored the curious object that had appeared in their home. A mated pair of mallards seemed to be taking an interest in me, or at least she was and he just seemed to be following her wherever she went. Clearly he needed to learn something about neediness.

Packing up, I took the shortest route for Staffordshire, looking for coffee and a better signal. The weather was cloudy with occasional breaks in the cloud leading to bursts of sunshine that were too warm for a linen jacket, unless you wanted to look like Alfred Molina playing Reverend Shannon in the *Night of the Iguana* at the National Theatre in 1992. (I only say that because I saw the production and he had a very sweaty linen jacket. Personally I would have taken it off but perhaps that wasn't an option for a disgraced priest, so what do I know? Obviously it wasn't real sweat but was painted on.)

At the start of the day my route took me down fine narrow lanes, along short stretches of main roads and then back onto single track lanes. Often I passed junctions with precipitous drops, down slopes into lanes deep with tall hedgerows either side. I did notice that I'd not seen grubbed up hedgerows for some time. Cheshire would include the odd fence instead of a hedge but that's just a part of the landscape. In the northernmost counties the field boundaries are almost exclusively dry stone walled. On trips into Wales in the past, I'd seen tiny fields bounded by dry stone where I'd been told that the walls served no purpose other than to clear the landscape of rocks. In some places the fields were so small you'd call them pens rather than fields. Of course whoever told me this might have been winding me up and they might have actually been pens.

Moving inland, drawing closer to the metropolis of greater Manchester and its satellite towns I passed through Middlewich (where I wondered if they have cuckoos) and Holmes Chapel, where I wasn't able to make misspelled references to literature other than a weak pun on Sherlock so I didn't. I had headed this way to figure out where I was going in Staffordshire and I had learned that a good place to do that is a supermarket with Wi-Fi and a coffee shop. My intention was to head for that part of Staffordshire that falls within the Peak Experience District National Park; Macclesfield was perfectly placed as a stopping off point.

However, before I could reach Macclesfield, while I was still trying to escape Cheshire, the next moment of serendipity struck. Suddenly there in front of me, above the tree tops and houses was the Lovell Telescope of the Jodrell Bank Observatory. Searching for a good signal to edit my manuscript, and to post a blog, it struck me that a parking spot within sight of an astronomical observatory ought be just the job, so I swung down a lane hoping to get a bit closer, with frequent views across a few rolling fields to the famous radio telescope. Surely people who work in such places would be clued up on all things technological and connected, and would demand a good signal from the mobile phone companies. Down a twisty lane with occasional views of the radio dish, I pulled into a wide farm entrance track, with a good view of the telescope. Plugging everything into the cigarette lighter I connected the spaghetti of cables and logged on to write a blog. For a few moments I gazed geekily at what is, even today, 60 years after construction, still the third largest steerable dish radio telescope on the planet. The thing weighs 3200 tonnes, which is pretty impressive when you think that it moves. It's 250ft across, is nearly 300 feet high at its highest point and takes 5300 litres of paint, which means when they've painted one end they have to start again on the other. Actually that last bit is the Forth Bridge and it's not true of that either. The Lovell telescope has performed surveys of extra galactic radio emissions, made observations of the sun, measured radar echoes from the planets, been used in measurements of gravitational lensing and carries the train from North Queensferry to South Queensferry. No, hang on… that's the Forth Bridge, which is an amazing feat of engineering but, then again, the Forth Bridge didn't discover the galaxy VIRGOHI21 which appears to be made entirely out of dark matter. Don't get me started on dark matter though, or dark energy, or inflation, it's not worth it, and clearly I don't understand the maths.

* * *

Physicists will talk about meaning and beauty in the equations in which they work. Einstein's theory of general relativity is said to be the most accurate description of the universe that we have, all wrapped up in an equation that could be expressed on a T shirt. They often use the word elegant to express the meaning that scientists find in such equations. But can any of us grasp the detail of that equation to access that meaning? I can access the significance of one of the great simple equations of Newtonian physics, F=MA (Force Equals Mass x Acceleration), but I can grasp the idea of force by hammering in a nail. I can grasp acceleration and mass by the size and movement of the hammer. All of this is my everyday experience but the concepts within the general relativity equation are out of my reach. Hell, I looked up general relativity to see if I could give an example of a difficult concept within the equation but I was beaten before I started. Right from the start it's all Greek to me and I sort of feel I understand the idea of general relativity but none of the detail.

* * *

Suddenly my reverie was interrupted by a dog, some sort of spaniel, barking enthusiastically at my open window. I say enthusiastically as sometimes it's difficult to tell the difference between enthusiasm and aggression, but I suspect that with spaniels it's mostly enthusiasm with a dash of curiosity and perhaps too much coffee.

Shortly, heralded by the spaniel, the owner appeared and I assumed I was talking to the farmer.

'You don't mind if I park here for a moment?' I asked referring to the end of the track where I'd settled myself. The end of the track was broad and I was barely off the lane so not really blocking anything. However I've come to understand farmers as being fiercely territorial and understandably so when it comes to townies abroad and I count myself in that category.

'Not at all,' she responded.

'It seemed like it would be a good place to get a signal,' I added.

'Oh it is,' she replied without a hint of irony as she walked on with about eight dogs in tow.

Ironically, when I later visited the Jodrell Bank website to check the spelling, I found a note asking that people switch off all mobile phones and electronic devices during their visit. It hadn't occurred to me that radio telescopes might actually be against the use of wireless communications lest they interfere with their sensitive instrumentation. However, I don't recall any reports of spurious mistaken first contact events triggered by my attempt to get a signal on my unreliable tablet.

* * *

Sometime later I pulled into the Macclesfield branch of Tesco. I've been vague about the supermarkets I've used so far, but now I feel this is worth mentioning. I was relieved to find a Tesco as they are a good bet for a toilet, a coffee and provisions for the next few days. Shortly I was sitting in the Costa Coffee in Macclesfield Tesco thinking I'd quickly check I'd caught all the typos on the blog I'd posted an hour or so before when I'd been entranced by Jodrell Bank.

So imagine my frustration, or worse, when I tried to visit the blog only to get a message saying it was blocked! I can't remember the exact term but it said that it was blocked because of possible illegal or immoral content. (It didn't say exactly that but it was one of those thought police, bluenose type statements.) I'd experienced this in Tesco in Aylesbury and at the time I was feeling so low about the sheer effort of keeping up the pace of travelling, blogging and exploring, that I was about ready to give up. Tesco blocking access to my blog, which was essentially nothing more controversial than an account of my camping holiday, very nearly destroyed me. So sitting in Macclesfield Tesco some two weeks later, I felt my mood collapse into something between frustration and depression. The sim card connection in the tablet was unreliable at best and some days wouldn't connect at all, hence me always being in search of a good signal. Coffee shop Wi-Fi was one of the reliable alternatives. Although the blog wasn't crucial, all in all, the sheer effort of keeping going each day was enough and I simply didn't need these frustrations.

* * *

Later it turned out that the reason Tesco had banned access to my blog was that at the time I was blogging through the Google service blogspot.com. In the same way that Scunthorpe had once been blocked by Google for having a rude word embedded within it, now known as the Scunthorpe problem, it seemed Tesco didn't like the fact that 'gspot' was embedded in Google's blogging service. There may be some poetic irony in the fact that Google, who had once banned Scunthorpe, were now being banned by Tesco for similar reasons. However, this irony was lost on me. Today, after similar problems posting blogs onto Facebook I've now moved to Word-press. The day that 'Dpress' becomes a banned term by some jumped-up thought police, politically correct censor, I think I'll give up and go live in a shack somewhere in splendid isolation.

***

Leaving Macclesfield I asked Kathy to take me to the only place on that map that was: A, in Staffordshire, B, in the Peak Experience District National Park, and C, showed a campsite. Hopefully there would be none of this searching through the Gargantuan Book of Campsites, trying to figure out which ones were in Staffordshire, phoning them up and going over there before I even knew what sort of location they were in.

The direct route to Butterton was an adventure in itself. Clearly my relationship with Kathy was improving as, climbing out of Macclesfield, she led me along country roads and up into the hills, all pasture bordered by the now typical dry stone walls as the road turned into a narrow lane, somewhere around mid-afternoon twisting up an increasing slope into the high country. Soon the climb was steep and highly enjoyable, keeping the Truck in low gear, the diesel growling up the slope sounding like something from a more primitive generation.

Just before I crested the hill I passed the Hanging Gate Inn where I decided to stop to take in the view. At this point I was still outside of the Peak Experience District National Park but it was a beautiful peak experience all the same. The view presented a patchwork of fields, varying in size and shape, irregular with hedgerows and lines of trees along boundaries. The landscape undulated into folds where water courses were clustered with small woodlands, chaotic but ultimately ordered by the outcomes of the forces of the natural environment so fundamentally ordered but an order that we can't discern without a certain degree of comprehension.

I really wanted to pop into the Hanging Gate Inn (with a name like that how could I not want to?) and it looked like it might be a nice place, but my campsite anxiety got the better of me so I paused only for breath before continuing. What with the stunning view (did I mention the stunning views?), the edge of the car park seemed to drop away to nothing and I imagined that handbrake fitters and businesses specialising in the recovery of cars from over precipices do a roaring trade in these parts, but probably not with many customers in common.

From here on Kathy directed me over high moorland, along tiny single track lanes with more dry stone walls than I could have hoped for. Some of the lanes were such that the wing mirrors barely fitted down the lane; the landscape certainly put the Truck through its paces. I'd not been aware that the Peak Experience District had areas of bleak high moorland such as I'd seen in Yorkshire. My perception of the Peak Experience District had always been exactly that, peaks, often with wooded slopes quickly descending on either side to pretty river valleys lush with foliage and dingly dells full of dappled sunlight and shade. However, it seems the Staffordshire side of the Peak Experience District is much more like the high open moorland of Yorkshire and the Pennines.

On one particularly challenging descent, down a steep stone-walled lane, I was glad to understand the value of engine braking, thus not over using the Truck's brakes, as the slope ran on steeply for a good half mile. On a previous trip, before I owned the Truck, I had a similar descent from the North Yorkshire Moors in an old estate car, overloaded with camping gear and African drums made from tree trunks. I'd not noticed the brakes overheating until I arrived at a sharp turn, just as someone came the other way, and I discovered I didn't have any brakes left. Barely missing the oncoming car I pulled into the first available flat space to wait for the brakes to cool. As I contemplated my near-miss I remembered, and finally understood, the high revving diesel engines on the buses in my childhood, as they descended the steep hills of my home town on a Saturday afternoon trip to the town centre.

After traversing the moors I eventually arrived in the village of Butterton, a tiny hilltop hamlet with a church and a pub, a few cottages and lanes descending in all directions. The place was deserted other than a couple of builders packing up at the end of the day, who directed me down one of the lanes to the campsite at Heathy Roods Farm, a name to conjure with if ever I heard one.

Cautiously, I followed the instructions to a farm house about a mile away that turned out to be the cheapest campsite I'd found so far, yet with possibly the prettiest facilities, being all whitewashed cottage stone with exposed beams and all that. I got a very warm reception from a guy who seemed quite interested to hear about my trip as he directed me to a spot with the best view overlooking the adjacent valley.

For the second night in a row I allowed myself a proper evening meal instead of cooking in my tent. The walk up the lane turned out to be a gentle stroll past fields of young bullocks beyond more dry stone walls. As well as the bullocks I found myself compelled to stop to look at some spectacular moss formations around the churchyard, feeling that I could afford to while away the time having now camped, with the whole evening to kill in the middle of nowhere and nothing to do apart from eat.

The Black Lion Inn turned out to be the liveliest pub I'd been in for some time, though this may have been due to the 60th birthday party that night, with people coming from far and wide. However, from conversations with the locals I got the impression that the place would have been humming on any Friday night. It seems the English village pub is not yet dead, you just need to know where to look, but you might have to climb dramatic slopes and traverse wild moors to what you might mistake for the middle of nowhere.

Day 18 - Staffordshire to Derbyshire

Saturday May 18th

Miles on Truck: 1374

It turned out to be a windy night on the hilltop at Heathy Roods Farm, but by the time I decided to get up it had died down a bit. There had been gentle rain on the way back from the pub, but fortunately the owner of the campsite turned out to be correct in that it was an easier walk down hill on the return journey, and possibly easier still being full of beer and lasagne. What wind that remained was blowing up the valley and straight in the door thus ensuring a properly dry tent by the time I was ready to pack up, but that's probably why the valley was put there in the first place.

The showers, pot washing and toilet facilities at Heathy Roods Farm were located in converted outbuildings that had an authentic farmhouse feel. The place was a welcome break from the commercial set-ups of the big caravan sites and the thrown-together make up of some others I'd visited. This sort of described the feel to the whole place, authentic country farm house on a small holding in the Staffordshire peaks, down the road from what seemed like a vibrant village at Butterton that may, just, have bucked the trend of rural decline. How much this was due to local people keeping the community going or to incomers, is anyone's guess but, I wonder if that's a process that's been going on throughout history.

* * *

I asked Kathy to take me to Dovedale, just across the border in the Derbyshire peaks. This was to be my shortest day's journey.

Now, at this point, I have to admit to being just a little bit of a cheat. I've said all along that I'd not had any plans for my destination, being a fan of serendipity, but that is not entirely true. Of course, it is true to the point that I never booked a campsite in advance, so much so that sometimes deciding on and locating my campsite had occupied my whole day. If those counties have been ill-served by my lack of exploration I apologise as that was never my intention, However, a trip such as this doesn't come with any training and I was making it up as I was going along. I had a bit of a plan in that I wanted to hit Derbyshire on May 18th.

Each year some friends of mine run a camp in Derbyshire on or around the middle of May. When I decided to make the journey I chose May and June, as the calendar for the rest of the summer was just too busy to fit in anything lasting six weeks. However, even May isn't entirely free as the May camp falls slap bang in the middle of the date of this tour. However, this is a camping tour and the May camp is a camp, so why not combine the two? So without making any firm plans or announcements, I worked out that it was entirely possible to start in Oxford on May 1st, travel up the Eastern counties, around the North and back down through Lancashire via my mate in Blackpool, and this should take me about 18 days, thereby hitting Derbyshire on the weekend of May 18th.

So from Butterton I set off for the Derbyshire side of the Peak Experience District National Park, about ten miles away. The shorter journey would be a welcome break from the relentless requirement to keep moving.

I will say this for the Peak Experience District. I've only seen bits of it before, and perhaps that's the point of this trip, to randomly discover parts of England that I've never seen, but I'm surprised by what I found. I've been to Buxton, Matlock and Matlock Bath over the years but that's been about it. Driving up into Butterton from Macclesfield was a bit of an eye-opener, crossing the high moorland that would have graced any episode of James Herriot or scene from Wuthering Heights further north. I don't know what the figures are, or if the landscapes are comparable in terms of geographical definition, but the look and feel seemed very similar to that which I'd crossed around Whitby and on into County Durham. My point is that the Peak Experience District landscapes are as worthy of windswept romantic adventure as any in other parts of the country.

Coming down from the high moorland around Butterton, I descended into steep-sided valleys thick with woodlands, with tinkly waters, twisty little lanes and abrupt narrow stone bridges. The landscapes were dramatic and beautiful, as beautiful as anywhere in the country and I found myself thinking this would be the place would I come if I were to do some backpacking trips.

Thus, at about 2:00, somewhat to the surprise of my friends, I arrived at the campsite. There I spent the rest of the day in the company of pleasant people drinking beer and wine, attending a maypole celebration, walking a candle-lit maze and eventually sitting around the fire, making music, singing songs and forgetting the words, etc. Had I been here the night before I could have been doing the same thing instead of drinking beer and eating lasagne in Butterton, but that night I had an appointment with Staffordshire, today I had an appointment with Derbyshire, tomorrow I would have an appointment with Nottinghamshire.

The people I meet up with in Derbyshire each year are part of a community that express their connectedness to the natural world through camping, observation of the seasons and celebration. That's a bit of a simplification, and I'm sure many would take me to task on this, but it sort of makes the point. Their perspectives lean away from the rational that I've described earlier and seek to experience the meaningful connection that James Rebanks grew up with on his sheep farm in Westmorland. Unfortunately, few of us have that connection and we often find the meaning within the annual cycle of Strictly somewhat hollow. There are many such communities as this (I suspect I passed by one or two at Karma Farm in Cambridgeshire) and they are now arranging their own significant rites of passage. I've personally been to weddings and funerals as well as seasonal celebrations that are observed by these communities in the same way as the wider world celebrates Easter or Christmas. These communities do seem to have more parties, which can't be a bad thing, and they fulfil needs that are no longer catered for other than by corporations that are just interested in fleecing you of your hard-earned cash for the minimum overhead on their part. Of course, these communities may not be connected to generations of practice in the same way as James Rebanks is connected to his land in Westmorland, but these communities are now established enough to have second and third generations (sometimes more) and as such they have developed their own traditions that now go back decades. Those people who have invested themselves over years of attendance find meaning in that continuity, while newcomers might find immediate value in the experience of encountering a community with established traditions and practices that extend before their involvement. These new traditions might not be the centuries-old deep connections of the Westmorland sheep farmer but they certainly have greater significance than a TV series that will last until the viewing figures begin to wane, when it's more profitable to replace it with something with the same formula but a different logo. Of course, that's not to say that there are not people amid these communities with traditions that go back generations, but these are rare and valuable strands that are more difficult to access which is probably why they survive, hidden, to this day.

131

Day 19 - Derbyshire to Nottinghamshire

Sunday May 19th

Miles on Truck: 1384

Suddenly the missing summer had returned. The weather since about week two had been slowly deteriorating, becoming windy in Lincolnshire and up through Yorkshire, Durham and Northumberland, then getting wetter through Cumberland and Westmorland as the rest of the country descended into the chaos of unseasonal weather warnings. The southbound journey had been drier but still windy until yesterday. Saturday at the Derbyshire campsite had been cold, cold enough for extra layers even when sitting around the fire; but Sunday morning was gorgeous, too gorgeous to be sitting in a tent that was turning into an oven. Despite the later than normal night with the campers around the fire, later than normal for this trip at least, I had to get up to stop myself baking.

The campsite we attend each year (really just a farmer's field) is bounded along one side by a river, the other side by a gully that runs off of the river at either end of the gully. It's not a stream as such as it really has no flow, filling up from both ends, but at times of high water the gully floods from each end and meets in the middle. At worst the site can necessitate wellies to get to the loos but it does have the rather nice feel of being on an island even if not a proper one. Every few years though, coming to the island, if the weather had been very wet in the previous days, people might have difficulty driving up the slope on the other side of the gully. Leaving the campsite reminded me that this particular camp had been the reason I bought the Truck in the first place. A few years before, one of my previous cars had lost bits of its protective plastic underside as I tried to get up the slope so I decided I really needed a 4x4. Since then I'd secretly justified my ownership of the fifteen year old gas guzzler with the fact that a few times a year I need to be able to carry large amounts of camping equipment and a few musical instruments across occasionally muddy fields and across this particular gully. These days I justify the increase in my carbon footprint by the fact that I've reduced it by a greater amount by not having had any children.

* * *

Looking for somewhere in the East, to take me towards Nottingham-shire, I asked Kathy to take me to Chesterfield. Unfortunately I typed in 'Chestfield' so for a while I was heading for Kent. By the time I realised, I'd probably missed the most scenic route, but perhaps that's the nature of blind faith, be it in technology or anything else. Many of our decisions in life are based on nothing more than dodgy statistics, which might as well be blind faith.

Eventually I looked at the map and made a more realistic decision. I'd only selected Chesterfield because it was in roughly the right direction; that and the fact that I am a particularly proud owner of two of their rather nice sofas. Basing your navigational decisions on your preferences for furniture isn't a particularly rational thing to do but I feel some decisions can afford to be non-rational, if they are fun, and so long as the result is fairly inconse-quential. If I made a non-rational choice to place a dreamcatcher above my bed because I think of it as a nice piece of art, what does it matter if I have a vague thought that I would like it to catch bad dreams, even if I don't really believe that? The same thought process might go with the choice of plaster ducks—what the hell do they catch? Nobody would think anything of plas-ter ducks other than to think that they are either bad taste or ironic retro. I hasten to add I don't have a dreamcatcher above my bed as I think they are a bit too cutesy for me but that's just a matter of taste and interior design, preferring Chesterfield sofas which don't catch anything as far as I'm aware.

Deciding to be more sensible than to drive to Kent on a whim, I asked Kathy to take me to Mansfield, what with it actually being in Nottingham-shire, so at least it was better from that point of view. However Mansfield didn't make much of an immediate impression on me and there weren't any brown signs to tempt me from my default choice for Nottinghamshire, so from Mansfield I headed to Edwinstowe.

Before I set off from Oxford I'd had an ideal that I'd not do the obvi-ous thing in each county and that I'd seek out interesting and original things to do. However, the vagaries of poor internet connections, campsite neurot-icism and general disorganisation led me to dump idealism for quick solu-tions and in Nottinghamshire that meant Sherwood Forest.

The mobile internet connection in Nottinghamshire seemed particular-ly poor so I reverted to my ancient road atlas and spotted the Sherwood For-est Visitors Centre. Therefore, taking on the full mantle of the tourist, I headed off.

Passing by a cricket match I wondered if I'd made the wrong decision and should watch the match instead; however I thought sitting watching a Sunday afternoon cricket match, while romantically appealing, would probably bore me after a few minutes what with me not having a bloody clue about what was going on. Having a compatriot and a few cans of beer to sit and watch the match with might make a difference but I'm not entirely sure one is allowed to drink beer in public any more. Being at a cricket match might make public consumption of beer permissible but I was on my own and had to drive to a campsite at some point so I gazed longingly (however briefly) at the gentlemen in whites and continued on to the visitor centre.

* * *

The Sherwood Forest Visitor Centre was the usual mix of a café, gift shop and toilets. The gift shop contained the expected combination of toys for kids and books for academics and those interested in Robin Hood, the history of the forest and anything loosely associated that could be shoehorned in as merchandise. I'm sure they sold Robin Hood cheese, or Sherwood Forest honey or some such. I know the shortbread was delicious looking and equally expensive. Had they actually sold Robin Hood cheese I might well have bought some, what with the way my breakfast habits had been developing. At Beeston Castle, a couple of days before, I'd seen the same mix and treated myself to a pencil sharpener in the shape of a working medieval catapult; something that to this very day gives hours of pleasure lobbing tiny balls of paper at my mate Harry, who consistently smiles back at me with an expression of mild amusement, boredom, and the sort of sympathy usually reserved for those with some tragic excuse for their lack of mental prowess.

Having arrived late, as usual, there was just about an hour before the car park was due to close. What would be the consequences if I missed it? Would I be locked in; would it matter if I was locked in? Could I camp in the car? What would happen if I tried to put up my tent in the car park, perhaps just after dark and just long enough to get enough sleep before packing up again in the morning?

Putting my anxieties to one side, I strode off to see the sights of Sherwood Forest in a little under an hour. Doubtless this was an impossibility. I doubt you could see the sights of Sherwood Forest in a month or even a year. I'm sure there are real ruddy-faced outdoor types that will tell you they've spent a lifetime in Sherwood Forest and still find parts they don't yet know. Such is the nature of the outdoors and such is its attraction. On the approach across Nottinghamshire from Derbyshire I'd seen signs that I was in the vicinity of the forest not only from the signposts but from the views across fields—swathes of trees lining the near horizon with patches of forest occasionally closer to the road until, after passing the cricket match, I found myself in the thick of it.

The visitor centre recommended I see the Major Oak and told me about various options for nature walks, ecological study and the like. Being a bit of a tourist and deciding that a nature walk might feed my parking anxiety, I opted to have a look at the Major Oak, a twenty minute walk from the visitor centre.

The Major Oak is said to be the site of Robin Hood's camp with his band of merry men. The truth is that the tree is estimated to be between 800 and 1000 years old so it is contemporary with Robin Hood. This is all assuming that the legend of Robin Hood was seeded by some 12th century malcontent during the years when people were still pissed off about the newcomers during the Norman Conquest. If he ever existed it's likely that he's from somewhere other than Nottinghamshire, possibly South Yorkshire, probably not a dispossessed noble but someone in the artisan class, possibly a yeoman. The earliest references do seem to mention others in his group including some of the names we are familiar with today. As far as the whole robbing from the rich thing goes it seems that's a modern invention going back no further than the Victorian period. (The Victorians are responsible for so much manipulation of our perception of history.) What is interesting and somewhat synchronistic is the historical existence of Robin Hood games associated with May Day as early as the 15yth century. Considering the fact that I'd left on May 1st and had been at a maypole dance the day before, that all seems rather fitting if somewhat unplanned; accidentally meaningful perhaps?

When I got to see it, the tree was impressive. It's about as tall as you might expect a mature oak tree to be but the trunk is truly massive, at 33 feet around the base. The tree is thought to weigh about 23 tons although I have no idea how you weigh a tree. It's actually thought that it might be several trees fused into one trunk such that after hundreds of years you simply can't tell the difference. Another theory for its size is that it was pollarded (pruned back to harvest the wood), and this has caused it to have a heavier trunk that has given it longevity. Whatever the case, it's unlikely that an oak would survive for this sort of period without human intervention as most oaks will live for a few hundred years before succumbing to winter storms or the ravages of disease and rot.

Today the Major Oak is supported by an unfortunate arrangement of scaffolding that rather spoils the effect but without which it would probably have been lost centuries ago. Back at the hippie camp in Derbyshire, someone had been telling me that recent attempts to keep it alive had involved pumping the wood full of silicone, presumably to stop it splitting. I don't know how literal this description was but the leaves did look a bit on the brown side and the whole tree was looking somewhat decrepit. My hippie friend's point had been that if the authorities are having to do this sort of thing to keep it alive, perhaps it's just had its day and should be allowed to die. She may have a point and there does seem to be a difference between the sort of intervention that involves pollarding and pumping it full of silicone. I suppose that if it had died a few years before I'd arrived I'd have been disappointed to have missed it, so perhaps we are preserving it for future generations, or that's what we are telling ourselves.

Incidentally it's only known as the Major Oak after it was named thus by Major Hayman Rooke in 1790. (Clearly he was a humble man naming the tree after himself.) So it was notable over 200 years ago, but whether it would have been any different to any other tree in the time of Robin Hood is doubtful, as it would have been somewhere between a sapling or any normal mature tree. Whatever the case, if Robin Hood lived in Sherwood Forest, South Yorkshire or didn't even have the decency to exist at all, the tree we know as the Major Oak is unlikely to have had a connection with our favourite outlaw, but it's an interesting specimen all the same. One might say that the idea of the tree is a romantic notion and the world is better for it; if we lived in a world of facts and facts alone it would be a Gradgrindian existence devoid of legend, flavour or spice. People find meaning in art or dance or music, while others seem to be able to live without them altogether; who has the right to criticise a life flavoured by romantic notions? In a world of variation and live-and-let-live, it takes all kinds.

✳ ✳ ✳

Before returning to the Truck I spotted a large white sheet strung between two trees with some people in front of it. When I say large I mean large, perhaps twenty feet across, so not a bed sheet. Walking over to investigate I found two guys in proper living history medieval costume giving archery lessons. At a few quid for five arrows I grabbed my chance. After being reassured that it's still possible to exit the car park even after it's locked, I hung around for my lesson.

I had a bit of a go at archery a few years ago but that was with modern sports bows, all composite materials and high-tech-looking. Having some experience of rifle shooting as a teenager, I'd managed to achieve a good grouping and began to home in on the bull, though I never actually hit it. A few years later, when I came to chop down a yew tree that I'd planted too close to the house years before (are we keeping track of the timelines here because there's a test later?) I kept the wood in the hope that I'd be able to make my own longbow. Here, then, was a chance to get a close look at a longbow and see if I was any good at it.

I'm not.

Day 20 - Nottinghamshire to Leicestershire

Monday May 20th

Miles on Truck: 1442

The following morning the Khyam was covered in blossom as I pulled the pegs from the sandy soil. I hadn't bothered to put the guy ropes out, relying on the pegs that support the structure of the Igloo but the soil was so sandy and loose that they would hardly have made any difference. I headed south from Robin Hood country towards Leicestershire. I'd seen Melton Mowbray on the map and wasn't entirely sure which county it was in, but I decided I was going there anyway in search of the world's greatest pork pie.

The landscape was open, with hedgerows obscuring an undulating horizon. The day was hazy, with windmills unmoving in the distance, barely visible through the haze. It had the feel of a potentially hot day if the haze cleared, sort of Schrodinger's scorcher. The roads were fast, often straight with lots of speed cameras and signs telling people not to die horribly on motorbikes.

After stopping for coffee and fuel at the first available petrol station, I struggled to find the road to Melton Mowbray once more. New roads had been built with massive new junctions that Kathy simply didn't recognise. Above me there was an enormous embankment with crash barriers at the top where the roofs of vehicles could occasionally be seen speeding past. I made an immediate decision to avoid this superhighway, preferring the wiggly to the straight. Exploring on my own initiative, I found my way back onto my preferred road despite Kathy's protestations that she had no clue, but soon found myself at another unmarked junction with no idea where to go. I faced a sign saying 'Do not rely on SatNav.' How prophetic, I thought, but then found myself wondering 'wouldn't maps be out of date too, after all maps don't download updates?' I wondered what we were expected to rely on, seaweed?

Eventually I relented and joined the superhighway, all very fast with only gentle curves and clean lines stretching out of sight as if built by invading armies, but a trifle unsatisfactory as a driving experience compared to the winding roads I'd come to love. After a short stretch Kathy suddenly seemed to know where I was and she advised me to get off the superhighway, which I was in complete agreement with. However, she had one final twist in store for me, sending me back on myself, presumably on the old road that the superhighway had been parallel to. If the old road was still there why had I not been allowed to drive it? Was this Kathy working against me or were we both ignorant of our surroundings?

After many delays and diversions I entered Leicestershire on wonderfully wiggly roads amid more signs not to die on motorbikes in horrible ways. It struck me that these signs are to persuade people not to seek an elemental experience when the superhighway of life is so soulless. Many of us go through life in a clean sanitized existence only to end up dissatisfied with the experience, seeking something more meaningful. But meaning can come with a cost; sometimes it's inconvenience such as a slower route from A to B, sometimes it requires extra effort to find your way but in the process serendipity steps in to add value. Sometimes it's a greater cost and it seems bikers have died in that pursuit. Whatever the case, it seems the superhighway of life gets us to the end but we end up looking back and wondering if there might have been a better journey.

* * *

Finally, a little later than I would have liked, I arrived in Melton Mowbray which did indeed turn out to be in Leicestershire. Not really knowing how to begin my search for a locally-grown pork pie, especially under my time constraints, I found the Harboro Hotel which had a bar and convenient parking right outside.

'Hello, I'm searching for a Melton Mowbray pork pie,' I asked standing at the bar hopefully.

'This is Melton Mowbray,' came the reply from the friendly girl behind the bar.

'So can you do a Melton Mowbray pork pie as a lunch?' I asked.

'We don't do a specific lunch of a Melton Mowbray pork pie,' responded the bar maid. (Are we still allowed to call them barmaids? Should it be bar assistants? It's certainly not waitress. Perhaps they're beverage engineers?)

'Oh, that's a shame,' I replied. 'I'm touring the country and I'm hoping to have a Melton Mowbray pork pie in Melton Mowbray.' My disappointment was apparent.

'We could do you a ploughman's,' responded the nourishment purvey-or. 'That includes some Melton Mowbray pork pie.' I cheered up at this. 'It also includes Stilton.'

'Oh, is Stilton local as well?' I asked, perking up some more.

'You bet your ass it is!' exclaimed the sustenance vendor. (Well actually she didn't say that at all as she wasn't a character from a bad country and western film but then again she probably didn't say any of this in so many words. I don't go around the country recording the conversations of the people I meet, you'll be relieved to learn. But the conversation largely followed the points I describe from a starting point of Melton Mowbray pork pies, through Stilton to electricity supplies, only with a slightly less bantery style and fewer opportunities for silliness.)

'Then that's what I'll have,' I replied. 'And a cup of tea please.'

'Certainly.'

'And do you have anywhere I could plug in my little computer?'

* * *

At 3:00, late as usual, after a lunch of locally made pork pie and cheese on hot fresh bread with plenty of butter, I left Melton Mowbray feeling satisfied and full of flavour. Lunch seemed to have been meaningful and filling, what with my enjoyment of local food. Is the meaning of life simply hidden in that which we like or is there more to it than that? If someone spends their life indulging in the pleasure of food or sex or any sensual activity that might be described as pleasure, is that the same as meaning?

* * *

Somehow I'd noticed that the National Space Centre was in Leicestershire and I'd often seen the signs from the M1 wondering what it was, so I decided that this would be a good opportunity to satisfy my imagination. I didn't really know what to expect of such a place but I thought that, what with the long and glorious British tradition of space exploration, the British expeditions to the Moon and Mars, the many world-beating firsts achieved by Britain, the many British astronauts, and all that, I thought the National Space Centre should be included on my tour. There should be meaning in space if anywhere and if it could be found in lunch then it should be true for space too.

Hoping that 3:00 wouldn't be too late for a late afternoon visit, I set off for Leicester to the strains of Road to Nowhere on the stereo. I had to ask myself what was the symbolism of the song title? Was it about my relationship with Kathy and her ability to take me by more interesting routes, if only I had faith in her; or was it that even faith in Kathy cannot avoid the soulless experience of the superhighway of life? In the end I needn't have asked as the symbolism was plain to see; the National Space Centre was closed for the day.

The Space Centre seemed to be a largely inflatable building containing a few second-hand rockets. One might assume that second-hand rockets are rockets that have never actually been used as they tend not to do too well in the aftermarket, pre-enjoyed stakes, tending to move into the smoky, burned and twisted scrap metal or even largely vaporised category. Admittedly the clues had been there all along in that the National Space Centre had a brown sign from the M1 indicating that it was more of a tourist thing than a science thing. However, the same might be said of many science locations that fancy installing a gift shop in the hope of raising a few quid and selling some foam rubber rockets in the same way English Heritage sell foam rubber swords.

* * *

Wandering off in search of somewhere to camp, I found myself in rush hour traffic going nowhere fast. Clearly Talking Heads were still meaningful. Passing by a discount tyre centre, and aware that the Truck was in need of new front tyres, I decided to stop and try my luck. In the process of fitting the two new tyres they told me that my front brake pads were on the way out and asked if I wanted to get them done at the same time. Thinking that a proper brake centre would be better than a bunch of blokes with a shed full of tyres and trolley jacks, I thanked them and said that I'd deal with the brakes in my own time; however, I did now have something meaningful to do in Northamptonshire.

Day 21 - Leicestershire to Northamptonshire

Tuesday May 21st

Miles on Truck: 1534

So morning came, and after breakfast I bugged out and headed off. In the process I was struck by the difference in the soil between South Leicestershire and the day before in Nottinghamshire. Whereas Nottinghamshire had been sandy and wouldn't hold a tent peg, the Leicestershire soil was dark and sticky, such that it gripped the pegs and stuck to them when they came out.

Travelling south, the countryside seemed more undulating than the day before, deeply rolling landscapes where I could rarely see to the horizon unless I was at the top of a rise. The fields were full of oilseed rape and the hedgerows were full of cow parsley. I remembered seeing the cow parsley come out in Norfolk but I'd not registered seeing it since. Cow parsley is one of those plants (well let's call it a weed because that's what it is) that sort of sneaks up on you. It can be invisible one day and then the next it's everywhere. I've always wondered how it does it; does it sprout up over night? I suspect it that it's less dramatic than that and that you simply don't notice it until the flowers open, which probably does happen overnight. However, it's so ubiquitous that if you are not paying attention you could go for days without noticing it. Because much of the roadside landscape seems to be made up purely of cow parsley I suspect that, for the non-weed-inclined, there are many people who have never noticed it in their lives. Anyway, I've always taken the presence of cow parsley as an indication that the summer has properly started. Of course it's no guarantee but it's probably as reliable as the other famous sign of summer, 'Naer cast a clout 'till may is out,' which translates as don't put away your winter clothes until the mayflower (hawthorn) is in bloom.

* * *

For a few days I'd been feeling a little ambivalent about this project. The experience in Derbyshire and the thoughts of SatNav as an analogy of modern living had seemed inspirational for a day or so; then I started to question the validity of the symbolism. Had I got it the wrong way around, does Sat-

Nav represent the modern world and do the twisty little invasion-proof roads represent a more satisfying experience of life, was this all nonsense? Have other people come up with these ideas before and said them, or worse, rejected them? It wasn't really very helpful that since Sherwood Forest I'd not found anything very interesting and I seemed to have returned to the behaviour of bugging out in the morning, being too late to do anything during the day and going straight on to camp that evening. Okay I'd had a bit of pork pie and stilton in Melton Mowbray, but was that really so special, and the Space Centre had been a total disappointment?

I'd decided that after the tyre place in Leicester had condemned my front brake pads, I'd better get them done. I'd also forgotten to get bread and cheese the day before so I decided that Northamptonshire would be about looking after the logistics of the trip. Sorry Northants dwellers, but even if you have the greatest historic treasures, beautiful landscapes and the like, I wouldn't have time for them.

Driving into Market Harborough I spotted Tanvic Tyre and Service Centre so, biting the bullet, I pulled in for the brake pads and to get the tracking checked. The guys behind the counter seemed sensible enough and I sat down to wait for the bill. It took at least a couple of coffees before they came out with my old brake pads to tell me that they didn't need to be changed. Apparently they were barely a third of the way through. I asked if I still needed to pay but they wouldn't take my money. I'd not wasted their time as the tracking needed to be set so I paid for that, but that was a quarter of the price they could have charged me if they had just changed the brake pads and said nothing. It seemed the guy in Leicester had been mistaken or perhaps spinning me a line. No, let's say he was conning me. The whole experience sort of restored my faith in human nature, not that human nature was responsible for my dwindling enthusiasm for the trip; but I got back in the truck, put the MP3 player on and something loud and bouncy from early David Bowie came out. I drove on to Northampton in search of a supermarket, a coffee shop and Wi-Fi, with renewed vigour.

In Northampton, after spending an hour or so drinking coffee, eating a panini and a scone, I'd sorted out a campsite at Billing Aquadrome. Tesco still insisted on making internet access difficult so I reverted to the Titanic Book of Campsites and old technology, phoning up to see if they had a space. As it turned out Billing Aquadrome had plenty of space but that's a story in itself. I'd wondered about Billing Aquadrome for years having seen the brown signs on the motorway, so when I saw it in the Behemoth Book of Campsites I thought this was my chance to find out. It turned out to be easily the most expensive campsite so far, even considering the upmarket Sherwood Forest site I'd been to. However I thought it should be bristling with facilities, so what the hell. I had laundry to do and Billing Aquadrome seemed like the place to do it.

Kathy brought me in through the Northampton rush hour traffic with ease, though I was a little perturbed by the apparent smell of poo as I swung around the final roundabout. I suspected that it was just a local phenomenon, an unfortunately placed sewerage works perhaps, surely it wouldn't last, and besides, I'd already abandoned one campsite having paid for it in Keswick; I could always do that again, despite this one being much more expensive. Could I attempt to get my money back, the smell of poo not being written into any contract? To be honest I didn't fancy my chances so I decided that, if it came to it, I would cut my losses and run.

Swinging into the entrance I encountered numerous booths with red and white barriers and white lines painted on the wide approach road complete with areas of scary hatching. Stopping dead in my tracks, I noted signs declaring one was for owners only. I was clearly not an owner, whatever that was, but I suspected that, had I been an owner, I would know that I was one. One lane was closed and, being a frequent user of supermarkets, I knew not to waste time on that one. The fourth lane was for people leaving and a long history of life experience told me that I should ignore that lane. I did note that there were three times as many lanes for people arriving as there were for people leaving and I wondered about there being some Tardis-like effect going on here. A campsite that is bigger on the inside than the outside would certainly be an interesting place to spend some time, though I'm sure the novelty would wear off eventually.

I picked the only remaining option that wasn't closed, that wasn't for owners, that wasn't for people leaving or anything else that didn't describe me. Pulling up to the gate I found myself talking to a nice man seated in the booth at the controls of the red and white barrier. I say at the controls but I don't know that strictly. We've all been through entrance gates, toll booths, security barriers and the like but how many of us ever actually see what you might imagine to be the array of controls similar to the early models of the Starship Enterprise. Of course, the reality is probably that they have two controls, Up, Down, and Drop-the-barrier-on-the-car-before-it-can-get-through, otherwise known as the sudden death button. I know that's three but, hey.

'Have you been here before?' asked the nice man with all the buttons.

'No, it's my first time,' I smiled at the nice man at the controls.

'You need to pull into the layby.'

'The layby?' I looked around but couldn't see the layby from my position close up against the booth.

'Over there.' He pointed through the Truck and out the other side beyond the rear nearside roof pillar.

I craned my head behind me to see the distant layby through my rear passenger window, across the closed lane, the owners' lane and the lane for days when there is an R in the month. 'Over there?' I asked. 'Is it okay to reverse over there? There's all the things painted on the road, white lines and all that scary hatching.'

'That's okay, just reverse over there.'

I pictured reversing right across the road, across multiple lanes of oncoming caravans and owners, whatever they are, with all sorts of massive 4x4s bearing down on me.

I didn't fancy it.

Putting the Truck into reverse, I started to withdraw just as a Land Rover started to approach from behind. Being as this was the only open lane, assuming that he wasn't an owner, whatever that was, and he wasn't leaving at the same time as arriving in some weird Mobius strip-type phenomenon, he probably had no choice than to approach the booth where I was currently causing a blockage.

Fortunately, the Land Rover stopped, as did I, but going backwards was clearly no longer an option available to me. So, there, in the only available lane, in the full view of the nice man at the sudden death button and the driver of the Land Rover, I proceeded to perform a fantastically well executed seventeen-point turn (or some such but it was hardly an elegant display of precision driving). Driving back, I crossed all the white lines, and the hatching where you might imagine there are booby traps for those that venture out of the safe zone lest you claim to be an owner, whatever that is, and pulled into the layby. A moment later I climbed out of the Truck with something of a sense of relief, noticing a slight smell of poo.

In the booking-in office it turned out I was expected, as the receptionist had been notified of my arrival. This was quite impressive or a little scary,

I'm not sure which, since I'd booked my night's stay via a call centre somewhere else in the country. I say scary because most of the campsites I'd been to consisted of fields with sanitation tacked on; many didn't have gates, some may not have had a telephone connection and the one at Happisburgh didn't even have a fence to stop you falling off the cliff into the North Sea. (Actually they may have had a fence at one point but it was probably floating in the North Sea by the time I visited, but I might have mentioned that before.)

There was a high counter with a friendly girl sitting on the other side. She had all sorts of scary documents prepared for my arrival. There were printed out things with my details for car parking, for access to the facilities, one with my arrival details including my postcode, number of adults, children, awnings, children with awnings, gazebos, children with gazebos, etc., and one with my leaving date in massive type about ten times as big as anything else on the page. This is all very efficient, I thought, and I was quite impressed. She gave me two maps and drew on it where I could choose my pitch, so it was all nice with plenty of choice, unlike some campsites that will allocate a spot just big enough for your tent. I was even more impressed when she showed me a flyer detailing how I could get a meal and a pint for about seven quid. I say about seven quid as she showed it to me but didn't give it to me so I can't remember the exact details. (You may want to bear that last bit in mind for future reference.) I asked about the laundry and she told me that there indeed was one and that she thought it was open into the evening, eight or nine pm she thought. That was great; it sealed the deal; I wouldn't go elsewhere despite the smell of poo because I could get my laundry done this evening instead of having to wait around in the morning like I did in Northumberland. She told me it took real money so I didn't need to buy tokens so I was good to go (or should I say ready to wash?). When I left the reception even the smell of poo didn't seem that bad; perhaps the wind had changed or perhaps I was being over sensitive.

I drove in, past the nice man at the gate (for that is what he was and none of this was his doing and I'm sure he never has cause to use the sudden death button). I followed the instructions the friendly girl had drawn on the map and soon found the bit where I had a massive choice of pitches. I had so many choices that I was able to change my mind a couple of times before I started. This was a good thing as what seemed like the best positions, next to the water, seemed to have a bit of a poo problem, not the smell of poo but poo on the ground, and I suspected that there was a problem with large waddley birds of some sort similar to that I'd experienced in Rutland.

After pitching the tent, which with the wonderful and sturdy Khyam Igloo takes no time at all, I decided the best thing to do, before even having a cup of tea, would be to walk along to the laundry and see if I could get a cycle in while I got the contents of the tent sorted out.

The laundry turned out to be a five minute walk away and it was at this point that I realised just how large Billing Aquadrome really is. The place is the size of a small town. You might say village but comparison to most villages doesn't do the place justice. I'm sure if you looked it up you'd discover some statistics about acreage and the like. The place has lots of open spaces with rows of pitches for tents and caravans that were mostly empty in May. There were rows of caravans that looked like they were unoccupied but the sort of caravans where owners (ah, that's what owners are!), could leave their caravans instead of dragging them around the country getting in the way of Jeremy Clarkson. And there were rows of those sort of static caravans that aren't really caravans but small wooden houses that could be moved if you went to a great deal of trouble but you'd have to have a lorry and be really motivated. I suppose the latter category might be owners or renters. As I walked around the site it all began to make sense. There were lots of lakes, hence the aquadrome theme and sort of rivers, except that they weren't really rivers because they didn't have any flow so they were more like canals or long thin ponds. The whole site was very flat apart from the excavations for the water which were most probably man-made; there were trees and on the whole it was quite pleasant. The place had some sort of a fun fair with rides, and boats to take out on one of the lakes and a small steam railway that went around the site. It was all very agreeable really, if a little quiet. If there was any downside it was that the areas close to the water's edge seemed to have a duck poo problem but I suppose that's mother nature for you.

Continuing to walk to the laundry I passed a restaurant, so I thought I'd ask about the meal and a pint for about seven quid which the friendly receptionist had told me about. The restaurant was an isolated wooden building beside one of the many small roads that crisscrossed the site, the sort of roads that people walk along where there are 5mph speed limits, yet everybody drives at 15mph because driving at walking speed just seems wrong. I say the restaurant was isolated but that's not strictly true as there was a chip shop tacked onto one side of it but, apart from that, it was isolated in that it wasn't part of a cluster of buildings. Trying the door, the restaurant was dark inside with no sign of life. I'd not had a cup of tea since arriving and I needed to get my priorities straight so I continued on toward the laundry. Still it was early and there would be time to eat later as the place picked up, no doubt; it was May after all.

Arriving at the laundry I found that dark too, having closed at six, but it was good to establish that it would be open at eight the next morning.

Walking back past the restaurant, the lights had been turned on in the chip shop since I'd gone past.

'Can I help you?' said the nice man from behind the big stainless steel counter.

'Hello, do you know about the meal and a pint for about seven quid?' He looked at me a bit confused. 'The receptionist told me that there was a meal and a pint for about seven quid deal that I qualified for.'

He looked at me some more with that expression you might imagine if someone had landed from another planet. 'I'm sorry I don't know about any meal and a pint for about seven quid deal, we do fish and chips or sausage, battered or plain.'

'I was thinking she might be referring to the restaurant next door.' I gestured toward the dark and forlorn establishment through the wall.

'We're not open this time of year, there are not enough people,' he replied. The campsite clearly did have a lot of space hence me being able to pick my pitch. 'We do curry.'

'No thanks,' I responded. 'I was told, by the girl on reception, there is a meal and a pint for about seven quid deal.' He looked at me with the look of a man who is unable to help so long as there is the chance he can sell you a portion of fish and chips, so I made my excuses and left.

Leaving the chip shop I'd convinced myself that I really wanted to sit at a table and eat in a civilised fashion. I'd done a great deal of sitting in my tent and I'd not had a meal sitting at a table for a few days but with all the miles it felt like longer. Stepping away from the chip shop I found myself amid a genuine gaggle of geese, apparently having a bit of a dispute with some ducks; presumably one group or the other were the culprits of the poo problem, so I gave them a wide berth and let them get on with their conversation, thinking that passing off the blame onto each other wasn't really helping sort out the mess.

Back at my tent I dumped my as yet unwashed laundry, thinking the next priority would be to find out where the meal and a pint for about seven quid actually was. The girl had given me the phone number for security telling me that they would be able to answer any questions out of hours. Standing by my tent I phoned the number and spoke to a really helpful guy but he didn't know anything about the meal and a pint for about seven quid. However he did tell me how to get to the club house where perhaps I might find my dinner.

Looking at the map the club house looked like it was a ten or fifteen minute walk. There was the leisure complex that might sell food but that was a ten or fifteen minute walk in the other direction. Taking my map I walked back past the chip shop, past the laundry and on to the end of the street. There were various streets known as Duck Avenue and Swan Way or something. Many said Residents Only at which point I realised that people actually live here.

Halfway down Goose Drive, or somewhere, I asked for directions amid the large static caravans and I eventually found the club house. Inside it was a bit like the working mens' clubs I'd spent parts of my youth in when my father dragged me out with him of a Friday and Saturday night for two sets from the band with a session of bingo in between.

Walking in, it was quiet. There were just a few people inside and I felt like a stranger in a western once more. I wouldn't say it went quiet as I entered as it was quiet anyway and, to be honest, the locals didn't really take much notice of me. I did feel a bit self-conscious though, but that was probably me feeling as though I was walking into what is effectively a closed community. I told the barman about the girl at reception and the flyer she'd briefly shown me and how it described a fabled meal and a pint for about seven quid nirvana. The guy behind the bar said they had a deal on Thursday but I explained that I had been on the road for three weeks and I would be somewhere in Shropshire by then. (I didn't know that I would be in Shropshire but never having been there it sounded far enough away to make my point.) For the first time in the last three weeks, as I explained the trip, he was totally unimpressed or even uninterested. He spoke to his compatriots behind the bar and they did say that I might find my meal and a pint for about seven quid down at the leisure complex, another ten minutes in the opposite direction they were very vague and seemed unable to tell me what to expect down there.

So, rather dejectedly, I walked back to my tent, picking my way by a different route amongst all the lakes and streams, ponds and the like. I walked up caravan drive and past caravan island and eventually found myself outside the laundry. Still, at least I would be able to find it in the morning.

Eventually I found myself passing the chip shop once again so, in the same spirit of surrendering to travel on the superhighway (otherwise known as giving up), I relented. Ten minutes later I was back in my tent with a portion of pie and chips, sitting on the floor. I'd really wanted to sit at a table and use a knife and fork but Billing Aquadrome seemed determined to stop me. Northamptonshire had not quite been an unmitigated disaster, as the day had been saved by Tanvic Tyre and Service Centre but even that, I later discovered, happened to be just over the border in Leicestershire. If I could get up at eight the next morning to do the laundry before I left, everything would be okay.

Day 22 - Northamptonshire to Warwickshire

Wednesday May 22nd

Miles on Truck: 1580

The launderette opened at 8:00 sharp so I got up at the crack of 8:15 to catch it as soon as it opened. Surprisingly the launderette was a delight, all modern machines that were quick and efficient.

For once I was organising things properly and multi-tasking. The process necessitated multiple trips to the laundrette to load the washing machine, back for breakfast of bread and an over-ambitious sausage left over from the pie and chips from the night before, back to unload the machine and load the dryer, back to have a shower and take the tent down, back again to empty the dryer... you get the picture I'm sure.

To walk all of this each time would have added unnecessary delays so I found myself driving around the site obeying the one-way system marked on the map; but I seemed to be the only person doing so. I half expected the helpful security man I'd spoken to the night before to leap out from behind a tree having spied on me from a security camera hidden in a duck or something. Whatever the case, I got a few strange looks as I took unnecessary detours down to the entrance, via the mini railway, past the go karting, the pedalos and all the other jazz that would probably be fun if you were here for a few days with a group of friends with plenty of beer.

The day was overcast and quite windy so there was no smell of poo in the air, although there were lots of geese and ducks harassing me, presumably with security cameras hidden in them. Some of them might actually have been security guards disguised as ducks, there to check on appropriate use of the one-way system, though why they weren't flagging down other drivers I don't know.

* * *

Leaving Northampton I passed through Little Houghton, where I was struck by the colour of the stone buildings, golden honey-coloured cottages and a matching church, almost orange or terracotta and unlike anything I'd seen in the rest of the country. The Cotswolds clearly don't have the monopoly on chocolate box villages and this rich colouring is distinctive in comparison to the paler limestone of the Cotswolds further south and west.

Driving into Warwickshire, the sun suddenly came out for what became a pleasant day with white fluffy clouds and a bit of a breeze so not too hot. I suppose you could say that Warwickshire is the heart of England, though so many places make that claim. It seems that almost anywhere that isn't a coastal county might claim to be the heart of England.

It was almost as though someone had switched on the summer. The cow parsley was everywhere although there seemed relatively little hawthorne in flower which you might reasonably have expected to see three weeks before, what with it being called the May flower.

Arriving in Warwick the city was stunning. I'd been to Warwick Castle before, although I don't remember any of the town, having headed straight for the castle. My plan had been to do the same as a default but, fortunately, I didn't find the castle straight away. Being somewhat devious Kathy brought me into the town from the east, through Royal Leamington Spa, so I came past the castle from the north. As a result the first significant building I saw was the Lord Leycester Hospital, but my how significant it was! This is a complex of medieval buildings dating from the late 14th century, not like your Tudor half-timbered buildings from later; these are as they would have been built in the time of Richard II (he who left his treasure in Beeston Castle) and the end of the age of the chivalric knight, forty years or so before the battle of Agincourt and the time of Henry V. I made a mental note to reward Kathy some time and buy her some new batteries, or something.

I was actually looking for a café where I could get some coffee and lunch but I forgot all that when I found the hospital. Not realising I would be able to get inside I started taking pictures until I met one of the residents on the reception desk. It turns out the word hospital stands for hospitality rather than the modern sense of the word and it still operates today as it did in the 14th century. It's a sort of retirement home for elderly service men similar to the arrangement for Chelsea Pensioners, though the residents at the Lord Leycester Hospital will be sure to tell you in what ways their arrangement is different.

This was one of those serendipitous events that I'd been hoping for, so for the next couple of hours I spent a wonderful time wandering around the medieval buildings, in the 12th century chapel which sits atop the Norman gateway, in the galleried courtyard, up and down the covered staircase, in my lady's chamber, along the gallery eventually to rest in the Brethren's Kitchen having the lunch that I'd been seeking. (Actually there wasn't a lady's chamber nor were there any geese, of which I was glad after my experience at Billing Aquadrome.) If you are ever in Warwick and looking for something to do I urge you to take a look at the Lord Leycester Hospital as it's a marvel. The website rightly describes it as, 'The Hidden Jewel in the crown of Warwick historic buildings.'

Leaving the Brethren's Kitchen tearoom, sated by a ploughman's with goat's cheese cheddar and a great cup of tea with a slice of cake, I felt I'd had a good day having achieved something instead of just travelling from campsite to campsite. Of course seeing the countryside was often enough, but discovering a seven hundred year old building still operating some way close to its original use makes for such a more meaningful experience.

I had to move the Truck as the street parking was limited to two hours. It struck me that two hours free parking was unusually generous and quite sensible for a local authority when so many want to squeeze every penny out of visitors, so well done Warwickshire or the Borough of Warwick or whoever you are, you did good and I spent money in your community and I recommend others to do so. Had you not facilitated me in such a way, I would never have stopped and wouldn't be recommending that people visit in the future. Yet some local authorities wonder why their town centres suffer lack of footfall.

I wanted to have a look at Warwick Castle, even if I only got into the shop at this time of day so, asking the locals, I found a backstreet with an hour or so free parking. As I moved the Truck it was just after 5:00 and the Radio 4 PM programme told me about the murder of Private Lee Rigby, viciously attacked in the street by a fanatic. I'd not seen any TV for over three weeks and it would be another three weeks before I saw any, so I didn't see the footage of the blood-stained attacker until a year or two later. Radio 4, however, kept me informed of what was going on in the world and I'll never forget where I was when I heard the description of the attack. I'd been living a sort of parallel existence while I'd been on the road, but probably more in touch with people than when I was at home in my daily routine. However, the people I'd meet would only ever be transient faces, generous smiles and greetings. It had been a gloriously sunny day and, as I heard the news, there was hardly a cloud in the sky over the tiny backstreet in Warwick by the outside wall of the castle grounds. It all seemed so far away somehow, yet inescapably close as though passing through the gate in that wall would lead me into a different world again.

After another coffee in the castle café, buying a cardboard cut-out model of the gatehouse for a pound, I sought out a campsite, finding one in Coughton close to Stratford upon Avon. To access the site I had to cross a ford, which was exciting even though I was driving the Truck, but the water turned out to be only inches deep and thus a tad disappointing.

As I arrived the farmer was just cutting the grass, which I had almost to myself, so I was able to shelter from the predicted winds in the corner under the hedge and watch the sun shining from behind me, illuminating the landscape that was my view for the evening. Sometimes I feel that evening light with the sun behind you is more beautiful than the sunset itself as the golden glow brings out the colours, giving them a rich saturated hue such that you might imagine from a Photoshopped image. My companions for the evening were five or six curious chickens until they were called away before darkness fell lest the creatures of the night emerge, as I withdrew to my tent, zipped the flap against the darkness and crawled into my sleeping bag full of camp food and red wine.

Day 23 - Warwickshire to Worcestershire

Thursday May 23nd

Miles on Truck: 1648

The radio predicted a cold few days ahead and there was a possibility of rain throughout Thursday. So I set off through the ford and in the direction of Worcester in search of coffee and inspiration for something to do in the dry.

***

On the way to Worcester I spotted the first fields with the characteristic rich red soil that I'd seen before on visits to this part of the country; however, it was the weather that most caught my attention, at times feeling like I was driving into a squall. My plan when I'd first heard about the coming weather was to make the first thing I did to find a sheltered campsite and worry about any other activities later.

***

In Worcester I was pleased to see some sensible parking options next to the bridge over the River Severn where I had the opportunity to stop and take some photos. The parking was short term but free and it gave me a chance to stop while I assessed my options.

The river was fairly populated by swans, dozens of them, clustering beneath the wall on the eastern side of the river, leaving three quarters of the river clear. The only traffic on the river was a couple of coxless four rowing teams. As I watched, one of the teams steered toward the bevy of swans. Admittedly they weren't going very fast and, without a cox, they couldn't see exactly where they were headed, but they had the whole river to play on and the swans seemed comfortable to mostly stay close to the bank. However, sure enough, as every horrid child with fantasies of mild animal cruelty would imagine, they steered right through them such that the swans had to scatter. I'm sure the swans weren't hit by the boat or its considerable oars but I thought at the time that if anybody is allowed to drive their boat through swans surely it's only the queen or one of her representatives.

With the weather looking less positive than it had been the previous few days, I found longer term parking and was unable to resist the pull of Worcester Cathedral. I say unable to resist but that was probably due to the fact that nowhere else was pulling me. The cathedral was a safe bet for somewhere to go for a couple of hours with no danger of being caught in a shower and my unreliable Internet connection, even in the centre of Worcester, meant that I couldn't think of anything else. I could understand how poor reception might be an issue in the deepest countryside but here in the county town of Worcestershire, surely that shouldn't be the case. So I gave up and headed for the cathedral simply because I didn't need a tourist web site to know it was there.

* * *

'Hello welcome to Worcester Cathedral.' The nice man greeted me just inside the entrance with a handful of leaflets and a badge saying Friends of Worcester Cathedral or some-such. 'Have you been to the cathedral before or are you a regular visitor?'

'Err, no,' I hesitated to respond. 'I'm touring. I just like to look at cathedrals, and it's looking like rain,' I added not sure if that was an appropriate thing to say.

'That sounds interesting, where are you touring? Are you particularly interested in cathedrals?'

Not sure how much to say I replied. 'Well actually I'm about half way through a tour of the Historic Counties of England. I was in Northamptonshire yesterday, I think its Staffordshire tomorrow, although I'm not really sure from one day to the next. I did visit Ely Cathedral but that was a few weeks ago now.'

'My, that's fascinating and it sounds like it would make a wonderful subject for a book.' At this point I wondered if he'd been talking to the bloke at Heathy Roods Farm, that or I really was onto a winner.

'Well I'll need to see about that. I'm writing a blog as I go but after that I'll have to decide.'

Taking a leaflet I mooched off to spend a few happy hours wandering around in total awe of the engineers that built these places.

I suppose Worcester Cathedral is much like any other cathedral unless you are a particular cathedral aficionado. Even to my untrained eye there was plenty to fascinate me. You might imagine that the organ pipes, suspended above the choir, required considerable faith from the engineers that built them so that they didn't tumble down to crush the choristers below. I wonder if, in medieval times, there was a certain amount of guesswork and perhaps cautious over-engineering when it came to structural building, more of an art than a science.

You can imagine how these structures evoked wonder and awe in the population whose homes were ramshackle timber built with nothing but a fireplace at one end and their livestock at the other. Was this ambitious construction deliberate, with the wonder prompted by these structures prompting a sense of awe? But then again isn't this what cathedrals are all about? Aldous Huxley in The Doors of Perception, his essay on his experience of taking mescaline, suggested that to the uneducated medieval viewer a stained glass window, in the otherwise darkened interior of a cathedral, would be a mystical experience made all the more wondrous by a lack of understanding of the physics involved. Certainly, in my case I was awestruck seeing these massive constructions of organ pipes, apparently levitated above the choir, where they provoked a sense of awe despite the fact that I understand engineering: load bearing structures, the difference between struts and ties, cantilevers and all that jazz, or in this case probably all that Bach.

Apparently Worcester's organ pipes were actually erected in 2008 but when I saw them I didn't know that, so that's what I imagined. Is this a deliberate act even to this day, to invoke a sense of wonder, an attempt by the religious authorities to awe people into submission? If it can do that to someone with a modern education, what did it do to the medieval? Medieval worshippers wouldn't have been in awe of the organ pipes as they didn't exist, although organs in general have been installed in cathedrals since the early part of the European Renaissance, presumably closer to the ground. Of course the 2008 engineers weren't relying on faith as they had pocket calculators, but when you learn how many cathedrals did suffer catastrophic failure, you begin to realise that there was a certain back-of-the-parchment approach to their construction.

An eclipse provokes reactions of fear at the misunderstanding of the two minute blotting out of the sun with no warning; understanding celestial mechanics explains the experience. Seeing an apparently levitating organ or an amazing window blows away a medieval peasant (although they may have been better informed than we might give them credit for). However, understanding the physics doesn't negate the sense of awe.

For true cathedral aficionados the choir boasts a fine set of misericords, ornate carvings beneath fold-up seats in the choir. Members of the choir might be required to stand for long periods and thus much misery was endured by the elderly or infirm. The solution, or 'act of mercy' being the literal translation of misericord, was to equip their fold-up seat with a smaller shelf-like seat beneath, that would be at bum height when they were standing. Therefore they could stand in the act of respect but be supported by the raised seat. Ancient misericords are often ornately carved with biblical scenes or images of folkloric creatures. Many of those at Worcester Cathedral date back to the 14th century, just a couple of years before the peasants' revolt and the time of Lord Leycester Hospital. They are well worth seeing if you are into 700 year old carvings.

* * *

Beneath the cathedral is the 10th century crypt which is open to the public. It's a small chapel now and as a non-church goer I find myself wondering when all these little side chapels ever get used. Some will have been built by or dedicated to some ancient bishop or obscure saint. Usually there's a small chapel each side of the main chancel where the main altar is situated. Often there are multiple altars, perhaps one behind the main altar, chapels on either side of the nave, sometimes at the ends of the transepts on either side. In the case of Worcester they have one in the crypt. Do they use these at different times of the year or days of the week, how does this all work? I know I've seen small chapels dedicated to the local regiment where the fallen are commemorated. Do they use specific chapels for specific purposes? Do the faithful have favourites? I imagine I would if I were so inclined. It's almost worth becoming a Christian to find out.

Well okay, that last bit's not true, I had enough of organised religion during my ecclisifringical upbringing, as my friend Malcolm in Herefordshire puts it, so nothing would tempt me back, but I do find the ritual of it all fascinating. However, if that is where you find meaning in life then that's okay, so long as you allow others the same freedom.

Of course it's often in reference to religion that we think of *the* meaning of life. I remember Graham once interpreting this idea with the statement that people think, 'I'm so important there must be something more!' It's always struck me that this is the best interpretation of the concept of *the* meaning of life as it's commonly understood rather than *finding meaning* which might not be a single specific experience.

Anyway, the chapel in the crypt of Worcester Cathedral is fascinating and atmospheric, all pillared and heavily vaulted in the Romanesque style, plain and free from decoration as, I suppose, the dead didn't really demand decoration. Of course that may not be the case, as places of worship were stripped of almost all their decoration during the Reformation. The crypt is worth it even for the stairs up and down, the treads worn down by hundreds of years of footfall, disappearing around corners through subterranean archways; it's a medieval delight.

Eventually I ended up in the café where I enjoyed an excellent jacket potato and a cup of coffee served in a cup and saucer as you might expect from such an esteemed organisation as the Church of England. You'll have picked up the subtle hints that I'm not a religious man, contrary to what some people may imagine, but these ancient monuments are worthy of respect as are their refreshments, especially when served in a cup and saucer, though generally I prefer a more utilitarian mug.

* * *

Back in the car park I searched for a campsite in Worcestershire. These searches always proved challenging as the Monster Book of Campsites, was arranged by ordnance survey sheets (which is very sensible under most circumstances), representing sites as dots on a tiny map, with other dots representing a few local towns. I didn't know which towns were in which county, and in my case the counties were important to me, so there was much flicking back and forth, making notes in margins, crossing out notes and all sorts of confusion. Often I found myself phoning up and simply asking, 'Which county are you in?' which is probably only one step away from the scene in sci-fi moves where the time traveller asks which year it is. Well it felt like that anyway. I'm pretty sure most people thought I was a bit of an idiot, especially if the county didn't exist anymore.

It was only as I left Worcester that I first saw the Malvern Hills. Now I've lived in England for harrumph/cough/avoid the detail years, since birth at least, but there are many parts of England that I've never been to and the Malvern Hills is one them. Okay, so I'd never been to Whitby or the Lake District until a couple of weeks ago but that was the point of this trip, to discover parts of England that I've never seen and, as it turned out, perhaps find some meaning in the experience. So I'm sort of ashamed that the Malvern Hills came as such a surprise, but then again I'm not.

The point is the Malvern Hills are remarkable. It's as if someone has scooped up a chunk of Wales and plonked it over the border in the Southern West midlands. When I say remarkable, to be honest, I don't know why they aren't called mountains. Okay there is probably some specific definition in terms of height that means they are not mountains, but by comparison with the landscape around them, surely, they would qualify as mountains. The Malvern Mountains; doesn't that have a ring to it, or perhaps the Mountains of Malvern? By comparison I live in the Chiltern Hills, but they don't have the same majestic grandeur that the Malvern Hills (sorry mountains) have. They both have the same name, Chiltern Hills, Malvern Hills, but there the similarity ends. You could drive through the Chiltern Hills and not really know about them. Okay you go up and down a bit but you sort of get caressed up and down the slopes. You might use third gear if you drive through the Chilterns but with a run up, and in most places you can get a run up, then you probably wouldn't even drop out of fourth. But the Malvern Hills, now they mug you as soon as you see them. They are so out of place in the surrounding landscape that they can, surely, only be mountains and that's without mentioning that they have those pointy angles that you only get on mountains, not the soft rounded profiles of hills.

Anyway, I was impressed.

So, early in the evening I pulled into the Kings Green Caravan Park and set up. Strictly speaking the campsite wasn't really in Great Malvern, as I had to drive what seemed a considerable distance away from the town to get there but then the Windermere Caravan Park wasn't anywhere near Windermere and Sherwood Forest Caravan Park wasn't really in the forest; however, that might depend how you define a forest or a lake or a town for that matter. Anyway, I'd come to expect a bit of artistic licence from campsites over recent weeks so it was all good.

The Met Office had issued a severe weather warning for strong winds so the very helpful owner found me a spot in the L shape of two hedges with a caravan on the third side. I had the opportunity of parking the Truck across the front but I decided that might be a bit excessive, short of a hurricane and that almost never happens in southern England. If anything it was likely to be challenging when bugging out the next day. Otherwise the campsite was unremarkable other than the fact that they required you to have a key for the toilets. In my travels I've seen all sorts of arrangements including toilet roll holders locked so you couldn't steal the paper (other than a few sheets at a time I presume), various payment systems as I've described and buttons that you have to keep pressing every thirty seconds, but I'd not yet seen a key required for access.

The one thing that was remarkable about my stay in Worcestershire was, however, nothing to do with the campsite and entirely down to me.

When I arrived I'd been so relieved to have been on time, just a few minutes before the 6:00 arrival deadline, that I completely forgot to ask for an electrical hook-up so I was dependent on my own power supply. In this situation I would run the computer and the phone charger from the battery pack that I'd been lugging around the country for the last three weeks, trying to keep it topped up by plugging it into a caravan hook-up whenever I could and, as a result, hardly ever needing the battery pack. You may have seen these battery packs; they are primarily intended as a way of starting a car when it has a flat battery but they've developed from that with useful bits like fluorescent lamps, pumps for flat tyres, three-pin plugs and even USB connections for charging phones.

Now the Khyam Igloo is an excellent tent in all respects and it features a handy little ring that dangles from the inside of the dome and I'd got in the habit of suspending an LED lamp for general illumination. The only issue with this arrangement is that I tended to sit in the middle of the tent with my equipment around the edges and this included my toolbox-cum-writing desk. Sitting arched over the toolbox, the illumination from the dangling light cast a shadow over the desk and I'd not yet switched on the other lantern I used to illuminate the keyboard. I had, however, poured myself a generous glass of wine, as had become my habit.

It was in this situation of gloom, with a glass of fine Australian Shiraz from the supermarket in Great Malvern, in the shade of the Mountains, that I reached across the top of my writing desk and caught the glass a perfect swipe on the side, knocking it from the flat shelf on the end of the toolbox directly onto the battery pack that was providing the power to all my equipment.

The wine landed directly on the mains voltage three-pin socket into which my computer was plugged. The fan in the battery pack immediately went into overdrive. I'd come to learn that the louder and faster the fan, the more current was being drawn and now it was screaming. For a few seconds the fan whirred away as I tried to move so as not to cast a shadow over the thing. Then suddenly I didn't need to move out of the way of the light as there was, for a fraction of a second, plenty of illumination as a flash and a loud bang came from within the battery pack.

Anybody walking past would have heard a curse followed by a high-pitched whine followed by a bang and possibly a flash visible through the tent followed by further expletives and a certain amount of fumbling around as I hastily disconnected everything. I'm guessing that there wasn't anybody walking past as it was a dark and stormy night unsuitable for being abroad unless you were a character at the beginning of a bad novel or had a key for the locked toilets. The electrical bangs and flashes would indicate a literary genre in the gothic horror category or perhaps science fiction incompetence.

However, if there was anybody walking past they didn't enquire as to my state of electrical shockedness, come running with a fire extinguisher or even a replacement bottle of wine.

Day 24 - Worcestershire to Shropshire

Friday May 24th

Miles on Truck: 1699

The rest of the night passed without further incident, apart from at least one visit to the loo without remembering to take the key. Clearly I'd drunk enough wine before spilling it all over the battery pack. While lying awake I'd figured out that I could live without the battery if I could just guarantee a hook-up every night. Often I'd only ever been keeping the battery pack topped up and some nights I'd even left it in the Truck. If I could manage to keep the computer connected to the cigarette lighter as much as possible, and do the same with Kathy, then I could keep them both charged without too much fuss.

The wet battery pack was a different matter. The charge indicator LEDs showed it as still fully charged so the bang would have been the fuse blowing. It came with a spare fuse but I wanted to know that it was dry before experimenting with that. I did think that if we had a hot day the battery pack would be able to bake in the warmth of the Truck in the sun, but we were hardly having a dry summer. I wasn't sure if there were any implications of allowing it to get too warm but I sort of figured out that a bit of heat might drive the moisture off. You hear that when people drop their mobile phones in the sink they are often told to let them dry out in an airing cupboard and I wondered if the foot-well of the Truck with the heater blowing on it might serve a similar purpose. I didn't really want to leave the battery pack in the back of the Truck as I drove; after all it was still full of rather a lot of amps and I was worried it might burst into flames at some point should a drip migrate to somewhere sensitive. Of course, rationally, I knew this was highly unlikely but in such a situation the non-rational brain can take over until time reassures you that things are okay. Putting the thing in the foot-well would mean that if anything happened I'd have a chance of noticing before I was consumed in a conflagration of biblical proportions.

After a short detour around the Mountains of Malvern I set off for Ironbridge, hoping that the heart of the industrial revolution would turn out to reside in Shropshire. It seems Telford had declared its independence from

the rest of Shropshire some time in the second half of the 20th century and
I hoped that Ironbridge, wherever it was, would qualify as something to see
in the English historic county of Shropshire. I certainly didn't have time to
go hunting around in libraries or speaking to Honorary Secretaries.

The journey to Ironbridge took me through Kidderminster and
Bridgnorth, where I'd have liked to have stopped to explore but, as usual,
didn't have time. There were deep cuttings and dramatic cliffs of deep red-
brown sandstone, with beautiful woodland giving way to broad landscapes
of fields of a similar colour, looking as though someone had been scooping
up chunks of Herefordshire in much the same way as they had with the
Mountains of Malvern.

The weather seemed to be deteriorating. I found myself constantly
switching the wipers on and off, but mostly on. Throughout this trip I
seemed to have been dodging the severe weather or just on the periphery. In
Northumbria and Westmorland, when the South was caught in a deep depression, I was just on the edge of it and descended into Lancashire as the
snows came, the only place not awarded a yellow warning or worse. This
time the South East was back in the depth of winter with good weather in
Northern Ireland. Here I was heading northwest away from the worst.

By heading to the Malverns I'd really come too far south, but my route
snaked through the midland counties, possibly with no alternative. Ironbridge was one of the few places I could think of to visit without having to
resort to research on my frustratingly untrustworthy tablet, so I wasn't going
to spend another day going from one campsite to another if there was something to see.

However, the journey was worth it. Kathy brought me down into the
Ironbridge Gorge and I happily ignored her instructions, instead following
the signs for the Ironbridge Museum. Pulling into the car park in sight of the
bridge I spent a frustrating hour, with an intermittent and slow internet connection, searching out a campsite while I could take advantage of the electrics in the Truck. Meanwhile the troublesome battery pack sat quietly in the
passenger foot-well looking at me with that enigmatic expression that says.
'You have no idea what will happen when you switch me on.'

After securing somewhere to spend the night I had an hour or so left
on the parking, so I spent the rest of the time wandering around, back and
forth across the bridge, down the steps and back up again, taking photos of

the iron bridge from different angles and eventually deciding that the first picture was the best.

The bridge itself is an impressive thing. Built between 1779 and 1781 by Abraham Darby III (though the initial design came from Thomas Pritchard who died before the bridge was finished), it's 100 feet across, arching over the River Severn that flows gently, perhaps fifty or sixty feet below.

Eventually I headed back to the Truck and off to Coalbrookdale in search of a coffee shop. Coalbrookdale, a hop along the Severn Valley from Ironbridge, is the place where they cast the components for the bridge before it was erected a mile or two away. This is the significance of the iron bridge, as it is said to be the first factory-made civil engineering project.

The conventional understanding of the iron bridge at Ironbridge is that all the components were designed on paper before it was constructed as a kit, which is sort of true. A number of scale wooden models were made to work out the construction process, though these do not survive to this day, and it is likely that the remaining models were made after the bridge was constructed either to celebrate its construction or to market the bridge and its designers to the wider public.

The bridge is often portrayed as the first example of a construction project that set the way for our modern construction process of standardised components and interchangeability. However, the actual process probably involved a certain amount of on-going decision-making and, despite the fact that the major components had been made before construction began, it is likely that alterations were made as it was built. Neither was it the first iron bridge made, as a bridge was attempted but abandoned, due to costs, in the French city of Lyon about 20 years earlier. A smaller iron bridge is also said to have been constructed in Yorkshire about ten years before.

It's one of those all too common historical injustices that the bridge is commonly credited to Abraham Darby who, while he was an entrepreneur working in cast iron who had perfected the casting process, was actually assigned as treasurer, whereas the greatest responsibility for the design for the bridge lies with Thomas Pritchard, who didn't live to see it built and seems to have been written out of history in the process.

If the settlement of Ironbridge is easy to identify because it's not so much a museum as a whole village centred around the bridge, then Coalbrookdale is the opposite. You know when you've arrived in Ironbridge but Coalbrookdale is more difficult to identify. I know that sounds stupid but this might be a clue to the local council or whoever is responsible for tourism these days. If you are local then you know when you've arrived but if you are looking for somewhere how do you know? (Is that a philosophical truth stated by accident or just so much new age mumbo jumbo?) I'd driven to Ironbridge, pulled into a car park and I was immediately aware I was in the right place due to the sodding great bridge across the gorge; Coalbrookdale was not so easy.

Driving along the valley I found myself in Coalbrookdale before I expected, the two villages running into each other, having been pretty much absorbed (invaded) by Telford. A sign directed me to the Coalbrookdale Museums but I couldn't see where they were. My understanding is that Coalbrookdale is awash with industrial heritage and the like but I missed the lot of them. Please don't misunderstand me, I missed every single one.

On the other hand, somewhat pleasingly, there were actually working businesses in some of the premises; a car workshop here, some metal bashing somewhere else, that sort of thing, so the place isn't one of those museum ghost towns that heritage centres can become. But it is possible to imagine how every time a factory or workshop ceases to trade it becomes just another museum.

Once the heart of a gritty industrial community complete with dark satanic smokestacks, my guess is that the village is now populated by what you might assume are those with good jobs in the Midlands cities, or people who live further afield and use the place as a weekend retreat. I may have that wrong but the whole area has the feeling that what was once industrial hell is now quaint, and only the affluent can afford quaint.

* * *

I'd booked a campsite so I had no real time pressures and I'd have loved to wander around some grimy workshops that were the origin of the Gittins Steam Bypass or the Hotchkiss Sally, or some such. The work of those pioneering engineers is fascinating, paving the way for all the technology that followed right up to the invention of Kathy and beyond. However, I drove through Coalbrookdale and simply couldn't see where to stop. Most of the tourist centres I'd visited, and just about every ordinary little town, has some central location perhaps with shops and the like with, at the very least, a pay and display car park. But if Coalbrookdale offered such a centre I missed it. In the end I found myself a kerb to pull up against a few yards along the road from a small coffee shop where I was able to sit for an hour and drink coffee and biscuits, if you can drink a biscuit, but I'm sure you get my drift.

So I left Coalbrookdale without really seeing it. Ironbridge had been a joy but I couldn't help thinking that Coalbrookdale was missing an opportunity and, while it might be open to planned visits and those with good internet access, casual visitors were simply not encouraged. Perhaps people who live in *quaint* would rather not have visitors at all.

Heading to my campsite, further north I passed along a long straight road that I mused must surely be evidence of the uprising that caused the split of Telford from Shropshire. Later, when I checked the map, the road turned out to be the A5, so probably Watling Street and therefore a genuine Roman road. That night I went to bed satisfied that I'd received confirming evidence for my theory of straight roads and invasions.

Day 25 - Shropshire to Herefordshire

Saturday May 25th

Miles on Truck: 1776

It was cold on the Friday night, but that may not have been helped by me opening the tent at midnight to try to take a picture of the full moon. The photo was okay and people on Facebook seemed to like it, but it did let all the carefully preserved heat out of the Khyam. Fortunately though, I managed to not spill anything during the night. The morning, by comparison, was glorious. The air was still and the birds twittered as I washed up, with the sun warming my back in a way I'd not felt for days.

As I drove south towards Herefordshire the sun shone brilliantly and I tried to position the battery pack so the sun would warm the plastic and help evaporate any remaining red wine inside. This might have been a long shot but I was prepared to take any solution considering the battery pack had been a major part of my plan from day one.

The fields around were full of oilseed rape glowing bright yellow so much that I almost felt I needed shades. Clearly I had been mistaken about the hawthorn as there was almost none of it apparent in the hedgerows in this part of Shropshire and, where there was, the mayflowers seemed less obvious. Now I wonder if there is some regional variation; perhaps it's less common in the North hence me not seeing it in the previous weeks, or was it actually late flowering because of the long winter and continued cold snaps we were having? Perhaps I'm influenced by my home area where I frequently drive between Hertfordshire, Buckinghamshire and Oxfordshire where hawthorn is very common. The cow parsley, by comparison, is almost brutal in its ubiquity on the verges across the country. I do appreciate that cow parsley is considered an invasive species, but to my mind it doesn't do any harm and I enjoy seeing it throughout the summer everywhere I go.

* * *

Driving back along twisty invasion-proof roads, back into Bridgnorth, the road was bordered by a steep cliff, sometimes wooded, sometimes exposed terracotta coloured rock, with a strip of farmland on the other side and a hint of the River Severn meandering along just out of view.

Kathy turned me right, and then left, to guide me away from the road I'd travelled out of Worcester and I found myself heading towards Ludlow. At one point I was needlessly, and aggressively, overtaken by a Range Rover Sport, just to be in the small gap in the traffic ahead of me. I always presume this is just because I'm not tailgating the car in front. I have a particular opinion of Range Rover Sport drivers that I should keep to myself but I'm sure you can figure it out. They don't have a spare wheel on the back as the Truck does so there!

More invasion proof country roads took me south, at times barely more than single track roads with a bit of aspirational white lining down the middle, the sort of white lining that is intended to encourage you to drive on the left but doesn't really give you any prospect of doing so, the road being so narrow that you can't really help but straddle the line while you hope there isn't a Range Rover Sport coming the other way around the next bend.

In the distance I could see a line of hills that I thought might be Hergest Ridge, made famous by the Mike Oldfield album of the same name. The road was practically deserted so, pulling across a handily located field entrance, I stopped in an attempt to take a photo. No sooner had I stopped, a large tractor, of the massive wheels at both ends variety, approached from behind and I watched him advance on me thinking it would be extremely bad luck if he wanted to get into this particular field at the very three minute moment that I blocked the entrance. Sure enough the tractor slowed and indicated that he wanted to pass right through me so I had to make an undignified and hurried exit. I didn't see the scowl on his face but I'm sure I felt it as I did my best to get out of his way. Later I discovered that I was still far north of the Shropshire-Herefordshire border and it seems I was actually looking at Clee Hill. I didn't have time to visit either and they've both been added to the list of places I really must visit properly someday.

* * *

Driving though Ludlow, with quite a few black and white timber frame buildings, I passed into Herefordshire. I'd been seeing more such buildings for a day or so but there is a preponderance of black and white buildings in Herefordshire, so much so that the locals have defined a route known as the Black and White Trail. I've never travelled it as I'd only ever visited Herefordshire to call on Malcolm and he's not really into taking visitors on two or three day circular bike rides, but you could forgive him for that. Also he doesn't have a bike. The Black and White Trail circulates through ten small towns and villages of Northwest Herefordshire, described as the picturesque setting for a large number of timbered and half-timbered houses, some dating back to medieval times. The whole route is dotted with country pubs, village shops and tea rooms perfect for the weary but happy traveller gorged on a diet of timber frames, wobbly beams and the odd thatched roof. The landscape is one of orchards and hop-yards set against a backdrop of rolling hills and scenic farmland. Strangely Ludlow isn't one of the towns listed on the trail but the point is that this part of England has a very large number of such buildings and some marketing genius has managed to come up with a circular route through the area. The other point is Ludlow is in Shropshire and perhaps they were concerned not to tempt invasion if Ludlow were assimilated into the trail.

Leaving Ludlow I passed through what I could only guess was a country park landscape in the style of Capability Brown, all wide open spaces in a broad valley dotted with majestic oaks and horse chestnuts, a few sheep grazing in pastoral fashion and on the distant upper slopes more dense patches of woodland blending into the far horizon. The brilliant sunshine with the occasional fluffy white cloud served to make the scene more beautiful, spoiled only by the line of traffic of which I was a part. Clearly Heisenberg was right, being in a position to observe something changes its nature. Asking Malcolm later, he suggested that the country park was the former grounds of Berrington Hall, though I don't recall seeing the house.

The black and white buildings became more common as I passed into Herefordshire, through Leominster, and further southwest. For the first time I got a view of the line of hills on the southern bank of the River Wye including Bredwardine Hill rising, heavily wooded, out of the horizon. As I approached the Welsh border I could see the Brecon Beacons in the distance but they are in Wales so they don't count for this trip; perhaps the next if some forward looking (westward looking?) publisher wants to make a deal.

Eventually I pulled into a drive and parked the Truck under the shade of a fine oak tree in Malcolm's garden.

For the rest of the day we talked of many things, fools and kings, but probably not about pigs with wings for Malcolm isn't really into that sort of thing. Actually we talked, instead, of second hand books, old guitars and ukuleles, for Malcolm buys and sells such things, being the proud owner of some fifty acoustic guitars, including several romantic parlour guitars dating back to 1830. Indeed, he had found me a second ukulele to add to the one that I was already carrying.

The conversation had a marked leaning toward the rational and away from the illogical and specious that I'd enjoyed in Blackpool a week or so earlier.

If Graham was able to lend himself to ideas outside of the rational, suspend his disbelief perhaps, then Malcolm was firmly in the camp of the rational, preferring only those ideas that come from a theoretically sound, plausible perspective.

Before the trip we had been discussing Malcolm's suggestion that he might want to sell part of his considerable library of books on various non-rational ideas and philosophies. You see, although Malcolm cannot lend himself to anything that lies outside of the strictly rational view of the world, he has a fascination with non-rational ideas and the people that hold such beliefs. (Of course he wouldn't beat about the bush and he'd use the word irrational.) However, he'd being thinking of moving on to other areas of interest and retaining only those truly rare and fascinating books. I, however, was interested in acquiring such a collection of books, particularly the not so rare, in fact, the common-or-garden books of hippie philosophy that might have found their way into his collection over the years. I wanted these books not because I was so interested in reading them, but because I'd been thinking of setting up a small second hand book stall known as the Two Box Book Shop where the stock would fit entirely into two boxes. I dreamt of spending my summers taking the Two Box Book Shop around the country, from camps to festivals, amid curious hippies and more curious beatniks, selling second hand books and slipping my own works among them while drinking cups of tea with visitors, as you see in the trendier café bookshops of the world.

As we drank whisky into the early hours we talked of my trip over recent weeks, notable adventures and discoveries such as the Tees Transporter Bridge, various castles and Iron Bridge the day before. I described visits to Graham in Blackpool and my friends in the field in Derbyshire where we'd performed the maypole dance and such goings on. Malcolm's response to the shenanigans in Derbyshire was fairly dismissive as he asked how I could believe such nonsense. Of course you don't have to believe in the maypole dance to take part, after all you don't have to believe in a waltz. Either he didn't see the relevance of that point or I forgot to mention it at the time, probably the latter; but I do find myself wondering if he objects to the apparent irrationality of dancing around maypoles, or whatever, when it's not really that irrational, it's just dancing. It's almost as though any possibility of irrationality is like a red rag of foolishness to an analytical bull... or something.

At some point, I can't remember when as by then I was at least partly full of whisky, he argued that received wisdom eventually becomes literal truth. This may have been the next morning as the debate about rationalism vs experiential non-rationalism continued over breakfast. His thinking was that a society that knows no better seeks an explanation for phenomena such as the rising and setting of the sun, the reason some years have a good harvest or the fact that the universe is expanding faster than we expected. (Well let's face it, dark energy is irrational rather than thinking that some people got their sums wrong!) Whatever account takes hold soon becomes the explanation told to children, becoming the literal truth for the generations that follow. Received wisdom, the wisdom from earlier generations, is received by younger generations as truth told by their wise elders. In other words, in a society that respects its elders (presumably one that hasn't yet invented denim or rock and roll) any nonsense spouted by the previous generation is taken as gospel despite it being unknowingly based on a falsehood.

For example this is the situation with creationists. For anyone other than a creationist, it is quite easy to see that evolution, as an explanation of the complexity and diversity of life on the planet, is a much better explanation than the suggestion that some white-haired old geezer in the clouds created people and that the whole world is our playground. However, to a creationist, an eye or a flagellum (a spinning protuberance that allows some types of organisms to move) seems so complex that it could only be designed rather than have evolved. The creationist doesn't understand that there are earlier, less complex, stages of development of the organism that each step back incrementally to the beginning of time. These simpler stages in the development of the organism, such as a shadow-sensing light-sensitive patch on the skin or the same light-sensitive patch in an indentation that allow for direction sense of shadows, negate the need for a designer. The creationist's received wisdom is that complex mechanisms, such as the eye or the flagellum, are so complex that they couldn't have come about other than with the help of some intelligent intervention thus proving, in their terms, the existence of God. However, they don't understand how evolution could explain these organisms in a step by step process. This is the same as a hunter gatherer not having enough knowledge of celestial mechanics to understand the rising and setting of the sun in any way other than the idea that the great sun god is chasing the moon goddess across the sky.

* * *

So what's going on with people who appear to cherish beliefs that lie outside Malcolm's logic only view of the world, particularly his objection to people dancing around maypoles in fields?

I've met a lot of people with all sorts of views of reality but I don't think I've ever met anyone who believes in the literal idea that the sun and the moon are in fact a god and goddess that chase each other across the sky. Many people will talk of symbolism and metaphors, where the sun and moon are expressed as deities or some other view of reality, but I'm pretty sure that most people don't believe that the moon is actually a goddess looking down on us. People have been to the moon and walked around on it. However, people may just be using language in a different way from the mainstream. In almost every situation there is a degree of metaphor in these ideas.

Here's an example from a meme that I came across on Facebook attributed to Gary Zukav:

> *'Every intention sets energy into motion whether you are conscious of it or not.'*

Now at first glance that sounds like so much new age mumbo jumbo. In the context of this sort of statement I have no idea what people mean by the word 'energy'. However, if you substitute 'energy' for 'events' it suddenly makes much more sense:

> *'Every intention sets events into motion whether you are conscious of it or not.'*

That seems to make some sense. Now this may not be what Zukav intended and I'm not here to defend his writings other than to say that he is one of the few writers whom I've found could explain special relativity theory in such a way that I could understand it for more than an hour after I put the book down. Part of the problem seems to be that words like *energy* are used so casually. Energy can mean atmosphere, as when people say they can feel the energy in a place. Of course that's subjective but there is often some agreement between people so presumably it's not completely made up. We've all been to dull parties that you might describe as having no energy. Alternatively people might describe negative energy, which really sounds irrational. But what about somewhere that seems have a lot of tension? Conflict zones would be a good example but other situations such as households can exhibit the same phenomenon and many of us will have experienced that. In this case energy is a metaphor for social tension. But in scientific terms tension stores energy, so the term isn't completely nonsensical. (Student households may want to look away at this point.) In social terms the energy is only released when someone finally mentions the fact that someone hasn't done their fair share of the washing-up or cleaned the bathroom. Energy can also mean effort which is closer to the scientific term and, in that sense, as in the first example, it could mean events, if you think of things moving over time. In some situations it might even literally mean energy as in the ability of a system to perform work.

Here's another one:

> *The universe is not punishing you or rewarding you. The universe is responding to the vibrational attitude that you are emitting.'*

I have no idea who wrote that but according to Google it's all over the web. I really struggle with the word *vibration*, more so than I struggle with the word energy. So how about this rewrite?

> *People respond in kind to the type of person you are, perhaps in a similar way that dogs are said to respond to people who are nervous of dogs. So a kind loving personality might receive (on aggregate) a more positive response from people because they are relaxed and feel that they don't need to be competitive.'*

Not a mention of vibration but perhaps the original writer meant *manner* or *approach* or simply *attitude*. In fact if you take the original phrase and remove the problematic word vibration you are left with:

'The universe is not punishing you or rewarding you. The universe is responding to the attitude that you are emitting.'

Change the word universe to world, or perhaps people, then it almost sounds like common sense.

So language is problematic, especially when we start to delve into the realms of popular philosophy. It may actually be the case that some people aren't as irrational as sceptics imagine, they may just not be using language in the same way as it is used elsewhere. These might be people engaging in philosophy with little or no training. The problem is that few of us are trained in philosophy; but what are we going to do, ban amateur philosophy, no thinking beyond certain limits? Who sets those limits? Or should we ban colloquial use of language? Should we say all sub-cultures have to subscribe to the Oxford English Dictionary? Actually I'd quite like that last bit because I have a soft spot for the OED but I know I can't have the world the way I would like it, but then again neither can anyone else.

Of course this is a bit of a straw man argument-no rationalist is suggesting that we ban anything, but we might be in danger of discouraging exploration of ideas that lies outside of that which is measurable.

However, if we said the issue isn't language, what else might it be? What about the possibility that people who are perceived as irrational hold these apparently irrational beliefs (belief in impossible things) only insofar as those impossible things affect themselves. In this case I'm talking about internal psychological mechanisms. An individual who performs what they might describe as a spell, or a small ceremony, or even a full blown ritual with clouds of incense in a darkened room lit by nothing but a few candles, with barbarous words spoken in guttural tones, might have the intention of getting that job they really need, or finding true love, or gaining enough motivation to become successful. At first instance this seems like a highly irrational thing to do but is it really? If the result of that moment of concentration, perhaps fired by a bit of belief in some deity or spirit of nature or whatever, is to change the outlook of the practitioner, then where is the supernatural impossibility? Getting a job, we are constantly told by some politicians, is just a matter of trying a bit harder. What if it's a matter of self-belief? Finding true love is almost definitely a matter of self-belief as needy, desperate people who are interested in a relationship with every person they meet are deeply unattractive. People who are successful in business will always say that they believed in themselves and worked hard, which was the route to their success. So who is to say that spells or ceremonies don't generate self-belief? As a personal development exercise this seems quite legitimate. If you consider the idea that such a practice is really reliant on driving the idea into the unconscious mind, then the practitioner who uses all the apparently irrational paraphernalia with clouds of incense in the darkened room is really making a dramatic impact. It's like participatory theatre or even self-developed psychodrama.

The final interpretation of these apparently irrational practices, for now at least, is that they are doing this as celebration. Dancing around a maypole is something you only do in May, associated with the arrival of spring in the same way as the choristers do in Magdalen Tower in Oxford on May Morning. Of course Magdalen College has a couple of thousand years of religious practice to legitimise their efforts, whereas people dancing around maypoles in Derbyshire are involved in something that may be a bit of a revivalist movement. That's not to say the maypole dancers aren't getting something more from their dance. There is definitely a sense of community and belonging at such events (especially if people come back year after year). There may be elements of rites of passage for people who do this for the first time; or on a more personal level there may be elements of personal development attached, perhaps an escape from self-absorption, away from our tendency to be wrapped up in our lives and personal problems, such things that they simply haven't shared with the wider community.

*** ***

That night I slept in a bed for the first time in nearly four weeks. I know that it sort of feels like I was breaking the rule by not camping and I did consider camping in Malcolm's garden but it seemed silly to decline his hospitality especially after a few glasses of scotch and a decent meal. His house was a magnificent medieval residence and you don't pass up the opportunity to awake in ancient magnificence when it's on offer.

Day 26 - Herefordshire to Gloucestershire

Sunday May 26th

Miles on Truck: 1841

After breakfast and coffee I set off from Malcolm's for Gloucester-shire. I hadn't really considered the bank holiday weekend, but the campsite in Shropshire had been busy on the Friday night so I started to have some trepidation about finding somewhere to camp. Here I was though and I had to get on with it. Although I'd mentioned the second hand books a few times, we never got around to properly talking about them so I drove away empty handed, other than with a brand new second hand ukulele, which I was probably happier with.

I'd taken the opportunity to stand the battery pack in the sun the day before so I thought, while I was somewhere with another responsible adult I'd try putting the fuse back and see what happened. I'd inspected the fuse and it hadn't blown during the original spillage, which sort of made me think that the bang had come from the insides. This made me wonder if the insides might actually be fried. Of course my memory of the incident was fading as the days went by and I had been drinking at the time so I was beginning to doubt myself.

Taking my life in one hand and the fuse in the other I inserted it with trepidation (the fuse, not my life). The fuse went in, I pushed it home and nothing happened. I flicked the switch and nothing happened for the second time, apart from a tiny beep. However, the important point was that there were no explosions or pyrotechnics. Just to be sure I pressed the button for the battery charge indicator... it was fully charged. I went to the Truck, grabbed my phone and its charger, plugged them in and lo the phone started charging from the battery pack.

Driving away I wondered about the bang I'd heard a few days before. Something had shorted out and it was loud enough to sound serious. So far I'd tested the output through the three-pin socket and that seemed okay. I'd tested the lights on the unit, they were fine. The battery itself was holding its charge. The only thing that I could think of was the charging circuit which was on the same panel as the three-pin socket. I decided to hold the unit in reserve and use it if I needed it but try to not put any more charge into it for as long as I could. I had a little less than two weeks to go and I surmised that, if I was careful, I might be able to get back home without recharging it. After all, it's a dirty great 12 volt battery with 20 amp hours, it should be able to do a few charges of the tiny batteries in a tablet and a phone. I'm not really up on the science but if you consider the physical proportions between the size of a tablet battery and the battery pack, the two things simply don't compare. Of course my simplistic understanding of electricity and battery sizes might be an example of a limited understanding of the physics involved that can lead to a misunderstanding of the universe and its properties.

***

I asked Kathy to take me to Gloucestershire. For some years I'd known about the Severn Bore, where the tidal flow of the massive Severn Estuary is constrained by the very narrow, shallow, channel of the River Severn. On the incoming tide the difference in the volume of the estuary to the volume of the river channel causes a considerable wave to run up the river against the river current as far as Gloucester, some twelve miles upstream. It's a natural phenomenon that is becoming rarer. There used to be a bore on the Seine in Paris but someone had the idea of dredging the river and, as I understand the situation, it's never happened since. There are tidal bores in other parts of the world but the Severn Bore is one of the most renowned.

I say it's getting rarer because interventions, such as dredging, can make a considerable difference. However, a bigger difference would be caused by the proposal to build a tidal barrage across the Severn Estuary to generate electricity. There has been a great deal of comment on this idea such as the likely impact on wetlands and the marine environment but I've not heard anyone mention the fact that it would undoubtedly put an end to the Severn Bore. If you want to see it, see it now, and I can recommend just the place.

A temporary occurrence of an internet signal on my tablet gave me the opportunity to search for information on the Severn Bore and I was dismayed to discover that it only occurs on a few days a month around the time of the full moon. However, there had been a full moon a couple of nights ago in Shropshire and it turned out I was in luck. There would be a bore on Sunday evening and again on Monday morning.

***

Now here's a passing whimsy. Had there been a full moon that caused a moment of madness on the night of the wine spillage two nights before? Can the increased reflection of light onto the dark side of the planet cause a change in behaviour? Probably not but it's a fun idea to play with and it would drive Malcolm mad. Is it possible that thousands of years of light nights under the full moon have caused an association with people being out at night (when, perhaps, they should not be) along with associated nefarious activities? Is it possible that those nefarious activities have been spun by someone, anyone… many people, as madness? Perhaps it's possible, but it's much more fun to imagine that I spilled my wine all over my battery pack and nearly electrocuted myself because of the full moon. Of course I don't believe it for a second, I was pissed, careless (perhaps carefree), I was casting a shadow over my writing desk improvised out of a toolbox and that was it. But isn't that a bit boring?

* * *

According to the website, the variation in tides, seasons, time of the month, height of hemlines and any number of factors can mean the bore is more or less impressive depending on when you see it. There are good years, poor years and all sort of variations. This has led to the development of a grading system between 1 and 5 and this time it was due to be a two star, not great but the fact that there would be a bore at all was an enormous stroke of luck. Whatever the case, I had to think of something to do in Gloucester-shire and I'd seen The Severn Bore Inn on the web so what the hell, at least they might do a Sunday lunch so I asked Kathy to take me there.

The journey took me along Herefordshire roads identified with signs saying 'Road liable to flooding', with the River Wye meandering just out of sight to the right. The land around was the classic floodplain, locally flat with hills rising away to either side sometimes near, sometimes far.

I drove through Hereford and on to Ross-on-Wye. After Ross the roads became about as interesting as they can be. Apparently there is a cul-ture amongst bikers where they share information on the best roads for mo-torcycles. I don't ride a bike but I understand that sweeping curves are the thing. The roads out of Ross-on-Wye are a bit tighter than sweeping curves, descending the hillside in deeply wooded hairpins and paperclips, perhaps not perfect for riding at speed unless you could guarantee a clear road around blind bends. On the other hand, though, it was all very lovely in my lumbering Truck, dropping in and out of third gear, at four miles a fortnight, with the revs high and plenty of torque. After some getting lost, a bit of an argument with Kathy, and some directions from a decent local guy working in his front garden, I found my way to the pub.

Now let me say clearly at this stage, as with the Tanvic Tyre Centre in Market Harborough, the Severn Bore Inn at Minsterworth is a thoroughly decent place. Arriving sometime after midday, I ordered a Sunday lunch, a coffee and a soft drink chaser. I couldn't drink as I'd have to drive to a campsite later in the day, a problem I'd struggled with every time I'd allowed myself a pub lunch. I was presented with a meal genuinely fit for a king, succulent meats and the finest vegetables as I've had in a long time. A proper roast, cooked on site, the joints (as there was a selection) I suspect from the local butchers and as far as I could tell not a microwave in sight.

I asked about the Severn Bore and I was told that there had been one early that morning but another was due between nine and ten pm. The guy behind the bar said they had flood lights for after-dark performances so I should give it a go. Asking if there was a local campsite, I was told that I could camp in the garden or on the river bank. The possibility of being able to camp here, access to a pub for the day and free camping with no stress of searching around for a site was no contest. Add to this the fact that the money saved on camping could be spent on beer and it was a done deal. Of course this was not even to consider the fact that this meant I didn't have to drive again for the day.

So I started drinking in earnest.

So it came to pass that, after a wonderful roast lunch and a pint of ale, I was pitching the Khyam on the highest point of the river bank, where I could get the best view of the river from the door of my tent, and conveniently close to the pub and the adjacent public car park. I was ferrying things from the Truck, pegging out the tent between setting up my tablet to charge as I wasn't going to a campsite where I might find a hook-up. In the midst of all this activity two guys whom I'd seen in the pub came out, climbed over the fence and descended out of sight down to the river watched by the other punters. I'd noticed they had life jackets earlier, the sort of thing you loop over your head all furled up and that only inflates when you pull the emergency cord. I'd not thought much about them other than to think, perhaps... canoes, or some such.

However they were now attracting an audience of ten or fifteen people huddled over the fence by the pub. Whatever was happening was clearly more interesting than pitching my tent so, ensuring there were some pegs in place for now as it was breezy, and leaving my possessions unattended in the Truck, I wandered over to see what was going on.

Looking over the fence and down the ladder I didn't see canoes, I saw a speedboat.

Now this wasn't just any old boat with an outboard motor that you might describe as a speedboat, taking advantage of copious amounts of poetic licence that someone had left lying around by the bucket load. You would be perfectly within your rights to stand up in court and say, 'your honour, it was a speedboat,' where you might get in trouble for fibbing. No word of a lie, it was one of those rigid hulled semi inflatable boats that sounds like a bit of a contradiction but means it's a hybrid of rubber dingy and a rigid hulled boat. It had inflatable sides (or gunwales) that add extra buoyancy for bad weather. You see them on TV used by emergency rescue teams and special forces with black balaclavas. This one had a cockpit position towards the back with a steering wheel and levers, lots of dials and gauges, and a seat that you could sort of perch on while standing up. Looking back on it all now, standing up in a speedboat doesn't really seem like a terribly sensible thing to do, but you know how things seem different in hindsight. However, the impressive thing about it was that it had not one but two fairly massive outboard motors.

I watched these two guys reversing away from the bank from my vantage point leaning over the wooden fence. They had moored up in a sort of vertical concrete cleft cut into the bank which housed a couple of storm drains designed to discharge into the river. Presumably this was the outflow of the drainage that ran across the floodplain either side of the river. There was a ladder that ran down to the water and a metal railing around the whole affair to stop people tumbling to their deaths five or fifteen feet below depending on the condition of the tide. Of course, on a sunny Sunday afternoon this made a handy location to tie up your speedboat while you are in the pub, and the vertical drop of the cleft was more suitable for mooring than the natural bank which was sloping and muddy and didn't have any handy ladders.

As I watched one of the guys looked up, 'Oh, bugger, I forgot to untie the rope!' A tangle of rope ran up the ladder and looped around the railing at the top.

'Hold on I'll untie you,' I said in a genuine spirit of helpfulness, being the nearest what with the other locals being on the pub side of a fence a bit further away. Before I'd finished my reply I was leaping over the wooden fence with all the grace of a middle-aged man who clearly thinks he's twenty years younger. Reaching the railing I untangled the knot of loops, half hitches, twisted knickers and general confusion that was attaching the boat to the ladder. Having unravelled it all, I dropped it down to them.

'Thanks for that.' He paused for a moment. 'You'd better come out for a ride then, in return for being so helpful.' Before you could say avast behind (I know pirates aren't on speedboats or the River Severn but just give me that one) I was down the ladder and stepping into the boat, watched jealously (I imagined) by the remaining onlookers. It was an impulse. You have to take your opportunities when they come and what could possibly go wrong anyway?

Once on the water I was immediately handed a life jacket that I slipped over my head and strapped around my waist. That was a good sign I thought, at least they were responsible individuals; after all I didn't know who they were and I'd only seen them talking to locals in the pub.

It was the sort of boat where you stand up, or at least they were standing up. There was a tall console with a steering wheel with all the levers and dials and the tall seat behind so that you stood between the two and perched on the seat. 'Let's get out on the river and we can get going,' said the first guy as he put his half glass of scrumpy in a handy pint glass sized niche between the dashboard and the rail that you hold on to.

'Hold on,' I thought. 'Scrumpy!' The glass contained a yellow cloudy drink that sloshed about as we bobbed toward the centre of the river, the engines just ticking over. As I perched on the seat next to bloke number one, he pushed the throttle all the way forward and the boat lurched up at a steep angle.

In some alarm I looked behind and found myself looking down at the water frothing through the two outboard motors as they roared away. I say I looked behind me looking down but at this point the definitions of down and behind sort of began to lose their meaning. What would have been behind, with the boat sitting horizontally on the water became a sort of down angle into the water. Other than the seat, that I was barely perched on, there was nothing behind me, or is that under me? Whatever the case, what had once been defined as ahead was now up as the front of the boat lurched up at an angle of about 45 degrees with the blue sky and white fluffy clouds all apparently ahead.

'You have to give it full power to start with so as to get the boat up on the plane!' shouted the second guy, whose boat it later turned out to be. It seemed his explanation was prompted by the look of sheer terror on my face.

'Oh, okay,' I acknowledged somewhat meekly.

A moment later we were racing along at high speed, bouncing across the surface of the River Severn leaving a wide wake behind us that spread to the river banks perhaps a hundred yards or more each side. This could in no way be described as a toy boat, Your Honour.

It was at about this point that two thoughts dawned on to me. The first was that it was entirely likely that these two blokes were quite pissed; after all one of them was openly swigging from a glass of scrumpy and the other one seemed quite happy to throw the boat around without a care for the preferences of Messrs Health and Safety. Still they'd not made me buy a ticket so I suppose no contract had been entered into, so any sudden death incidents would be on the basis of a gentlemen's agreement and health and safety rules didn't come into it. Rules on complete and utter stupidity might have some relevance.

The second thought that dawned on me was that I'd rushed over to see what the commotion was about on the river without thinking that I was going to be away from my tent for any length of time. The Khyam Igloo is an excellent tent in any wind and even better when there is someone inside it but I'd left it barely pegged down right on the exposed top of the river bank without any guy ropes out and the weather was just a little blustery. By the time I returned I could potentially find my tent in the river. However, that wasn't the important part of the second thought. (Or does this count as a third thought?) I'd been unloading my gear from the Truck reversed into the corner of the car park. The doors were unlocked, the front windows were wound down and the roof was open. I couldn't remember exactly but I was pretty sure my tablet and wallet were on the driver's seat and the keys were in the ignition. I'd really had no plans to go on any adventures when I walked over to see what was going on.

'Err, I'm not sure I want to be away too long,' I said over the roar of the engines. 'I think I may have left all my possessions unlocked in the car,' I explained.

'Oh it'll be fine,' said bloke number one, or was it bloke number two, I can't really remember as by now it's all a bit of a blur.

'No you don't understand,' I added. 'I think I left the windows…'

'Here, clip this onto your life jacket,' interrupted bloke number two, with no apparent concern for my anxiety. He held out a red plastic coiled lead with a spring clip on one end. On the other end was a small plug. I hooked the clip onto my life jacket as instructed. As I did so he shut down the engines and we came to a halt, flopping back into the water as calm reigned once more. For a moment I had a suspicion of what was about to happen. Bloke number one, meanwhile, continued to swig from his scrumpy.

'You sit here,' he gestured to the driver's seat. He plugged the other end of the cord into a socket on the console and explained, 'This is a cut out for the engine. It ensures that the engine stops if you fall overboard while you are at the controls.'

'Fall overboard!'

'It's only a precaution.'

'I'm really not sure about this.'

'Oh come on, it's easy.'

Moving into position I plugged myself in. Feeling somewhat insecure, I pushed the two throttle levers forward. The boat began to chug through the water gently and I pushed it a bit further forward.

'You have to give it full power when you start so you get the bow up and then you're skimming on the water,' encouraged bloke number two.

My reaction was to think that I'd be quite happy to not skim on the water at all. I'd once piloted a narrowboat on the canal at the age of thirteen at something less than walking pace and that was quite fast enough for me. It wasn't the fact that it might be dangerous so much as the almost total guarantee that, even if my valuables were still in the Truck now, they certainly wouldn't be after three days in hospital after nearly drowning. 'Man dies in terrible drunken speedboat accident, authorities appeal for clues of his identity.' It was all so obvious. By the time I was fished out of the water the Truck and all evidence of my identity would be long gone while friends and relatives would wonder if I'd been abducted by aliens.

Pushing the throttles further forward the bow lifted a little.

'Go on, all the way forward!' he encouraged.

I did as instructed. The bow lifted up to the scary angle again, behind became down and the water churned just where behind had been a moment before. As we gained speed the boat levelled out a little and we were riding on the water at speed, the wind in our hair, spray all around us.

After a while I began to become comfortable with the boat and found that I could steer easily and it responded with apparent agility. I really was driving a powerful speedboat with not one but two engines on England's longest river. I was advised where to steer, to avoid the occasional floating fallen branch or log that looked much like a crocodile. Apparently there was a line of submerged rocks across a point in the river that I had to avoid, which was an issue as the tide was on the way out.

However, no matter how comfortable I became with my newfound speedboat skills I was still worried. The further away we motored the longer it would take to get back and the gravity of the situation was becoming clearer to me. I was on the river with two total strangers in an extremely powerful speedboat, I had no idea who they were or whether I could trust them, I already doubted I could.

'I'd like to go back now please. Could we turn around?' We must have travelled at least two miles up-river. We'd passed around meandering curves back and forth, the landscape was totally unfamiliar. I was utterly at the mercy of these two guys and someone was probably making off with my wallet at that very moment.

It was at this point that bloke number two leaned over and took the steering wheel. 'You want to turn around?' He proceeded to flip the boat around and perform high-speed doughnuts in the middle of the river. The whole place was awash with waves from the wake as we spun around several times, leaning over at an extreme angle.

Just then bloke number one intervened. He must have seen that the general look of concern I'd been displaying had developed into one of abject terror. Sideways had now become down in the same way that behind had become down before. I felt as though I could have reached out sideways and touched the water and, in fact, I probably could have. 'Okay let's take it easy,' said bloke number one as he persuaded his mate to calm down and head us down river.

For the next ten or fifteen minutes we cruised back along the river at a very pleasurable speed, but at least we were getting nearer to my disembarkation point. No doubt there I'd find my belongings thoroughly rifled and the whole 39 counties project would come to a sorry end.

As we cruised we chatted about the life of an adrenalin junkie vs the life of a risk-averse now sedentary onetime adrenalin junkie. I think I managed to regain a shred of credibility when I told them that I had done two parachute jumps and flown a glider solo before I was 20. The fact that I had done neither since didn't seem to matter.

I remained at the controls throughout the return journey and even had my photo taken at the wheel, though the image remains on their camera where, I can only assume, they have a rogues' gallery of the terrified and the insane. At one point it was pointed out that I must be alright because I was wearing Ray-Ban Wayfarers so I must be some sort of cool dude. The fact that bloke number one felt he needed to point this out at all, in an attempt to bolster my status, must indicate that I had been behaving like a girl. In truth I was trying to do and say anything to increase my chances of getting back on the river bank as soon as possible.

Arriving back at the pub, it quickly became apparent that we had a problem. Well actually I had a problem, they were fine. It turned out that the reason they'd left the pub when they had was because the tide had been going out; the Severn is an estuary after all and the river level rises and falls as far up-stream as Gloucester, hence the Severn Bore. From down on the river the pub was barely visible over the raised bank that hold back the extreme floods. It turned out the concrete flood drain outlet they'd moored to had a shelf projecting out horizontally and this was now just below the level of the water stopping us getting up to the ladder. By motoring at high speed up-river and then cruising at a leisurely speed down-river, we'd been away long enough for the ladder to be out of reach. I couldn't get ashore the same way I had come aboard. Being two boatmen of the pissed variety, it seemed they'd not thought of this.

There followed a period of argument between bloke one and bloke two about what they should do. One suggested that I should scramble up the muddy bank where, I considered, there was a very good chance I'd slip and fall back into the river. The other option was to take me to the ski club, whatever that was, but apparently it was some distance away and I'd have to find my way back to my tent, my Truck, my recently purchased 300 pound tablet and my wallet, assuming they were there when I returned. That is assuming I'd be able to find my way back at all.

After some time, the scramble up the river bank was decided as the least-worst option and I was put ashore in a location that had the best ratio of long grass to slippery mud. I scrambled up the bank, displaying the same agility that I'd demonstrated jumping over the fence that triggered this whole ill-advised adventure.

Atop the bank I waved them off, glad to be ashore, not really sure if I should be grateful or relieved. I felt like I'd been gone hours.

The Khyam Igloo was still there, despite being pegged out with the minimum of peggage, but, miracle of miracles, so were all my possessions. When I got back to the Truck I discovered that I really had left the tablet on the dashboard and my bag was sitting on the seat with my wallet in full view. Both front widows had been left wound down as had the roof and the tailgate. Everything I'd been using to live over the last few weeks, plus everything I needed for the following weeks, had been sitting there totally exposed for nearly an hour.

After finishing setting up I spent the rest of the afternoon in the pub chatting to the locals about my adventure, discussing the rights and wrongs of their claims about the need to stand the boat on its tail to get it going, and hearing their opinions about the safety of the whole escapade.

* * *

Eventually, as dusk fell, a group of us assembled on the pub's viewing platform to watch the bore. Remember the bore? This is what I'd come for.

The River Severn is a slow meandering thing. A look at the map shows it snaking across the Gloucestershire plain, sluggishly making its way to the Bristol Channel with no sense of urgency whatsoever. The distance from Gloucester to the estuary proper is probably no more than six or eight miles in a straight line depending on where you consider the estuary to start. However, the course of the river is probably twice that. The river we looked out onto from the deck at the back of the pub was gentle and benign.

Then came the bore.

In the dusk it was hard to see it coming and, what with it being a natural phenomenon dictated by the vagaries of nature, we had only a rough idea of when to expect it. Squinting into the fading light we were unsure if that movement over on the far bank towards the bend in the river was the bore or just a shadow. Then we heard it. The first indication was probably the cracking of wood as low branches gave way to the inundation. Then we could hear the sound of the wave on the bank directly before us and on the far bank. It wasn't a roar, that would be unrealistic, but it was a considerable rush of water, a loud splashing which in itself doesn't sound very dramatic but it is when it goes on for some time. The wave wasn't big, a couple of feet high and not big enough for those that like to surf the wave. Apparently it was a two star, out of five, but it was impressive all the same. The sound of the water against the bank was considerable and the destruction significant, with sizable branches snapping off if they became vulnerable. What surprised me was that there could be any branches that were vulnerable if this was a frequent phenomenon, but I suppose with the constant erosion of the river bank and the changing landscape, trees would come into contact with the wave, become weakened and from time to time suffer such depredation to become damaged. Out in the river the wave was continually rolling, whereas at the bank it was broken and crested with white horses where it churned up the silt, causing a seething brown tumult occasionally carrying debris in its path.

Behind the first wave followed a group of smaller, less dramatic, waves with less destruction and beyond that the surface of the river was broken and choppy. What, moments before, had been a calm and tranquil waterway was now a fast powerful upstream flow, rising rapidly up the banks. Large assortments of debris, flotsam and jetsam were carried in the flow, sizable branches and pieces of wood discarded from god knows where, as well as all manner of other things that, I can only assume, spend their existence floating up and down the river on the tides. This continued for an hour or more, the level of the river noticeably higher than before the inundation.

The Severn Bore is an event that you'd be lucky to catch on the off-chance; I consider myself very lucky bearing in mind I was there for only one day. But even if you don't manage to see a five star event, it's still worth it to see the transformation in the river take place over such a short time. It's one of England's remaining natural spectacles that could disappear in the coming years which, as such, strikes me as all the more meaningful. If you get a chance take a trip down by the riverside, enjoy the beauty and take in the spectacle.

Day 27 - Gloucestershire to Somerset

Monday May 27th

Miles on Truck: 1889

I woke on the riverbank after a somewhat lumpy night. I'd been camped right on the brow of the flood defence, a ridge of earthwork about four feet above the natural riverbank and it wasn't too even. There was another bore due at just after 10:00 so I had breakfast, packed up and got ready for the spectacle.

When it finally came it was no more exciting than the night before, but with natural phenomena you pays your money and you takes your choice. I was lucky that it happened at all when I was there, and the spectacle of a wave travelling up the opposite bank occasionally snapping branches off was worth the wait. Speaking with another spectator he described it as just a surge, but that in itself was interesting and to be really awestruck you have to come back for one of the scheduled four stars that happen a few times a year or the fabled five stars that only happen once in a few years.

I started the Truck, asked Kathy to take me to Portishead on the way to Somerset and set off in search of coffee.

* * *

Another day, another floodplain. The River Severn was occasionally visible on the right-hand side, full enough of water that it looked fit to burst. Clearly it wasn't close to overflowing what with the small bore. Presumably the raised flood defences were built to withstand a large bore and extreme flood conditions on top. Away in the distance was Gloucester Cathedral on a promontory, similar to the way I'd seen Ely Cathedral rising above the fens three weeks before.

Passing through Gloucester, Kathy directed me right into the town centre where they've semi-pedestrianized it directly through the bus and taxi only part of town. Clearly she was getting her revenge for the disagreement of the previous day.

Driving southwest again I strayed on and off of the floodplain, occasionally rising up hills that gave me views inland or out across the Bristol

Channel, where the Severn Bridge and the imaginatively named Second Severn Crossing were gleaming white in the sun.

It's both amazing and not at all surprising that, if you choose not to take the motorways and you let a nice Irish lady be your guide, you discover so much more. I've only ever driven through Somerset on the motorway, unless I was heading to somewhere within the county. From the motorway you might imagine that Somerset consists of only the levels and little else apart from Glastonbury, Bath and Wells and all that baby-eating-bishop nonsense. Perhaps the lesson here is that it shouldn't be at all surprising that you discover more if you come off the motorway, but we do that so infrequently that we are amazed at what we find.

Somewhere around Almondsbury, shortly after stopping to view the Severn River Crossings from afar, too far away to take a photo without a lot of telephoto lenses, the phone rang. It was Graham from Blackpool.

'I'm just phoning to say goodbye.'

When I'd phoned him from Whitby he'd told me that he'd got a hospital appointment, and when I visited him he'd still been awaiting his test results. Furthermore he'd had the most horrendous hacking smoker's cough for years. His paroxysms would strike at any time, often amid a telephone conversation, and you'd have to sit there with the phone listening to him convulsing until it would stop as quickly as it had started. He'd make a brief apology and the conversation would carry on.

'What do you mean goodbye?' I knew exactly what he was saying but my response was more to say, *how dare you treat this so lightly.*

'I'm phoning to say goodbye.' He paused, 'I've had my test results and it's cancer, terminal.' None of this was a surprise, I'd been expecting it ever since he started talking about going in for tests when I phoned him from Whitby. You can't smoke roll-ups for five decades, have a cough that defies polite description for years, and not imagine the possibility. 'So that's it really. I've been phoning everybody to let them know.'

'Now hold on a minute.' Speaking into the hands-free phone I started looking for somewhere to stop. 'You can't just drop that on me while I'm driving!' My response was tinged with something close to anger. Taking the first available turning I threw the Truck off of the main road, finding myself on a side road that quickly diminished into a country lane. 'Just wait a minute while I find somewhere to stop so I can pick up the phone.' Somehow having a phone next to my ear feels more personal. Talking into a speaker phone, even in the privacy of a car, seems more distant somehow. Perhaps the perceived intimacy of the voice speaking directly into your ear brings the other person closer.

The lane turned into a single track road, recently resurfaced and still covered in loose chippings. Either side there were nice houses set back from the grass verge behind hedges with narrow driveways. There was nothing suitable for an emergency phone call. Pulling onto a grass verge it was right at the last moment that I spotted the white painted rocks hidden in the long grass. The nearside front wheel hit the rock with a bang and I swore as I pulled back into the lane to find somewhere else. The careful work of Tanvic Tyre Centre was quite possibly ruined. Graham was quiet on the phone as I pulled back onto the lane to find somewhere else as I swore at the hidden rocks.

A few moments later, which seemed like minutes, I skidded to a halt again on the loose chippings, sliding into a field entrance opposite some-one's drive. Three horses in the paddock looked at me with curiosity. Thoughts crossed my mind that if someone complained about my presence I'd explain that I was receiving a call from a best friend telling me he had ter-minal cancer and wondered how that might work out. Do people who own paddocks have empathy for such situations? Would they just see the scruffy truck, driven by a scruffy bloke with too many weeks of beard to even hear me out? Did anybody care that I had stopped in their field entrance? Had anyone even noticed?

Unplugging the phone from the cradle I put it to my ear. 'So tell me again, what did they say?'

'They said I've got cancer and it's terminal. There's nothing they can do.'

'So is that it?' I complained. 'You thought you'd just phone up and say that while I'm driving.' That might have been a little unfair of me, whenever he phoned me I was going to be on the road for the next few weeks. I'm not sure how else I expected him to handle it; it's the sort of life event that we aren't trained to deal with.

'I'm letting everyone know,' he explained.

'Okay,' I responded, not really knowing what else to say.

'To be honest most people are a bit irritating, treating me with kid gloves and avoiding the difficult conversations.'

'Well I'll not do that,' I replied. 'I'll still treat you as the same self-cen-tred git you've always been.' I sort of felt that the statement might have been a bit strong as the words came out.

He laughed. 'Oh thank you!'

Graham always had an apparently self-regarding nature but people with that perspective can often have hidden motives that are actually more gen-erous than you might expect. And who doesn't have a self-regarding nature anyway? Just some people are better at hiding it than others. Of course that's not to excuse total gits and sociopaths lacking in any human empathy, often see pushing in front of us in Range Rover Sports. Graham doesn't drive a Range Rover Sport.

For a while I sat in the field entrance learning the details, just how much he didn't know, would he make it to Christmas (why is making it to Christ-mas always considered such a milestone?), how many visits would I be able to fit in before he falls off the perch, that sort of thing. In the meantime the horses looked on and I continually craned my neck to look out for irate lo-cals complaining that I shouldn't be parked in their field entrance. Eventually the anxiety of the situation with the horses and their owners got the better of me. When you've known someone for 30 years, who for a time counted as your best mate (when you used to hold to such concepts), there's only so much you can say when they tell you they are on their last legs. I had to get on with the trip so I promised to stay in touch and set off again.

* * *

A few miles further on, in brilliant sunshine with just enough white fluffy clouds to make the day seem brighter as the sun shone off of the clouds, I passed under the Clifton Bridge, which is probably better than pass-ing over it as you see more of a bridge from below; something I learned when I stopped to look at the Humber Bridge. A set of red traffic lights enabled me to sneak a sly photo with the steering wheel in the foreground as I sat beneath the bridge. From below it's quite a sight. The Avon Gorge is dra-matic enough as you drive alongside the river with 300ft cliffs and the river meandering by, but add the 86ft towers on either side with the 700ft span and the whole place takes on a different quality. Because the towers are built out, away from the edge of the gorge, the west tower constructed on a massive 100ft abutment and the east side the tower standing on a near-vertical outcrop, the whole structure has greater presence still.

* * *

For some weeks now I'd lost track of the days of the week. Of course we all know that the days of the week are arbitrary. A cat doesn't know it's Friday or a dog doesn't know it's Shrove Tuesday in much the same way that I didn't know it was Spring Bank Holiday Monday. However someone had pointed out the fact and I began to wonder if I might have trouble getting a pitch for the night. Consequently, when I arrived in Cheddar my priority would be to find a campsite.

Eventually I found myself on smaller roads descending through the Mendip Hills, down nice twisty wooded curves until, suddenly, I was at my destination. Strangely Cheddar struck me as very similar to Keswick or Ambleside. Perhaps it's the influence of the tourist industry, the maze of narrow village streets in local stone, thronging with holidaymakers and the inevitable services of cafés and pay-and-display car parks. Interestingly, it was the very lack of such convenient facilities, in an identifiable centre, that led to my confusion with Coalbrookdale and actively discouraged me from spending any time (or money) there. The place just didn't seem geared up for tourists despite the supposed preponderance of industrial heritage museums that I couldn't find. I'm still convinced I wasn't really welcome.

Arriving in Cheddar I parked in the first available spot, at first not finding the village centre and car park, and asked in a charity shop. The girl in the shop directed me along the road in the direction of what she described as 'the entrance to the gorge', which of course meant nothing to me in a vaguely *over there* sort of direction.

Parking in the pub, I had my second ploughman's of the trip, again complete with local cheese (this time without any pork pie), and searched for a campsite. Sampling the local cheese, as is compulsory in a village named after cheese, I managed to locate a campsite in Rodney Stoke, a few miles out of Cheddar. So I ignored the gorge, imagining that it wasn't going to go anywhere; it's been there for 1.2 million years or so and it wasn't going to fill in in the next few hours. The only danger was that the gorge might be closed to visitors after 5:00 as with some of the places I've arrived at late in the day. Never having seen even a picture of the gorge, I had no idea if that was even a realistic possibility. Could such a landscape feature be fenced in somehow, some ancient landowner reserving the right to restrict access, save for an entrance fee or membership of some sort, perhaps even former membership of an Oxbridge college? Stranger things take place in this land of ancient customs and privileges. Clearly I had no idea what was to come.

I found campsites in Cheddar, as you really would expect there to be, but they were all of the Caravan Club variety and not of the Caravanning and Camping Club variety that describes itself as 'The friendly club'. Make of that what you will, but do remember the smug bloke in his awning in Rutland. Finding Rodney Stoke, with the campsite conveniently in the back garden of a pub, not to mention spotting Glastonbury Tor in the distance, I quickly set up and drove back to Cheddar to see if I could find the fabled gorge.

Of course the gorge isn't a secret, but you could so easily miss it if you didn't know it was there, and had I not got out of the Truck and looked at the notice board I would have missed it. Honestly, you would expect there to be a massive slope or rolling hills in view but down in the village there's nothing. If you face the right way you can see a bit of hillside ahead of you, which I suppose might be a bit of a clue but it doesn't give it away.

However, if you take a particular turn off the roundabout by the Riverside Inn (where they do a fine ploughman's with Cheddar cheese) follow the road towards the unassuming hillside that you wouldn't notice unless you knew it was important, cross the bridge and pass the information centre on your left, follow the road as it narrows through all the tourist traps, which begin to give you a clue, follow the road as it opens out and weaves right then left and then right again… and then you see a bit of a stone cliff on your right. When I say a stone cliff I mean a substantial stone cliff, proper vertical, right down to the pavement, with overhangs towering above you. Then you might then have an inkling of what you are heading into. But as the road narrows again, only to open out a bit to allow another stretch of tourist traps with more cliffs on your right, it's only as the road swings to the left and you spy the first cliff on that side of the road that you can see that you are in a gorge and you get that moment where you understand the true meaning of the word awesome, realising that you are in an utterly transformed landscape.

There's a great deal of misuse of the word *awesome* going around these days. I remember a friend once ticking off someone, in the nicest possible way, for describing something as *awesome* when, really, she just happened to like it. His point was that an erupting volcano is *awesome*. However, if we use *awesome* to describe a great rock band or a nice pair of shoes then we will have no word to describe an erupting volcano, unless we resort to the phrase *trouser filling*, which might be appropriate. In this case Cheddar Gorge *is awesome*, it inspired awe in me with its first appearance.

If you haven't seen Cheddar Gorge it is something to behold. (I must have missed the school trip if there was one.) I've said before that I was awe-struck by the Mountains of Malvern but the Cheddar Gorge leaves them cold. Sorry Malvern, but the awe levels just keep rising, though I feel that with the Cheddar Gorge they may have reached their peak.

I grew up not seeing pictures of Cheddar Gorge and, as a result, I sort of imagined a valley getting wider as it sloped up, perhaps wooded, but roughly straight, and for some reason I imagined there might be a river at the bottom. That conception is utterly wrong and utterly inadequate.

As you ascend away from the last of the cafés and gift shops, the road doubles back and doubles forth in short stretches with small car parks and phalanxes of coaches on either side; but above you the gorge proper appears, sometimes towering up sometimes sloping away either side, all limestone grey in angular shards broken by platforms supporting green slopes and deeply wooded thickets.

Soon the road becomes all invasion proof (the Romans would surely have hated it, twisty and convoluted), becoming steeper, but so as you don't notice because you have to change down for the bends. So the Truck creeps up the incline as the landscape opens out with terraces on either side and it begins to look as though it's all over. Then suddenly you swing around a bend to the right and you are in a narrow gorge with cliffs down to the road either side and you can barely crane your neck enough to see the daylight over the top, 450ft above (taller than the Avon Gorge and the Clifton Bridge towers put together). The road continues up twisting slopes, sometimes with wooded slopes either side, sometimes with cliffs dangerously close to your front wing as you try to avoid oncoming traffic enjoying the curves in the opposite direction.

Of course a sensible person would walk the gorge but I was, as usual, pressured for time and I had no idea how much there was to explore so I drove the length and worked my way back down, stopping in the many small car parks indicated by signs that warned that rocks could, and probably do, fall at any time, where parking is possibly going to involve an insurance claim against an act of god, or at least an act of geology. Stand close to the bottom of one of the cliffs and look up and you really do get a sense of impending doom when you imagine the size, weight and speed of anything that might topple over the edge leading to instant death in a way that would make it into the papers in an alarmist, *Cheddar Gorge Should be Banned to Protect Our Children* sort of way.

Layby-hopping my way down, going out for little walks, I soon discovered how steep the hill really is, or at least how weak my calf muscles had become since I'd stopped any regular long-distance walking. Clearly the correct way to experience Cheddar Gorge is to get out and walk but you probably need a full day to do so, so it's been added to my list along with Whitby, the Mountains of Malvern, the bleak moors of the Staffordshire Peak Experience District, the whole of the Lake District and a few others. I'm told that the gorge is even more impressive from above than below. Certainly the aerial photos on the web do give a better impression of the sheer drop from some of the cliffs, but if you haven't visited the place I urge you not to research the pictures because you really don't want to take away from the impact of the experience. I'm told there are steps cut into one side called Jacob's Ladder (after the biblical stairway to heaven) although it seems that the name has been given to numerous cliff steps and paths around the world. Of course there are many other features not least the caves which I didn't have a chance to look at, what with the driving, the camping and the hearing about old mates dying of cancer.

Day 28 - Somerset to Devon

Tuesday May 28th

Miles on Truck: 1988

Back at the campsite I'd spent a very agreeable evening in the excellent Rodney Stoke Inn with a couple of pots of tea, pints of Old Gorge and a very reasonable pizza. Eventually I dodged the raindrops back to my tent and settled in for the night. By the morning it became apparent that the rain had no intention of stopping so I put the Khyam away in the rain for only the second time on the trip. The rich red Somerset soil stuck to the tent pegs in much the same way as it had done in Northamptonshire.

Having spotted Glastonbury Tor the day before, I asked Kathy to take me to Glastonbury; being a bit of a beatnik myself, I thought it worth passing through hippie central on my way to Devon. Soon my trusted Irish navigator directed me down a tiny, narrow lane alongside the pub which looked like it pointed right in the direction of the Tor on the far horizon. Faithfully, I turned carefully down the lane, feeling the front wheels descend at a considerable angle from the main road. This was looking good; a cross-country route, all twisty, narrow and up-and-downy, direct towards Glastonbury, through unknown lanes, trusting in my electronic guide; just the sort of serendipitous adventure I was looking for, finally proving that it is okay to trust in technology as we once trusted in God. Here the cow parsley brushed the sides of the truck and in places the long stalks almost met in the middle of the lane. I could happily drive like this for miles not knowing where in Somerset I was. The only other evidence of traffic on the lane was that of horses as the narrow road twisted slowly left and right and back again I found myself surrounded by overhanging trees, abundant cow parsley and long grasses. Had I met anyone coming the other way, reversing would have been a nightmare, what with the constriction in the twisty, steep lane, such that I might still be there today trying to see over the spare wheel on the tailgate. Under Kathy's watchful eye I passed over a little brook and through a couple of junctions, where I had to crane my neck to see around the high hedges to spot if there was anything coming. I enjoyed the adventure, letting Kathy guide me on, knowing that I was headed, however slowly, towards the hippie capital of England.

Eventually, I found myself climbing a steep hill with tight hedges still on either side and shortly the lane emerged onto a larger road. The road crossed ahead of me from left to right (or from right to left depending on where you might be going), and the hedges either side restricted my view of oncoming traffic. The road however was flat and as I inched forward, the front wheels of the Truck slowly clawed their way off of the steep incline of the lane onto the level main road. Fortunately, as I emerged the road was quiet, and I turned right as directed only to notice that the road seemed familiar.

I was still in Rodney Stoke! It turned out that bloody Kathy had driven me around in a circle and brought me back to the same main road a few hundred yards from the pub. Clearly the mad woman was still not happy with me and I began to suspect revenge. Trust in SatNav? My trust was being toyed with.

* * *

Sitting in the Truck, looking at maps, trying to get a signal on the rubbish tablet and making notes, I found myself returning to the revelations of the previous day. After hearing about Graham's imminent demise, the gloomy rain seemed somehow appropriate, although that seemed like such a cliché that I wondered if I was just being maudlin. In the end I asked Kathy to take me to somewhere in Exmoor just to see what it looked like. However, the best made plans, and all that, had other ideas. Deciding to at least get a better view of the Tor, and perhaps take a picture, I ignored Kathy's protestations and tried to follow my instincts towards the Tor. Naturally, being a bit of a fan of more creative, shall we say non-rational, approaches to life, my intuition is as reliable as a slide rule without an instruction manual. Unfortunately I'm of the generation where I owned a slide rule but never learned how to use it and, as a result, I got lost. Instead I found myself passing a pay and display car park at the bottom of Glastonbury high street, and it seemed a shame to waste the opportunity so I decided to stop for an hour.

The high street presented me with a fine collection of buildings variously from the 18th century on. Some may have been earlier but I'm not an expert and many older buildings will have been improved or changed beyond recognition. Whatever the case, there's a wonderful selection of Victorian gothic revival buildings with turrets and crenulations that, I'm sure, many people imagine are medieval. Some of the stone buildings do look extraordinarily weathered so who am I to say? I don't get to Glastonbury very often, and it had been a good fifteen years since I was last there, so it's always interesting to visit. What I don't remember from previous visits is the number of buildings that are painted in bright colours and pastel shades. I don't know if this has always been the case or if I spent my last visits looking at the pavements as I did in Louth. Of course Glastonbury contains the usual collection of shops bristling with the apparently irrational, all ancient mysteries, divination and the sort of thing that would put Malcolm's back right up.

Spending a happy hour or so, to the limit of my parking, I browsed up and down the high street looking at various trinkets, considering how many incense sticks I'd already got that I hadn't used, looking for pieces of hematite in interesting shapes and sizes and generally being fascinated by it all.

'Hello,' said a guy with dreadlocks as I picked up a dreamcatcher.

'Hi,' I responded a touch non-committally, turning the dreamcatcher over in my hand. It seemed to be made of a wooden hoop with what looked like string in a web shape. I'd seen lots of these before and this didn't seem the best example.

'I bought one like that last week,' he informed me.

'Oh?' I replied. He must be a local I thought or he was on at least a ten-day holiday. 'Any good?' I found myself wondering what there was to do in Glastonbury for more than a day or so but then I'd only ever been a day visitor and should probably give the place a bit more of a chance. I sort of felt that all the hippie paraphernalia would be too much for me if I spent too long there, a bit like *kiss me quick hat overload* in old seaside resorts.

'It's brilliant. It catches all my negative dreams.' He paused to see if I would respond but I let him continue. 'The feather ensures that the good dreams float down to you and the bad dreams are caught in the web.' I raised my eyebrows attempting to make a sort of, *oh really, that is fascinating and completely believable* expression, but I suspect I just looked as though I had an unfortunate case of indigestion.

'Oh okay,' I replied, not really feeling I had anything to contribute.

'Mine has a turquoise at the centre for protection.'

I put the dreamcatcher back hoping for an opportunity to exit politely. I simply couldn't bring myself to share his enthusiasm but tried to hide my true feelings.

'And it came with a certificate of authenticity.'

This was the breaking point for me so I made my excuses and left. To be honest I thought it was a piece of tat, and at the time any suggestion that some certificate gave it provenance was stretching it a bit. Glastonbury is a fun place and I love the Tor; the tower and the views from the top of the Tor are striking, after all they had attracted me all the way from Rodney Stoke. The climb makes the Tor all the more meaningful; perhaps you have to put effort into something before it can have meaning. The somewhat tawdry nature of some of the things sold in the town represents all that Malcolm dislikes, and stops him seeing beyond words like *energy* and *vibration* to see that there might be some useful meaning for people. Claiming validity by attaching a certificate of authenticity represents just that; as, surely, quality will out. If you bought a dreamcatcher on a trip to a reservation in Nevada, or wherever, then so be it but then you'd not need a certificate to reassure you. Presumably if you were a Native American living in England, then Glastonbury would be the place to make a decent living and certificates of authenticity would be the way to go. Whatever the case, it was clearly very meaningful to him and he was very proud of it.

Later it struck me that there was a parallel here with those blokes who play their car stereos at full volume with the windows open. It always seems to be dance music and it always seems to be a bloke. But they never seem to realise that nobody else shares their enthusiasm for that particular piece of music. It's as if they can't understand that we won't be impressed no matter how wonderful the music is to them. In fact the rarer and more esoteric the music, the less likely we are to share that feeling and think how cool the driver is. This also goes for his flash car and probably any other objects of desire he cares to display.

As it happened I do own a couple of dream catchers but they were nothing like his. They are made from very fine metal bangles with bright anodised coloured finish, one in red the other green. Each is strung with a fine web of fishing line, almost like gossamer; you can hardly see it. Each dreamcatcher has a single plastic bead strung on one of the strands, not in the centre but somewhere in an asymmetric position that seems to create a kind of creative imbalance. You'd imagine that such modern materials would invalidate them as dreamcatchers as they are usually made from natural materials, wood, leather and the like. But these are the most delicate things I have ever seen. They are rare, rather than mass produced, which is how I like my art, for art is what they are. They were made by a girlfriend just before a particularly difficult breakup which makes them all the more meaningful. Of course the guy in Glastonbury could never share that meaning as I could never share his, but that doesn't make it any less valid. You see, meaning isn't transferrable which is what makes it so very difficult to judge.

* * *

From Glastonbury I passed through Bridgewater and up into the Quantock Hills. I'd driven this route before on the way to Minehead for a weekend course in something I can't remember much about. The Quantock Hills were a bit of a surprise. When I came this way before it was on a Friday night in the autumn so it was dark. Though the road was pleasantly twisty I'd not been aware of the outstanding beauty of the place and the occasional surprise views of the sea.

I came down into Dunster and resisted the temptation to go and look at Dunster Castle. I could see a sizable tower or keep on top of a quite significant wooded hill, perhaps half the size of the one that Beeston Castle perches upon. I wanted to push on into Devon as I'd considered I'd given Somerset its day and I'd already stayed too long by stopping off in Glastonbury.

Turning left off of the Minehead road, I passed through Dunster village, a place where the streets are so wonderfully narrow and twisty that most of its length is controlled by traffic lights to allow a flow of traffic in one direction at a time. It was really quite a discovery and, again, I'd have liked to stop but I pushed on, adding it silently to the list.

Beyond Dunster the road climbed steadily, curving left and right up the side of a wooded slope, not tight curves but sweeps that were a real joy in third gear where the Truck's power and acceleration lie. I thought I felt my ears beginning to pop as I ascended onto Exmoor. Soon I passed a sign saying I was entering Exmoor National Park. From Wheddon Cross Kathy, now being more cooperative, took me west across the centre of Exmoor.

The hedges bordering the road grew tall and thick. The bushes and trees had been cut back neatly lower down, but higher up the branches had been left to grow so that, in time, they might grow together and eventually arch over the road. The hedge was so impenetrable that almost all of the landscape was hidden, and for some miles I struggled to get any view of Exmoor at all. For a while, up here, it seemed to be raining less than earlier, though with the lack of a view there seemed no discernible benefit from the improvement. I'd had visions of landscapes similar to the bleak high moorlands I'd witnessed in Yorkshire and Staffordshire but from what I could tell the high hedges here were just hiding farmland.

Shortly I descended into Exford, describing itself as the heart of Exmoor. I thought it might be nice to get an inevitable souvenir, perhaps a T-shirt declaring that I'd been to the heart of Exmoor or some-such amid the preponderance of camping shops and cafés catering for Exmoor walkers and seekers of fine Devon cream teas.

Much to my surprise, the heart of Exmoor contained nothing but a pub, a post office and a general store. I missed the wonderfully named 'Farmers Den' which might well have catered for the requirements of those in need of a tent peg or two, but might just as likely have supplied only widgets for your forage harvester and the like. It seemed while Exford has discovered its identity, the rest of the world hasn't and unlike Keswick and Cheddar, Exford is not yet geared up for tourists, which was sort of reassuring though it didn't help in the T-shirt department. Whatever the case, it's surprisingly unspoiled and despite my interest in camping shop browsing, they might just have the balance right.

Hiding the Truck amid a dishevelment of farmers' scruffy 4x4s, I checked out the village shop in the hope of finding something useful for the remaining camps, and ended up buying some locally grown muffins which turned out to be a joy over the next day or so.

Beyond Exford there were more high hedges that served to block the view, and at this point I began to wonder if this was actually deliberate, a conspiracy perhaps? Is Exmoor proud of its natural beauty and stunning landscapes but also comfortable with its lack of tourist traps and T-shirt sellers? Is the place trying to hide itself from passing travellers? What did strike me, as I drove through, was that there seemed to be very little uncultivated moorland, although it was difficult to tell because of the effectiveness of the hedge conspiracy.

Further on I passed through Simonsbath and out again in the blink of an eye. Strangely Simonsbath was on the map but there seemed to be nothing of it, whereas Exford actually had a village centre but wasn't on the map. There were some very strange things going on with Exmoor, and secret government installations come to mind. The hedges beyond Simonsbath had been allowed to grow high over the road on both sides as I'd imagined back across the moor and the trees were beginning to form a tunnel so perhaps this was the plan of the conspirators as I had surmised.

The weather was taking a turn for the worse with beating rain blowing onto the windscreen, when suddenly I had a shock. I passed a sign saying 'Welcome to Devon.' Since climbing up onto Exmoor, ears a-popping, I'd believed I was in Devon as I'd assumed that's where Exmoor is. I thought I'd once seen a map showing Exmoor in Devon but apparently I have been labouring under a misapprehension. For miles now I'd been stopping to get shots of the rare views through the high hedge or photos of bleak tumble-down shacks, all bleached wood and rusty hinges, and posting them on Facebook with captions saying Exmoor, Devon. Now I felt a fool, well more of a fool than usual. Was I mistaken or was there something more going on? Perhaps the whole hedge conspiracy was linked to an incursion from another county or some group from further afield; maybe rebels from the conflict between Westmorland and the upstart county of Cumbria had set up an enclave in the South and were using the hedges as cover. After all, who would suspect a people renowned for their dry stone walls to hide behind mere hedges? But twenty-foot high hedges that form into tunnels, that might be different.

The passage out of the enclave was confirmed as the hedges in Devon were cut low and trim, as the people of the county were clearly proud of their landscape and wanted travellers to see it. Soon I was descending from Exmoor west towards Barnstaple. There, in the distance, there was a flash or light through the clouds, not sky blue but clearer perhaps, clear enough to brighten the evening or even offer a sunset over the sea.

I dropped down through steep-sided valleys, a patchwork of irregular fields and dense woodlands as the road snaked back and forth towards sea level. I found myself in a conveniently slow convoy that allowed me to take in the landscape as we meandered around switchbacks, hairpins, paperclips and knicker twists reminiscent of the drunken looping knots on the speedboat mooring on the Severn. Again I found myself struck by the staggering beauty of the landscape, forested slopes, too irregular to cultivate, with dappled light cascading through the trees, vistas across miniature timbered valleys, their undulations hiding landscapes out of view but enticing enough to make me want to stop and explore. Of course there was nowhere to stop on these narrow precarious roads clinging to the side of the valley and I had to push on, as usual, anxious to find out where I would be sleeping. Finally I crested the hill to see bright sky on the horizon, sunlight streaming through the clouds, with the sea visible down the valley to the west as though Barnstaple was some promised land after passing over Exmoor in the rain.

* * *

Barnstaple, however, was not the promised land I had hoped for, despite the light reflecting off the sea. I couldn't find a town centre with a conveniently placed car park to welcome visitors and their wallets. Instead I drifted into a car park beside a muddy estuary next to a police station. Looking at the helpful map drawn in cartoon fashion I couldn't even locate where I was and it seemed to bear no resemblance to the town I was in. It strikes me that, especially in the SatNav age, people might visit places in just this way, heading for a town without so much as a hint of a plan saying, *hey, let's be spontaneous and just wing it*. In Thame or Cheddar, Whitby or Ambleside you know when you have arrived. You can park and see immediately where you go to spend money into the local economy. I may have missed the signs but Barnstable, like Coalbrookdale seemed to be useless without local knowledge. I couldn't see where to stop so I ended up in a car park away from the amenities or shops, there wasn't a cream tea to be bought for miles as far as I could see, and I *would have* bought one as I considered my options, so I got back in the Truck and drove away. Granted, I could have wandered into the nearby police station but as this isn't the 1950s I decided they would probably have better things to do and I didn't want to waste a pound on an hour's parking only to discover I was in the wrong place and move on in ten minutes.

So I moved on, found myself in a stream of traffic passing the pedestrianized town centre (no wonder I couldn't park) and ended up on an industrial estate where I could stop to work out my next move. Are we beginning to see a pattern here? We've closed off all the town centres to traffic, out of town supermarkets and the Internet have taken all the trade away from town centres and thus they are full of empty shops and derelict shells of once vibrant communities. Meanwhile visitors are shunned because there is nowhere to stop unless you are a local and know where the secret car parks are. In which case you are probably on your way home from your dreary job and unlikely to want to buy a bloody cream tea anyway! So passing visitors end up in dreadful industrial estates and laybys on main roads and move on seeking somewhere more inviting.

Eventually, from my grimy industrialised rest stop, I was able to locate a campsite in the nearby village of Croyde and I headed over there hoping to find the Eldorado that Barnstaple had failed to be.

* * *

Returning from the on-site chip shop, a bonus if ever there was one, I spotted two more Khyam Igloos just up the field from me. The difference was that mine was the standard green whereas theirs were bright orange. I sort of object to all that camping gear in bright safety colours; bright tents are fine for festivals but bright orange tents in the wilderness just seem a blot on the landscape. However, it turned out these bright orange Khyams were the special editions made for the Land Rover G4 Challenge, a series of over-land adventure competitions a few years ago involving off-road driving and various outdoor sports like rock climbing, mountain biking, kayaking and other fun adventures that I swore I'd get into at some point in my life but only ever did once or twice.

I don't know what the relationship of the Khyam Igloo is to the event, whether they are provided as part of the challenge, whether you have to buy your own or even buy your own Land Rover (surely they don't give away such equipment for promotional purposes) but there are pictures of orange Khyam Igloos in the Arctic, in deserts, up mountains, and deep in various jungles around the world looking all intrepid and generally orange, with orange Land Rovers parked nearby looking equally intrepid. My Igloo isn't orange, or very intrepid, but it has been as far as Cumberland and it was quite windy, what with the severe weather warning, so perhaps that counts.

It only occurred to me later that the fact that I chose a Khyam Igloo for a 39-day continuous camping trip where it was erected every day and had to reliably serve as my only shelter, being used in all weathers, sometimes being taken down wet, and yet performing perfectly well is in itself a recommendation for the tent. If there is such a thing as the Khyam English Challenge I was doing it!

So I got talking to these guys, all square-jawed and hunky with the two matching tents and an interesting 4x4 minibus parked next to them looking very intrepid in the fairly high winds blowing off the Devon coast. We started talking about our tents and general outdoorsy gear and it turned out they were in Croyde for the surfing, which when you look around seems to be the business of the place. We talked about surfing and tents with groundsheets and the like and they inevitably asked me what I was doing there.

I felt a bit cagey about mentioning the whole search for meaning thing as it's a bit irrational and I sort of imagine that if anyone is going to be a sceptic then blokes like these would be. I know it's a stereotype but we often rely on stereotypes. Another word for stereotype is heuristic, or rule of thumb. Such shortcuts in thinking have been the rules by which we have survived for thousands of years. They often lead to incorrect conclusions but when it's a matter of survival they can be useful. Not all snakes are poisonous but if you treat all snakes as poisonous then you might live longer unless, of course, you are snakeskin shoemaker but I don't suppose there was much call for snakeskin shoes on the African savannah when these heuristics evolved. Of course such rules of thumb can lead to ignorance of the facts, superstition, or even prejudice if you are taught that all outsiders are competitors for resources; but for tens of thousands of years these heuristics had survival value and it's entirely possible that we are hard-wired to develop these non-rational or mistaken ideas. Is it possible that a sense of meaning attaches to these ideas to encourage their use and so aid survival? Is meaning in heuristics part of evolution?

So we chatted for a while and they came to the conclusion that I was doing a bucket list trip, which might have contained an element of truth. We had a great time swapping blokey stories about tents and I, briefly, sort of felt like I was one of those square-jawed hard core guys.

However, I now wonder if I was right to be so cautious. They might well have understood my quest and my fear of misunderstanding might have got the better of me. Granted it might have taken an evening of chat and the consumption of the bottle of rum given to me in Derbyshire, but a surfer might have known exactly what I meant by the search for meaning. Surfers often talk about something almost spiritual when surfing, though as with *energy* and *vibration* I really don't know what *spiritual* means. So who am I to say that these guys don't find meaning in surfing and possibly something more? They just might not think of it that way.

Day 29 - Devon to Cornwall

Wednesday May 29th

Miles on Truck: 2090

There is of course another possibility to explain interest in non-rational ideas in an apparently rational world; that is flavour. Non-rational ideas can just seem a bit more entertaining. Now this is a bit debatable, as any scientist with a good understanding of their field will talk with a sense of wonder. We've all seen Brian Cox, Carl Sagan or David Attenborough talking about physics, cosmology or evolution. Understanding just how atoms are made up of mostly nothing, or that a particular unique species came about through millions of years of chance mutations to occupy the perfect niche in the environment, does engender a sense of true wonder. You discover the nature of reality and you think *really? That's amazing!* That sense of wonder is flavour. You learn something amazing and it enriches your life to know it. But many people aren't into physics or cosmology or evolution; I wish they were but I simply can't have the world the way I would like it. So what about the idea that non-rational ideas are simply attractive?

* * *

Afraid of the apparently strict 11:00 deadline for leaving the campsite, fearful that they might somehow physically extort another night's fee out of me, I got up pretty sharpish and got breakfast out of the way as quickly as possible.

After a hurried breakfast I packed as quickly as I could and tried to get the tent as dry as possible. The construction of the Khyam is such that you can turn the whole thing upside down while it's still erected, so that it sort of ends up looking like a radar dish. While it dried properly for the first time in two days, I sat in the Truck for a few minutes and tried to figure out where I was headed. Talking to the G4 guys, I had mentioned Land's End as a destination and they suggested a place called Sennen. I'd never heard of it but it seemed reasonable.

Unfortunately Kathy led me right into the heart of Barnstaple, to parts of the town I might have been glad of seeing the day before when I was looking for somewhere to park. However, I didn't escape the town before she led

me right through the bus and taxi only area just as she had done in Gloucester. I was half expecting to arrive home ten days later to find multiple sum-
monses for driving in restricted streets and to have suffered numerous
sanctions for not having replied on time.

Driving in brilliant sunshine I crossed the Torrington Bridge to Bideford. The bridge is high above the estuary with striking views and I had to
wonder why it was built so high. Does Bideford get tall ships visiting on its
tiny estuary or is it just that the hills around are so high that it would have
been troublesome to build a lower bridge? Whatever the case I found it briefly entertaining in my own bridge-obsessed way.

Soon I passed into Cornwall on sweeping roads that would attract motorcyclists from far and wide but there was a striking lack of signs advising
motorcyclists not to die horribly on their visits as I'd seen in the Midlands.
Shortly I saw the first wind turbines I'd seen in over a week and, interestingly,
also a solar panel farm diligently facing the sun. (They've become more common since but at the time of writing they were quite unusual.)

Before long the ordinary main road I travelled suddenly bore the name
The Atlantic Highway which I felt might be a little ambitious for Cornwall.
Surely such a name would work for the east coast of America or even the
west coast of Ireland but is Cornwall in the Atlantic? Google describes the
waters off the north coast of Cornwall as the Celtic Sea, though I'd never
heard that before I looked it up. I suppose you can call something what you
like and if it sticks that's good enough. In that case I'm calling this trip the
Khyam Truck Challenge. On second thoughts, that's a silly idea, unless they
want to pay me or promote my book, and even if they do I'm not changing
the title!

The *Atlantic Highway* reminds me of the *Pacific Coast Highway*, a dramatic
stretch of road that runs along the California Coast from San Francisco,
through Big Sur to Los Angeles. From what I can tell, it follows cliff-tops,
alongside beaches and winding precipitously along hillsides almost defiantly.
(I say from what I can tell as I've never driven it but if a publisher wants to
fund such a trip you know where to find me, but you might want to line up
behind the publisher for the Wales trip and possibly Scotland.) You can sort
of imagine that the early 20th century engineers who built the Pacific Coast
Highway could have taken easier routes but they cut a (mostly) horizontal
path along the hillsides within sight of the sea where the mountains of Big

Sur rise directly from the ocean. You have to applaud their ambition and sense of place.

Of course the Atlantic Highway was nothing like the Pacific Coast Highway but, in its own way, it deserves the name. The Celtic Sea Highway just wouldn't have the right ring to it. Granted the views aren't all as dramatic as California might promise, the Atlantic Highway being inland in places for a start; but the sweeping curves and open landscapes with occasional views of the sea were a pleasure in the warm late May sunshine and I occasionally caught vistas such as the unexpected view of Lundy Isle, famous for its postage stamps from my childhood.

My plan was to drive straight for Sennen and find a campsite around there so that I could take in Land's End and whatever I fancied; however, serendipity was having it otherwise.

Malcolm had suggested that I have a look at Tintagel Castle and lo!, there, on the Atlantic Highway, was a sign for Tintagel village. So right turn, head for Tintagel, and I'd still have time to get to Sennen. For some weeks I'd thought I couldn't travel the country and not visit Land's End so it remained firmly on the agenda; however, driving to Tintagel was another example of serendipity's interference. No sooner had I decided to head for Tintagel than there, off to the right, was a sign for Boscastle, known for the infamous flood of 2004 and also The Museum of Witchcraft and Magic.

So on I pushed to Tintagel and I was glad I did. While it is clearly a tourist trap, full of gift shops and pink ice cream parlours, it's well set up for the unprepared visitor. Walking down the long path, I found the kiosk and handed over my recently acquired English Heritage card.

'I'm afraid this card is out of date,' said one of the two guys in dark green English Heritage T-shirts in the kiosk.

My immediate response was to panic. 'No!' My second response was to protest while continuing to panic. 'No, surely!' The word *surely* wasn't really appropriate as I knew it wasn't, or shouldn't be, out of date as I knew I was telling the truth but in times of stress your mouth tends to start working before you've had time to give it instructions. 'It can't be out of date, it's only a few weeks old!'

One of the guys showed the card to the other. 'It says it was issued on the tenth of May 2012.'

'No, that's wrong, it should say 2013! I've only had it a few weeks!' There must have been a clear sense of astonished panic in my voice as the two guys in the dark green shirts each looked closely at the card. 'It's only the temporary card as I've been on the road since I joined so I've not been home to get the proper card that comes through the post.'

They paused for a moment before I continued. 'You see I'm touring the whole of England, one county a day, and I was in Whitby earlier in the month so I won't get home to collect the card.'

As I wondered if I was going to have to explain the specifics of my trip in infinite detail, and hoping that it wouldn't sound so incredible that it seemed like I was making the whole thing up, they paused and looked at me before handing the card back and waving me through. Next time, I thought, I'll bring the receipt, which on this occasion was in the Truck in the car park, in the village back up the long hill, in the hot sunshine, where I knew I wouldn't want to walk all the way back down the hill again.

* * *

Once past the kiosk, Tintagel Castle was impressive, impressive in the same way that Beeston Castle was impressive. It was built in about the same period on an even more inaccessible rock, a pair of rocks in fact, most of which could only be accessed by flights of hundreds of narrow steps. In some accounts the location is described as a peninsular, in others an island.

The place is reported to have been inhabited by Romans though it's said no evidence of Roman buildings have been found. It's thought that the early medieval period (that many of us grew up describing as the dark ages) saw a local Cornish King, Dumnoia, using it as one of his residences. Later, in the 13 Century, Richard Earl of Cornwall constructed a castle that seemed to have been built more to impress the locals than for any other reason.

One might imagine the feeling of sheer horror felt by Lord Whoever's servants when he declares that he intends to build a castle in such an inaccessible location. It's okay for him but he doesn't have to drag everything up there to build the damn thing. Much of the stone might have been quarried on site but everything else has to be borne up there by some poor mug who doesn't get any say in the matter. Then, after a generation of lugging, dragging and humping impossibly heavy rocks up this pointless rock (that nobody in their right mind will try to invade anyway so why bother), not to mention the number of poor souls who fell off the bloody steps because Mr Health and Mr Safety haven't come into existence yet—then, after decades of doing all this, Lord Whoever moves in. From then on all his food and wine (can you imagine barrels being dragged up those steps?), furniture and all that crap, has to be brought in on a daily basis. You might send out for a pizza but some poor sod on a moped has got to deliver it up those bloody steps.

Utter bastard!

And another thing! Can you imagine getting your army mobilized? I was shagged out after walking back up the hill from the visitor centre to the village and I was wearing a T-shirt and a camping jacket. I carried nothing more than a man bag with a notebook and a tablet, a phone, a wallet, a bunch of keys and a ukulele tuner. Halfway up the slope I was thankful that I didn't buy anything heavy in the shop. Can you imagine marshalling your army from your castle and getting them up that slope? Most of them would be dead from exhaustion after half a day; I mean this was the age of chain mail! Sod that.

Utter, utter bastard!

To the modern castle fan, Tintagel Castle is nice; it's got lots of steps, a few walls and enclosures where you can see how big the rooms were but there's not much of it left. The overriding experience is one of steps, many of them quite steep and some of them narrow. A few of them are narrow and steep but it's okay if you like that sort of thing. Don't get me wrong, it is worth a visit, even if only to get a flavour of how exploited people used to be before they had employment rights.

Of course it takes time to write a book and the world moves on. Today Tintagel Castle has a bridge to allow visitors easier access. You could never describe the hundreds of steps down towards the water and then back up to the heights of the ruins as wheelchair friendly. I've not been back since but I wonder if the narrow steps are still available for the more adventurous and those, like me, who suffer with a bit of a sense of vertigo. The bridge does look very high.

* * *

From Tintagel I headed for Boscastle, thankfully only ten minutes' drive away and well situated for a combined visit if you start early enough.

Of course Boscastle is famous, infamous perhaps, for the flood of August 2004 when a series of relatively localised circumstances conspired to cause one of the most extreme flash flood events ever experienced in Britain. Heavy thundery showers on 16th August caused massive amounts of water to rush off the land into watercourses in Boscastle, Crackington Haven and Rocky Valley. Over the course of an afternoon seven inches of rain fell inland and it is said that at the peak one inch of rain fell in just 15 minutes. Rather wonderfully, though not for the locals, the unique Cornish weather conditions that can cause this are known as the Brown Willy Effect, named after Brown Willy, the highest point on Bodmin Moor. The high moorland is often responsible for precipitating showers out of the moist air coming from the Atlantic as it is caused to rise over the high moorland and condense out into rain. If you go walking on Bodmin Moor, take an umbrella!

Unfortunately Boscastle wasn't helped by its geography, with a narrow twisty river channel which is said to have risen by seven feet in one hour. This was made worse by the fact that the bridge across the river caused a bottleneck which trapped debris including rubble, cars, trees, caravans and the like. When the stone bridge finally gave way, a 10ft wave was observed as the choked water was released. It is estimated that something like 20 million gallons of water flowed through the village, causing considerable structural damage and washing away 75 cars, 5 caravans, 6 buildings and several boats. It is said that some 100 homes and business were destroyed, while seven Sea King helicopters from the Navy, Army and Coast Guard rescued somewhere in the region of 150 people from rooftops and other perilous situations. Miraculously nobody was killed or even seriously injured. Writing this today I find that thought brings a tear to my eye, that we support each other like this, and so it should, for we are a people of community and cooperation, and such experiences bring meaning to our very existence.

Descending into a deep valley, it was easy to see how the landscape had funnelled the torrential rain into a flash flood years before. The same terrain meant that the warm sunshine, cooled by a pleasant breeze when I'd been on the exposed headland at Tintagel, was significantly warmer in sheltered Boscastle. In the car park a quick change into shorts was required.

The Museum of Witchcraft and Magic is a fascinating place established by Cecil Williamson whom I've never really known anything about. His Wikipedia entry suggests that, as well as founding the museum, his Witchcraft Centre was part of the MI6 effort against Nazi Germany, back when that sort of thing used to happen. Perhaps that sort of thing still happens, perhaps MI6 and MI5 work with Mystic Meg and that astrologer bloke off of breakfast TV to track down terrorist cells. Perhaps they then get Derren Brown to convince them of the error of their ways, or at least that it's possible to make a coin land on heads six times in a row without having to do it a thousand times. Perhaps that sort of thing still happens, perhaps it never happened at all and it's just a lovely story that makes the world seem more colourful. A world where some things are a little bit in doubt just seems a bit more interesting, a bit like my garden seemed more interesting before I had the trees removed. Walking down the garden revealed hidden places beyond the trees where, only then, you could see just how extensive the pond was. Now the trees have gone, more for the benefit of the neighbours than me, the whole garden can be seen at a glance. This is nice in its own way, especially as you get the evening sun on the terrace, but potentially not as interesting from a point of view of undiscovered places. A world where there are some things we don't inspect too closely seems to have something of that which lies, metaphorically, beyond the trees, ripe for exploration or imagination.

I'd always been a bit unsure about the Witchcraft Museum, thinking that it could so easily be badly presented. Boscastle was all civilised and clotted cream, well set up and working as a nice tourist trap, if a tourist trap can be nice, and in this case it seems it can. Parking was accessible and the place seemed welcoming. I didn't do anything there other than visit the Witchcraft Museum but, on the whole, I was very impressed and I'd like to have explored the village further.

Stepping into the museum I felt the temperature drop significantly. This wasn't any spooky supernatural phenomenon; the museum is housed in an old stone building snuggled very close to the hillside and as such you can imagine that the temperature stays fairly constant inside. It wasn't cold but a bit too cool for shorts and I began to regret my decision to change when I'd arrived. However, in the true spirit of discovery I pushed on; I'd paid my money and I wanted to see what they had.

The museum covers an interesting mix of historic and modern practices from folklore to fact. They have many artefacts that describe folkloric traditions from across the world so there is a strong anthropological slant to the place. Visitors are led along a specific route which starts with the horror stories of historical abuse, social exclusion and downright torture. You learn that many people who were abused by the authorities or the church in centuries gone by were probably just the socially excluded, mentally ill or other people marked out by difference. Other people were scapegoated, victims of vendetta or malicious accusation. In a society where there is a perception of no smoke without fire, you only have to make a whisper in the right place to set events in motion that mean you can grab that piece of land or their prize livestock. Of course some were people who genuinely held differing religious beliefs and suffered horribly for it. Religious intolerance or general intolerance of others' belief systems is something that seems to trouble us more today than ever.

One rather impressive feature was the substantial stone circle they have constructed on the ground floor. By clever use of mirrors and lighting they have made a quarter circle of stones look like a full circle that appears, perhaps, 20ft, or more, across. (Talking to the museum staff more recently, it seems the new owners have removed this and are planning to rebuild it upstairs.) Otherwise the museum houses an extraordinary collection of artefacts illustrating the history of the occult and folkloric traditions both ancient and modern. Some of the displays upstairs look like they come from notable personalities of the modern world of occult subculture, if you but knew who those people were. I recognised just a few names, but by no means all of them, as it's a pretty specialised field.

Clearly on the scale of rational to non-rational, belief in magic is about as far into the irrational as it is possible to go. Belief in the possibility to effect change at a distance goes far beyond the scientific worldview. Believing in the ability to divine information, either about the future or the present, is also beyond science.

This is the extreme end of the scale as objected to by Malcolm, belief in the supernatural. Of course, many believers in this field would argue that they have an extended understanding of what is natural and there is nothing super about it. Others might have differing opinions of the structure of the universe or theories of the nature of reality that differ from the current scientific perspective, often picking on the idea that scientific perspectives change so why, they argue, can't their perspective be the correct one?

Alternatively some might compartmentalise their beliefs, as though it's possible to believe in something that you, really, know to be untrue just because you like it or it feels comfortable or some other personal motive. I know that sounds impossible but it seems many people compartmentalise their understanding of reality, otherwise there would be no scientists going to church, which there are. The concept of 'something else' is familiar to many people. In this case the something else is a different layer of belief from the understanding that the universe is governed by laws of motion, thermodynamics, death and taxes. Alternatively, in the compartmentalisation model, different, apparently opposing experiences of reality, which normally contradict each other, seem to exist side by side. A bit like metric and imperial, both seem to work for the user so long as they are kept separate. Rather like the common concept of the head and the heart.

The practice of performing an act with a remote, apparently non-causal, result is an anathema to rationalists. Causality, the clearly understood mechanism between cause and effect, is at the heart of science. If you can't point to a causal mechanism between two apparently unrelated events then science says it can't be real. Practitioners of magic might reply that the scientists don't understand the mechanisms they work with, and there follows a spiral of dismissive claim and counter-claim until someone says something rather unkind, everybody is offended, nobody learns anything about the other side and all prejudices are confirmed.

However, if the practices of witches and magicians are that of devotion, or reverence for something as simple as nature, or if the practice of ritual is for significant events in the same way that we have rituals for births, weddings and deaths, then what's wrong with that? It could be argued that such practices are of psychosocial benefit. It has been suggested that part of the problem with out of control adolescent males is that their life experiences lack the rites of passage that they might have had in earlier generations. Instead they have rites of passage facilitated by their peers that include antisocial behaviour or crime. To get to the top of the gang you have to actually stab someone. Ceremonies that make our youth feel a part of something, even if they are totally arbitrary, might give young people a sense of belonging that could begin to solve some of our social ills. (Of course you can't just impose such ceremonies because to someone unconnected they would be meaningless, for meaning is everything but it's not transferable.) This would define spiritual and magical practice as something akin to generating social cohesion. The people in the field in Derbyshire were, indeed, a community, albeit one that comes together at weekends.

* * *

Leaving the museum it was after 5:00 and I still had to drive the length of Cornwall. After I'd eaten a locally sourced Cornish pasty, Kathy suggested it was still an hour and a half to Land's End. Cornwall doesn't have any motorways, even if I'd been prepared to use them; however the A30 is as close to a motorway as you will get in the county. I had used the A1, under duress, in Bedfordshire and Northumberland so I thought it was permissible to do so again. I simply couldn't leave Cornwall without going to the end of the land.

At 7:00 I arrived at Land's End car park. I had no trouble finding it; there was nowhere else to go. When I'd come here as a child the whole peninsula had been cut off as a private estate. Regular people simply didn't get to see it, now we can.

From the car park you pass through an entrance declaring itself as the Land's End Hotel, which I thought was fair enough considering the location. On another day, and feeling a bit more flush, I might even be prepared to stay there. However, beyond, someone seems to have built a theme park. There was a little village (as they called it), shops selling Land's End related bits and pieces, all shut up but you could walk through the village, which seemed considerate of them considering how many places are gated these days. Beyond there were some buildings with what I can only assume were attractions or exhibitions, some dedicated to the air sea rescue service, the lifeboats and other Land's End type activities. The place was a little desolate, probably helped by the fact that I was the only person there. The whole collection of shops and attractions had a sort of end of the pier feel. If this was the end of the pier, does that make Cornwall the pier, and in that case what is the rest of the country?

Walking between the buildings, past the darkened shops and attractions, closed up bars and snack joints, I found myself on the cliff tops. At this point I wished I'd brought my compass which was safely back in the Truck. The point of Land's End is that it is the westernmost point, which is a bit odd when you consider that John O'Groats is the northern most point in Britain. I could see where the westernmost point was but having the compass point it out to me, to make that measurement myself, seemed as though it might have been more meaningful.

The actual westernmost point was clear as there was a path along the cliff top to a snack shop perhaps a quarter of a mile further. The sign said that was the actual Land's End and therefore, presumably, the westernmost point. Not having a compass seemed a disappointment. Is this an instance where a scientific measurement seems more meaningful than anything else? Is there meaning in the accuracy and hard knowledge of measurements? Hard facts (not necessarily Gradgrindian) may seem more meaningful than a vague understanding or even a distinct sign pointing west. From the point of view of a visitor, the sign was put there by someone else who might not have been completely reliable (though I'm sure the people who run the Land's End estate are as reliable as any). But is there something in the direct experience of making that measurement that gives meaning? Is this where science sometimes seems to let us down? We are told that such and such is true but we don't have a connection to the things science tells us. Science is, in modern terms, distant or too complex, out of our reach, for most of us to experience directly. Do any of us really know what goes on at the Large Hadron Collider or understand the complexities of genetics? Hell, most people don't even understand evolution and that's been around for 150 years; what chance do we have with physics and genetics? The people in the field in Derbyshire, the guy with the dreamcatcher in Glastonbury, or those generations of people represented by the Museum of Witchcraft and Magic, are all seeking direct experience of something rather being told that something is the case with no connection to the thing they are told about. The people who actually do the science, who tell us how it works, are as much gatekeepers as a priesthood, moderating the experience for the congregation. On the other hand modern people living in a world of superficiality seem to be seeking direct contact with something. To have my compass point to the west would have given me a definitive feeling of having reached a significant point on my journey. (Okay, I know compasses point to the north but you know what I mean.)

Managing to get a signal on my tablet, I posted a status on Facebook that said I'd arrived at Land's End, and started to stroll the last quarter mile along the cliff top path without another soul in sight. The path led to a whitewashed building, some sort of snack bar titled The First and Last Refreshment House in England, all closed up against the elements. I imagined that there could well be plenty of elements to be closed up against. The landscape was rugged, with jagged cliffs and a comfortable breeze blowing in from the Atlantic. The sun was setting in the west beyond Longships Lighthouse about a mile offshore; beyond that there is only America.

My lack of a compass bothered me. I'd thought that learning about the religious persecutions of witches would express meaningful experience. People persecuted for finding meaning in things that were not part of the established worldview seemed about as significant as you might imagine. Yet here I was feeling that the use of a simple scientific instrument, a magnetised needle pointing to the definitive north, showing me I had reached Land's End, that seemed to be as significant, as meaningful as anything else might be.

There was a response from a friend on Facebook: 'You've gone as far as you can, you have to turn around and come back.'

Day 30 - Cornwall to Dorset

Thursday May 30th

Miles on Truck: 2248

Bugging out on a blustery sunny morning I headed for Dorset at all speed, apart, that is, from a half hour stop at Penzance to take some pictures.

I'd stayed in what I'd imagined to be the first and last campsite in Britain, where I'd arrived after the office had closed so, as in Happisburgh, I picked a spot and got on with my evening. I wasn't interrupted by any talking legs during the evening but awoke to find a label tied to my tent in the morning, all without having been disturbed. Sure enough 30 days into the trip I was beginning to relax about the prospect of just finding campsites without booking in advance, in much the same way as you figure out how best to live your life long after you've made all the important decisions. The site wasn't actually called *the first and last* campsite in Britain but everything else in the area is known as the first and last; the First and Last Pub, the First and Last Café, presumably there's a First and Last Shoe Shop and a First and Last Launderette. Lower Treave Campsite was either missing a trick with its name or there was another campsite closer to Land's End that I'd not been able to find.

Leaving Land's End the previous evening, I'd followed the signs for Sennen Cove, as suggested by the surfer guys, but by the time I arrived it was late in the evening, the sun was just about setting over the Atlantic and the whole place looked shut up. Apparently it's a bit of a surf centre so, presumably, the surfers had all gone for an early night so to get the best start the next day to catch the surf and perhaps have one of those surfing mystical experiences I'd heard of. I must come here again I thought... yet again.

Heading out of Penzance, Kathy wanted to send me into the pedestrian maze, a labyrinth of potential collisions between machines and people, but having seen her play that trick in Barnstable and Gloucester I knew better and followed my initiative.

One problem with machines, such as Kathy, is that they have no insight, whereas people can make on-the-spot judgements based on real time information. The deep-level analysis that is the strength of SatNav is good for its own purposes, but reliance on such tools can easily lead us into a maze of errors that, if compounded, can result in misunderstanding, conflict of interest or worse. These days we are relying on big data for similar analysis and I find myself wondering if conflicts or errors might arise. There's certainly a conflict of interest between the needs of pedestrians and drivers. If we don't allow human judgement to have its place, might reliance on non-human systems lead to unintended consequences?

I'd been on the trunk road through Cornwall heading back east, but Kathy asked me to turn off toward Truro. Engrossed in the music and with the soft volume of her voice, I missed her advice to turn left. She nagged me to turn around when possible but there wasn't anywhere suitable so I pushed on. She would have to fit with my situation rather than dictate my every move. Turning around might be the logical move from the perspective of the deep analysis of her programing but, there, on the ground, I would have to continue.

At the next roundabout she came up with a new analysis and directed me down a tiny country lane. Suddenly I was in another world of shaded routes with bluebells and wildflowers, all serendipity and wonder. Masses of cow parsley and ferns grew on 5ft high banks on either side of the narrow lane, with bare red earth that looked as though someone had gouged a path through. All around birds twittered (and possibly blogged), the whole environment was full of flavour and richness because of a missed turning. Serendipity, a mistake and a total lack of measurement had served me well.

So perhaps deep analysis, sometimes combined with error or non-rationality can lead to a little bit of magic. I drove on, through a few miles of country lanes like I'd never seen before, all strewn with wild flowers of every colour, higher both sides than the roof of the Truck. The colours seemed almost hallucinogenic, as if someone had turned the saturation up on a Photoshopped picture, the detail of every spray, each leaf and petal there in immense detail, right by the window, brushing against the door mirrors. As I came out of the lanes I passed by another solar panel farm, and onto a new main road, otherwise with no idea where this took place.

Surfers sometimes speak of something spiritual, whatever that is. Malcolm used to talk of unifying the microcosm and the macrocosm but I've never managed to get him to explain what he means. I suspect the experience defies explanation and I wonder if he's ever experienced it anyway, even though, despite being an arch-rationalist, he apparently craves the experience. Appearances can be deceptive and the square-jawed surfer might be a deeply spiritual person. Perhaps those who espouse rationalism are also deeply spiritual people finding meaning in the science that they proselytize but unable to express it in the language of measurement.

* * *

After a long stretch of trunk road my serendipitous navigator turned me toward Plymouth. The new road took me down sweeping curves along precipitous edges and through shadowy woods with dappled sunlight, yet there were no signs advising bikers not to die horribly. Do the bikers and the guys on the speedboat in Gloucestershire seek the same thing? Often called thrill-seeking, you could hardly call it spiritual, but neither could you call it rational.

Eventually I crossed the Tamar Bridge, a suspension bridge which declared that it had been built in 1961. Clearly those who built it were proud of their achievement though it was certainly no competition for the Humber Bridge; however twenty years between the two might have made all the difference. For people who are only reading this book for the bridges, Brunel's Royal Albert Bridge, a lenticular truss bridge, stands alongside, all diagonal struts and braces with distinctive tubular arches above, opened in 1859 and carrying the railway into Cornwall. (Somebody might find it meaningful.)

On the other side I passed north of Plymouth, emerging onto the Devon Expressway; was this road named in competition with Cornwall's Atlantic Highway? I began to think that all roads should have names like this, though I suspect, Devon and Cornwall have used up all the best names. Warwickshire Parkway, North Sea Wetway, Lincolnshire Windyway? No, the West Country definitely had the only two good names.

The Devon Expressway was not a bad road, very fast and curvy, skirting to the south of Dartmoor, undulating through beautiful landscapes but mostly with views of tree-lined verges just like any other modern A road. But even so, when I stopped for coffee sometime later, just outside Exeter, all my nerves were jingling. (I'd spent a month without driving on a motorway. Had I become unaccustomed to the intensity of driving on fast roads?) The intensity of the Expressway had been constant whereas a gently changeable road with fast and slow stretches, hairpins and straights, so addictive to bikers, gives you variety. Is that what the superhighway of life does to us; nerves jangling because of the perpetual high speed, high efficiency, high information flow? The coffee machine that I'd stopped at was declared 'temporarily out of order' so I sloped back to the Truck disappointed and in need of a release from the stress of the Expressway.

* * *

Amid the mixture of boredom and my newfound inability to deal with motorway driving, I found myself thinking about the expected rationalist criticisms of the Museum of Witchcraft. Of course I understand that the rationalist, scientific understanding of reality governs much of our existence. There is simply no disputing science when it explains concepts like evolution, which is known fact with evidence (even if the processes are still being debated); I simply don't care what the creationists say in response, they are simply wrong. The argument for evolution is settled in favour of science in the same way we know that the earth goes around the sun and blood circulates around the body; whereas there would have been times when such ideas were not understood or disputed. However, seeking a life with something more than science-fact does not mean disputing all of science. But some rationalists in the media seem to think that people who seek experiences outside of the purely objective, meaningful experiences if you like, are also questioning the whole of science, which isn't necessarily the case.

Yet more rationalists will argue that anything that isn't objective is not worthy of respect or even human decency. This situation often seems to arise, particularly with some comedians but other commentators too, when their dismissal becomes almost offensive but serves to gain a laugh. They make cheap jokes then trot out the old argument of free speech while ultimately being abusive of people who are unable to respond. Okay, I might not see things in the same way as the bloke with the dreamcatcher in Glastonbury or a fan of crystals, but without being in their shoes I cannot know what they get out of these things. Of course that is not to defend the Glastonbury tendency to declare bread made under the full moon as magic bread, it's just bread! A crystal is a rock, it has beauty, but putting it out under the full moon (which is just reflected sunlight) doesn't cleanse it. If you want to cleanse a rock, wash it. If you want to ceremonially or symbolically cleanse a rock then that's different but let's not try to convince ourselves that anything physical is happing. However, ideas such as magic bread and cleansing crystals will be the things that arch-rationalists will focus on to support their arguments, to the exclusion of anything else that might have positive benefit. There is a difference between the right to debate belief and the right to abuse belief. If you express your argument through humiliation then you have lost the argument. Anyone who is offended by such abuse is then accused of trying to deny free speech by saying that they are using their beliefs to negate criticism. But lumping everything outside of science as equally bad, equally irrational, is ignoring the meaning that might arise from some experiences.

Of course some believers in non-rational perspectives, particularly some religious fundamentalists, will take offence to shut down debate. If an individual, or group, tries to shut down debate in this way it does not justify bullying or abusive behaviour of people who are simply attempting to have a more meaningful experience than is offered by TV soaps or recreational shopping. So I suppose I should be respectful of the magic bread brigade even if I can't see what they get out of it. I just don't have to eat the bread.

To many rationalists, anything subjective is just decoration that gets in the way of the study of the important facts. It's as though rationalists are misunderstanding what people get out of subjective experiences and can only see the apparently nonsensical. If they can never see past the magic bread or moonlit crystals they will never see the meaning. Having said that, I'm sure that there are many people who are into magic bread and moonlit crystals who think that's where it's at and, perhaps, they have missed the point themselves but who am I to say if an experience is subjective?

* * *

Setting off again, without coffee, the Alabama 3 came on the MP3 player with their song *Converted*. The speech at the start stated 'I've got to go somewhere and that place might as well be church.' He goes on to talk about repenting in that wonderfully ironic way, that gospel, acid house, country music style that only the Alabama 3 seem to be able to accomplish. It's the case that going to church used to be the default when we were troubled; that default no longer works as we have become rational beings no longer valuing non-rational beliefs. (Honestly, folks, this is just the way the music came out on the journey, you couldn't write it this way, but some people would identify meaning in these coincidences.)

Still hoping to get to the Jurassic Coast, I pushed on passed Honiton, and came within a spit of Axminster and Lyme Regis, though I saw none of them.

Soon I found myself driving through the beautiful hills that border the Dorset coast, though slightly less beautiful from behind a container lorry where passing opportunities were few. Had I taken the time to research the area I might have known that I passed within minutes of the Charmouth Heritage Coast Centre where I could have had my fill of the Jurassic Coast and all its fossilised wonders. Add it to the list.

I spotted a sign for Bridport, which might have been a mistake. It wasn't a port, as you might imagine, but considerably inland, though I'm sure that as towns go it's very nice being within a few miles of the sea. But with the name Bridport I imagined there might be an interesting harbour I could park up at and watch the fishing boats come and go. Call me a romantic if you like. Still, if the mayor of Bridport wants to invite me to visit and show me around I'll happily pop by and put the world right on the matter in all future writings on the area.

Following my intuition, which hadn't served me well so far today, I decided to head south, imagining that I would hit the sea sooner or later; and thus I found myself in West Bay, where there was indeed a tiny harbour with fishing boats resting on the mud.

There followed a frustrating hour attempting to get my tablet to download a series of tourist websites that never came despite me having five bars on the signal meter. I'd bought the tablet a couple of months in advance of the trip and it was turning out to be utterly useless despite extensive everyday use before I left. While I was waiting for the websites to download, there were intermittent heavy showers, sufficient to keep me sheltering in the Truck as I watched the incoming tide slowly lift the boats off the mud. The Samsung tablet was a complete mistake and I cannot recommend it at all.

What I can recommend, however, are the fish and chip kiosks on West Bay Harbour. Seeing three kiosks on the opposite side of the harbour, bemoaning the missed opportunity to try the local fish and chips at Whitby, I decided I'd not let that happen again. Risking a soaking I dodged the raindrops and scuttled around to the kiosks to see what they had. Market economics seemed to be working well as all three offered the same deal, all apparently doing a healthy business. Five quid promised a large cod and chips which I ordered with an ambition that matched my appetite. My ambition, however, did not foresee the magnitude of the feast that awaited me. Back in the Truck I unwrapped the paper package to reveal the largest piece of fish I have ever seen. Honestly it must have been over a foot long, perhaps even more than fifteen inches tip to tip. I found myself having to use my large wooden chopping board (an invaluable piece of camping equipment as it can be used for a multitude of purposes) just to put the fish on, as my vintage enamel camping plates were simply inadequate for the task.

Once full of fish and chips I located the Jurassic Coast-themed holiday park, a massive complex with chalets, caravans, tents and all manner of accommodations, bars, a club house, swimming pool, nightclub and all manner of distractions. It was quite unlike anywhere I'd visited. However, they seemed incapable of getting their act together with their computers so standing in the queue I found myself making the sort of calculation that you make when on hold to a call centre. I think accountants call it a sunk cost calculation, whether you consider what you've already invested in something or walk away and cut your losses. The judgement is complicated by the unknown factor of how much longer you will have to wait.

After what felt like 65 million years, but probably about half an hour, I bailed out and headed off in the hope I might find somewhere else and that they would still be open. This was the first time I'd taken the chance of finding a campsite this late in the day. Even in Rutland I'd managed to find somewhere before teatime; this time I was abandoning a site at about 7:00 and driving off relying only on the chance of seeing one of those brown tourist signs with a picture of a wigwam. I was genuinely prepared to wild camp or sleep in the Truck if needs must.

Leaving the Jurassic holiday park, I drove east along the coast road, up over chalk downland towards Weymouth. Passing over Abbotsbury Hill I stopped to admire the dramatic view of Chesil Beach stretching before me into the evening haze. The beach isn't like other beaches, as you might think, in that it's not a boundary where the land meets the sea. Chesil Beach is an isthmus that sits off-shore, parallel to the land, enclosing a lagoon. The white spit of shingle, just 200 yards wide, like an embankment rising out of the water, was clearly visible from the hilltop two or three miles away. The beach stretches for nearly 20 miles resting at a distance from the shore that varies from a hundred yards at its narrowest to a wide lagoon over half a mile offshore at its widest. It is a truly impressive sight, especially from the vantage point I'd stumbled across. After a day of nothing but driving, with nothing of interest to report other than the uninteresting Devon Expressway (which wasn't even in my target county), serendipity suddenly served up one of the greatest sights of my trip so far.

However, the day was running out and I had to find somewhere to stop, so I pushed on through Abbotsbury, all chocolate box pretty and on to Portesham where I stumbled across a dairy farm with a very pleasant campsite attached.

* * *

Checking in, I set up and spent an agreeable evening on a tranquil campsite with the sun going down over the downs to the west. The evening progressed, bathed in sunshine without a breath of wind, but with a large and noisy murder of crows in the nearby trees. The site was just busy enough to be noticeably fuller than the sites I'd been at a month before, but still with plenty of space between tents so that I didn't feel crowded.

In the still evening air the site had strange acoustics. Two families with a cluster of tents across the grass were talking at no more than normal volume, but I couldn't help overhearing most of their conversation despite being a good distance away. Their kids played with a toy rocket, propelled by setting it on a launcher and then jumping on the base with some sort of arrangement that fed air, compressed by the weight of the child, that launched the rocket. It looked like enormous fun. The altitude was impressive, especially when the bigger of the kids became involved. I'm guessing that Dad had already been banned from joining in lest he burst it, because I'm sure no self-respecting father would be able to resist otherwise.

Meanwhile, as the sun set, a lone camper fiddled with his motorbike at the very far side of the site. After a while he proceeded to start the bike and repeatedly rev the engine while apparently making adjustments. The bike was some large touring machine with a loud bass note and a low, slow firing pattern rather than those whizzy high-pitched machines that disappear over the horizon. All the noisy revving and fiddling seemed like a display, some sort of mechanical affectation seeking attention. I don't know that he didn't have a genuine problem with his fuel/air mixture or whatever, but if I was in that situation I'd make the adjustments in a layby in the morning, just before setting off for the day so that I could judge the results while riding and not disturb the peace of an idyllic summer evening. I found myself wondering about a guy like that camping alone and immediately labelled him an oddball, someone to be slightly cautious of, were I to encounter him, someone who I'd be concerned about if I had kids with a rocket and he showed too much interest. Watching from the shade of my tent as I cooked my meal (the massive fish and chips turning out to have been an interlude), I wondered if he was the sort of guy who doesn't make social connections easily, or he may have been a very sociable guy who just found himself in a position where it's not easy to be social, such as on a campsite where everybody wants a bit of their own time and space. Perhaps he just wanted to be alone.

On the other hand he may have been writing a book about travelling the 39 Historic Counties of England on a motorbike. Thinking about it, his book might well be more interesting than mine, with stories of his time on the road being much richer with an old Harley Davidson than they could ever be with a fifteen year old Truck and an Irish electronic navigator. Surely then, they'd invite him onto Radio 4 to tell the world about it. The point is, however, he's probably a perfectly ordinary, non-scary bloke, and perhaps I should be less eager to judge.

Day 31 - Dorset to Wiltshire

Friday May 31st

Miles on Truck: 2441

The next morning I soon discovered I'd left my shower gel in Cornwall so I had a shower with washing up liquid. I was pretty sure I'd heard of people doing this when I was a kid when people were less well-off, although perhaps there's more of that in our modern world of cuts and austerity. Whatever the case I guessed it was okay and, indeed, it was. For the rest of the day I was lemon fresh and squeaky clean.

I breakfasted on the remaining two Exmoor muffins, which required a spoon because they were still so fluffy therefore I can heartily recommend them. Trying to avoid the debacle that had been Dorset, I made a point of starting to think about Wiltshire as early as possible. I wanted to be out of the Truck and looking at something, interacting with people, at least by lunch time.

Despite the showers in the night the Khyam was nicely dry for the first time in quite a few days, so packing up quickly I asked Kathy to take me to Woodhenge, via Weymouth for wine, shower gel, food and fresh coffee. I'd been to Stonehenge many times so I didn't want to go there and Avebury is too full of sheep poo to walk without staring at the ground, and rather than watching where I'm walking I'd rather be taking in my surroundings.

Emerging from Weymouth I found myself on what appeared to be a Roman road heading towards Dorchester, arrow-straight and heavy with traffic. Researching later it seems I may have been mistaken about it being a Roman road, despite Dorchester being a Roman settlement and their quarrying for Portland stone directly south of Weymouth. You might also imagine the Romans would need easy access to the many nice caravan parks along the coast around Weymouth. Perhaps it wasn't Roman and was, instead, built by later invaders, possibly that bloke Norman.

The day was a Friday and the weather really looked as though it had finally turned to summer. The day before had been fine but with a band of heavy dark cloud that dumped its contents on everybody as it went over, but today looked much better and it seemed everybody knew it. People were out and about in shorts and T-shirts with a vengeance after the long winter and intermittent spring.

Passing a sign for Tolpuddle, I found myself wondering why I always imagined it to be somewhere in the North of England. Of course I'd heard of the Tolpuddle Martyrs and knew they were related to industrialisation or the rise of factories or something to do with workers' rights. To be honest I'd probably not be able to tell the difference between a Tolpuddle Martyr, a Luddite or a Leveller. I suppose my perception is that all of the outrageous slings and arrows of shameful mechanisation and the general exploitation of the multitude took place in the industrialised Midlands and North of England where there was coal and iron ore, as I'd discovered in Ironbridge and Coalbrookdale. Anyway, the Tolpuddle Martyrs were a group of six Victorian agricultural labourers accused of starting a union, which was then illegal, or at least very frowned upon. They were transported to Australia and they came from Dorset. So there, that's me told.

An interesting footnote to the story is that their case caused such an uproar that a march was organised which collected over three quarters of a million signatures and they were released and returned to England. The march was one of the first successful marches in Britain and is an early example of what people can achieve if they stick together against the oppressive baron.

Eventually Kathy turned me away from the fast main roads and onto quieter country routes, across the sort of downland I was expecting to see when I got to Wiltshire. I soon found myself directly behind a small motorbike as it peeled off from the main road onto a smaller country road. This wasn't the sort of bike that would tear away from you, such as one of those whizzy high-pitched machines that disappear over the horizon or one of those large touring machines with a loud bass note and a low, slow firing pattern. This was a one of those small bikes, 175cc at most, probably not very new and never very fast even when it was new, perhaps more comfortable cruising at about 50.

For quite a few miles Kathy kept me on the tail of this bike as it weaved around corners and up and down chalky farm downs. I stayed perhaps 200 yards behind, never closer than 100 yards even on the slower stretches, as the rider banked through corners and blind bends. He clearly knew the roads well and I was happy to let him take the lead. (Of course it could have been a her but I'm not going to do all that clumsy him or her nonsense in my narrative.) I quite enjoyed following him, always keeping him just in sight on the bends with plenty of time to slow if I saw his brake light come on. I swear that, occasionally, just for a moment, it felt like my consciousness was with him, leaning into the bends, sitting astride the tiny engine, rather than where I was in the Truck.

After passing through Salisbury there was a brief incident where I couldn't find my way out of a petrol station on the A303 at Amesbury, but after some direction finding, course plotting and triangulation I escaped. There might have been some celestial navigation but for the fact that it was daylight.

Never having been to Woodhenge, I found a series of post holes in concentric rings or ovals that were left over from the Bronze Age. Once excavated, the holes were marked by short concrete posts, perhaps two feet tall, that have been colour coded, painted on the top, so that visitors can see how the rings are associated. I'm sure I've read or heard discussions of whether it was a hall rather than a henge, with the post holes making the pillars but that theory seems to have been discounted. I'm sure the archaeologists know their stuff but the positions of the bigger holes looks like they might have been in the right position, halfway out in the rings, to bear a more structural load. If you wanted to build a large enclosed space, or you had built a smaller one and wanted to expand it, you might have to put in many groups of pillars because available materials wouldn't allow you to span the wide spaces we are used to. We would consider having all those pillars to be a problem because we are used to large halls, but if you've never seen a roof truss and you don't understand the forces in struts and ties, then this might seem the perfect solution. Anyway what do I know, I'm not an academic and I'm sure they've considered this, haven't they?

What does strike me about Woodhenge is that it's one of the few ancient monuments that children can climb on. Effectively there is nothing left other than the surface of the land. Someone had been there recently, presumably the night before, and had performed some sort of ceremony. There was a crushed pineapple (the significance of which I cannot imagine) and some purple flowers. This does go to illustrate that people still feel the need to use places that they feel are significant or have some connection to the past. Of course this is not rational, but when modern religions have failed us what else is there? As Alabama 3 said yesterday 'I gotta go someplace and that place might as well be church.'

As I walked away I passed a car pulled up by the gate. A teenage boy, looking a bit shaky, was leaning on the fence with, presumably, his mum putting her arm around him, helping him get over his car sickness or whatever was troubling him. However, the part of the scene that really told the story was the driver, still in the front seat with his seatbelt still on, with the passenger door wide open so I could see him clearly (at least he'd had the good grace to turn the engine off). From the look of the driver's body language he considered this stop a terrible inconvenience that he could do without. I wanted to tell him to take his bloody seatbelt off; even get out of the car for the sake of his son (if that is who he was, but the point still stands no matter what the relationship). Go sit with the kid, show some empathy, sit on the grass, perhaps even take ten minutes to walk around the ancient monument until the kid feels better, see if it takes his mind off his problem. Perhaps even take the opportunity to ask what he thinks it all means, what were those post holes? Give the kid something to take his mind off his troubles. Connect with the kid, support him and show some respect instead of sitting there with your seatbelt still on as though you can't wait to get away. None of this is necessarily rational, but it is the human thing to do in the situation and the kid will love you more for it. Then again, thinking back to the noisy biker on the campsite the previous evening, perhaps this wasn't the scenario at all and I shouldn't judge a scene without really knowing what's going on.

✳ ✳ ✳

I asked Kathy to take me to the Vale of the White Horse, the Uffington White Horse being something in Wiltshire I'd not seen. Unfortunately the Uffington White Horse in Wiltshire is something I will never see and neither will anybody else; because the Uffington White Horse is in Oxfordshire, where I'd started exactly a month before. Clearly my childhood associations with chalk carvings being in Wiltshire were mistaken. Whiteleaf Cross is in Buckinghamshire so why shouldn't the Uffington White horse be in Oxfordshire? Had I known this a month before I would have headed that way on May 1st. Add it to the list.

My search for a white horse of any description brought me to a car park behind some shops in Westbury which I put down to poor Internet access. There wasn't a white horse that I could see for miles around, although for all I know I might have been behind a pub of the same name. Normal people were coming and going on a hot sunny late Friday afternoon and I got a sense of being the drifter that I'd felt I was when I was unwelcome in Rutland. Somehow, looking for a white horse, I didn't feel I belonged here. Clearly Kathy cannot be trusted.

Day 32 - Wiltshire to Berkshire

Saturday June 1st

Miles on Truck: 2553

Next morning the English Heritage book showed one single entry for Berkshire, Donnington Castle, so having become completely bereft of imagination I decided I'd head there. I seemed to remember it was also a race track; what would that mean for a Saturday? The day was glorious again, and the weather man had predicted a good start to June, so I was keeping my fingers crossed for my final days on the road.

One thing I had noticed over the weeks was that people say good morning to strangers on campsites. Is there some sort of time warp going on here, or are people different when taken out of their normal community? Perhaps people actually become members of a community when they engage in a common activity and in everyday live we are not part of a community at all.

I'd stopped near Devizes on a campsite that required a four-figure combination to use the toilets. By this time nothing surprised me. I'd found sites where you had to fetch a key, others where you *went* on trust. Over the weeks the arrangements for showers had been equally varied, requiring anything from twenty pence to a pound for a shower or those buttons that stop the water after long enough. The best solution, I thought, was in Warwickshire where the site was more a field with a shed for the toilet and showers. The farmer, keeping the whole process quite low profile, had placed the shed behind some bushes so that all you saw from the road was an open field with the odd tent. You didn't need a key or a combination or anything. Stealth toilets are clearly the way of the future, whereas a combination lock could lead to considerable confusion in the night when a sense of urgency overrides short-term memory.

* * *

The roads east from Devizes were fast and almost straight, not Roman road straight but modern roads that cut through the landscape without bothering to go around fields. The fields themselves were wide open prairies with few hedges to block the view of ripening crops. Oilseed rape was still in the fields, gleaming yellow patchworks to the horizon. I'm sure rapeseed is normally harvested by this point in the year; was it late because of the weather or have I never really bothered to note when it disappears from the fields in the same way as it just seems to appear overnight. Is rapeseed a stealth crop? Is cow parsley a stealth weed? The landscape was peppered with barrow mounds, being the major feature of Wiltshire, that and Stonehenge, and of course Avebury, which I'd decided to skip due to the poo, stealth or otherwise.

I'd passed Stonehenge the day before and already decided that I'd seen enough of it, particularly on the annual summer solstice pilgrimage. However, I hadn't counted on Kathy working with serendipity and I was brought along the road straight past Silbury Hill.

I'd seen Silbury Hill many times too, but it has a special significance for me. Considering the nature of the ideas I've been exploring it's a strange coincidence of two serendipities that I passed Silbury Hill.

Those of you in the know, and you know who you are, will know that Silbury Hill is a large, late Neolithic earthwork thought to have been built a little less than 4500 years ago, and with estimates that it took between 100 and 500 years to build. However, that description really doesn't do it justice.

No seriously, any academic description doesn't tell you anything that direct experience communicates, and that might be a clue in our search for meaning after my experience with the compass at Land's End.

It's a hill, I mean a real, full-sized, hill! Now let me state that I hate the modern practice of using multiple exclamation marks (as I've previously talked about the use of awesome). However, Silbury Hill… is bloody awesome!!!!

It inspires awe.

It's an enormous artificial mound in the landscape 39 metres (128ft) high. At the base it's about 180 metres (590ft) across and 30 metres (98ft) across at the top. It's said to be about the same size as the pyramids of the same era. It makes you wonder just how much communication there was across the world at the end of the Stone Age and whether there was a cross-fertilisation of culture about how to build places of worship.

I say places of worship but we really don't know what it was used for. It wasn't a fortress, although it would have been easy to defend, but there is no evidence of a structure on top. It would have been a great lookout point but, really, why would you? If you wanted to know what was coming over the horizon you'd send someone to look rather than waiting hundreds of years to build a lookout. So, we really don't know what it was used for and the archaeological community then falls back on the old chestnut of 'ritual practice' to describe something they don't understand. Cultural practice might be a better term.

What I can say, for sure, is that were the hippies from Derbyshire allowed to hold their ceremonies atop the mound, and I'm sure that's been done by earlier hippies, then they'd find a use for it, or find it meaningful, or significant, or just very nice.

They might have trouble keeping the candles alight though.

Of course, Silbury Hill is in an ancient landscape that includes West Kennet Long Barrow, constructed over 1000 years earlier and visible from the top of Silbury Hill. (You are not allowed to climb it today as the hill is in a bit of a state with recent collapses after various excavations over the last 250 years or so.) Just down the road is the, also awesome, stone circle of Avebury at 300 metres (1000ft) across and connecting the two is West Kennet Avenue 2.5 km (1.5 miles) long. Actually, I've missed out The Sanctuary, another, smaller concentric dual stone circle that the avenue runs to, with Silbury Hill off to one side.

That's the point of this landscape, there's so much that you simply can't describe it in the context of a travelogue about England, it deserves a whole book and there are many. Wikipidilidido is a good place to start but really, if you have the chance, you just need to visit. Bring walking boots, and perhaps sandwiches and a flask and something to sit on, so you can park up and walk between the sites, and you'll have a wonderful day. There is a car park at Avebury and one at Silbury Hill but I have no idea of the charges and time limitations to check first. (What is this, a guide book or a search for meaning?)

* * *

I first saw Silbury Hill when I was staying at a children's convalescence home in Marlborough in about 1973. My parents had, briefly, been involved with the Jehovah's Witnesses and before that they'd had a connection to the Mormons. Malcolm once suggested I had what he called an ecclesifringical upbringing.

My mother, by then separated from my father, had been in hospital and, wanting to ensure my spiritual wellbeing, she'd made contact with the local JWs and arranged for a local couple to take me to the Sunday afternoon services. (I imagine it's okay to call them JWs as that's the name of their website.) They also took me on the odd day out. They took me to the occasional service, though I only recall going to one or two. I remember the services were held in a corrugated iron shed at the bottom of a farm track, so I suppose that makes it a barn. You can say what you like about the JWs (and most people do) but I believe they are well-intentioned. These days they have quite a few nice new chapels with clean lines, lots of natural light and carpets, but I've known them to worship in all sorts of shabby places, so the odd barn was probably not unusual. I sort of feel that this makes them a humble people in a smug, we've-found-salvation-and-we're-going-to-ram-it-down-your-throat-on-your-doorstep-whether-you-like-it-or-not, sort of way. Religion is full of paradoxes.

Anyway, apart from the farm shed services, which were very noisy indeed when it rained, they took me on a few days out including trips to Avebury and Silbury Hill, to the top as you were allowed to do that in those days what with the collapses not being known about. It is my honest belief that the Jehovah's Witnesses were responsible for awakening my interest in ancient history, folkloric traditions and the ideas and philosophies of cultures other than the Abrahamic faiths.

Like I say, religion is full of paradoxes.

Shortly after that I started to make up my own mind about religion (finding my personal meaning in other ways), but at the time I was still under the influence of my mother and it was her condition in hospital, rather than any pressing need for convalescence on my part, that led to me being sent away for a few months to Wiltshire.

For me the road to Damascus realisation came at an early age, when I couldn't reconcile the obvious facts of science with the obvious nonsense of God; you know that guy with a white beard in heaven and the existence of all the other paraphernalia such as Jesus rising from the dead, all those other miracles, the heavenly host and hellfire and damnation. I suppose I should call it my road to Cambridge realisation, as that's where Newton would have done his great work on classical mechanics, which was ultimately the reality of the world that I saw as un-reconcilable with all the God and miracle nonsense.

Of course today I understand that a great deal of the nonsense comes from sources that may have lost their origins and gained meaning through their repetition down through the ages. It's possible to imagine, for example, that an edict requiring an ancient desert community to always share their water might result in a water ritual of some kind but, thousands of years later or when the community moves to an area that has an abundance of water, they continue the water ritual because it's been performed for generations and thus has meaning. Yet the meaning of the water ritual is lost in that it is no longer necessary for the survival of all members of the community. What was a practice that had value intrinsic to survival has now become an arbitrary part of religious dogma. However, that arbitrary water ritual now has a meaning created by its tie to its ancestors and forms part of the glue that holds the community together. The water ritual might as well be a standing on one leg ritual if it's something that the community has been doing for generations. This arbitrary adherence to values would still fulfil the same function in the community. (I'm pretty sure this argument was the whole basis for the film The Life of Brian.)

So religious beliefs and practices can become disconnected from the origins which originally gave them meaning; in the end these practices have only arbitrary meaning but still have value to those who know no better. Today we live in world where many of us can only find meaning in arbitrary things, be they TV soaps or consumerism, society having applied Newtonian thinking to kill off the god that gave us meaningful experiences through ancient water rituals and the like. But the meaning found in consumerism, passed down to us by corporations, or the meaning in TV soaps and celebrity culture passed down to us by other corporations, is transient and arbitrary. Of course *all meanings are arbitrary for nothing holds intrinsic value.* The meaning from ancient religious symbolism, our water ritual for example, was so wrapped up in generations of repetition that its arbitrary nature was difficult to see, but even that meaning is, ultimately, illusory. The meaning wrapped up in modern experiences is equally arbitrary, but worse, the tinsel of celebrity or the gloss of consumerism is an illusion that wears off very quickly. It's almost as though the priesthood of ancient religions, who mediated the meaning in religion, had the authority of the establishment, but modern meaning is mediated by a priesthood of corporations who hold no such authority.

This leads us to an existential crisis where that which we value is ultimately meaningless yet that which had meaning from religion is understood to be, rationally, nonsense and superstition.

We used to live in a world where we believed that there might be something else, some afterlife or something more to our existence. But many of us now live in a world where we see that continuance of existence as nonsense after science has pulled that rug from beneath us so that this life is all there is. With that transition, something is missing for many of us, certainly all those of us without faith, and it might not be healthy to leave that void empty. Perhaps, in an existential world, finding meaning becomes the most important thing? Who are we to criticise where people find it?

* * *

Is there a middle ground between the rational destroyer of religious meaning and the irrationality of religion and superstition, and if so who will mediate that meaning, if not a priesthood and not the marketing departments of corporations?

The hippies in the field are having a go by deciding for themselves. They find their own meaning, in their case often in the natural environment but also reconstructed from folklore and myth. If the beginnings of religion are the shamanistic practices of early societies, throw in a little intoxication (or in some cases quite a lot) and the modern hippies might not be far from the beginning of the whole process. In Derbyshire anybody could make contact with the gods through dance and music, often simply rhythm, the primitive sort that doesn't require a great deal of training, for education can become a barrier and creates elites. Through these necessarily simple neoreligious practices, often made up or reconstructed, anybody can have a revelation or at least a damn good time with the same people each year and the meaning grows from there. However, if meaning isn't transferable, as with the guy who plays his music loud in his car, then what they do in the field won't mean much to anyone until they've tried it themselves a few times. You have to lend yourself to it and the rest follows from there. There's a phrase I've heard in these circles and it's that you've got to fake it to make it. Childhood *let's pretend* has a lot going for it.

I'm sure the Derbyshire hippies know that the world goes around the sun and that we evolved from ancestors common to apes, even if they only have a passing understanding of celestial mechanics or evolution. Having said that I know, over the years, I've also met experts in these fields in these fields... if you get my meaning? They take the meaningful bits out of ancient religious practices (or what they imagine them to be), usually involving community and celebration, while still having a rational understanding of the world.

* * *

The road to Donnington Castle, near Newbury, was, for the first time on the trip, thick with hawthorn, the mayflowers evident all around so, perhaps, it is just a South East thing. Is hawthorn more common in the Home Counties?

Unable to find Donnington Castle on my own, Kathy kindly decided to take me to a pub of the same name which, I thought, was probably a better deal. Over an impressive bacon and brie baguette I discovered that they don't have a problem with noise from Castle Donington race track because it's in the Midlands some 98 miles to the north… exactly to the north. I mean if you drew a line between the two it would be directly on the north/south line. What's that all about? Well it seems meaningful to me, or at least it feels meaningful to discover as a piece of randomness.

It seems that Donnington Castle was a medieval castle built in 1382 whereas Castle Donington is a small town in the Midlands not far from East Midlands Airport and the location of Donington Park Motor Racing Circuit. Why the names reflect each other as they do, and why they are directly north/south of each other is anybody's guess. There's probably no reason for it at all, but it's rather pleasing anyway and it seems sort of meaningful. Of course it's just a coincidence, but in evolutionary terms we are probably programmed to notice coincidences as they are a useful rule of thumb (heuristic principles) to discover things about the universe. Today we understand that not every coincidence is meaningful in a scientific sense but in a world devoid of religious meaning perhaps we crave such incidents. The fact that the Donnington Castle coincidence randomly coincided with that part of the trip where I was thinking about my childhood religious experience is another totally random coincidence, but it's a coincidence that's useful to illustrate the point.

Rational, scientific thinkers will point out that these events are just coincidences and nothing more; and they are absolutely right. There is no connection between Castle Donington and Donnington Castle or at least I've not been able to find one. The fact that they are virtually north/south of each other is also just a coincidence (Castle Donington 1.3373 degrees west and Donnington Castle 1.3383 degrees west). However, some people see significance all around themselves. People have been seeing significance or meaning in all sorts of things from the beginning of time. Rationalists will say that this is the brain engaging in magical thinking, seeing causality where there is none. But if we understand that is the case—there's really no connection between a civil parish in Leicestershire where there is a race track and a ruined medieval castle directly to the south—but we can't help seeing the connection because that's the way our brains work, then what's the problem with taking delight in that connection? To say ah, that's just a coincidence and berating any further meaning you care to enjoy is sort of like ignoring our innate programming, like sucking the joy out of the randomness of the world. Connection spotters are what we are. If connections like that give us a sense of wonder because that's the way we are built, then so be it. Is it actually irrational to behave in the way that we are programmed by evolution?

* * *

Incidentally, while checking all this I discovered that it would take sound eight minutes to pass between the two Donningtons (never mind the difference in spelling). That's not a coincidence but it is interesting to know, which is sort of fun and it takes quite a bit longer than you might expect. Why do I know how long it takes sound to travel 100 miles? In December 2005 I was awoken by the sound of Buncefield Oil Depot exploding. The explosion was so loud that it was heard in southern Holland about 200 miles away. However the Dutch didn't hear it until something like a quarter of an hour later. Of course to a scientist this is no surprise but in our world of apparently instantaneous communication it can seem strange that something as powerful as an explosion can take time to be heard at a distance. See, science can be fun too even if such little facts are not great scientific discoveries.

* * *

Donnington Castle was a delight even though there is so little of it left. It was built by one of the knights in the service of the Black Prince. As such it's from the height of the chivalric period and would have had plate-armoured horsemen and their peers riding in and out of the gateway that can be seen today. This is spot-on the classic schoolboy view of knights in shining armour. Only the gatehouse remains after the rest of the castle was used in a 20 month siege in the English Civil War and was probably destroyed during the slight of the castles after the Civil War to stop it being used in fu-

240

ture uprisings. Today it is possible to see the extent of the castle walls, where there would have been a small inner courtyard. It's hard to imagine any group larger than a dozen surviving for so long in such a small space.

* * *

After Donnington Castle, which offered an hour's entertainment at best, I looked for something else to do. The web sites waxed lyrical about Berkshire being a royal county and suggested everything from Windsor Castle to the childhood home of Kate Middleton, which I decided to give a miss. Other than that, the county seemed to offer everything as the playground for the well to do. I looked for a supermarket instead and hoped for inspiration along the way. In the end I went for a haircut and looked for a campsite.

* * *

In 1986 I'd walked the Ridgeway long distance footpath; well I say walked, I got drenched at Segsbury Camp, an Iron Age hill fort just on the Wiltshire border with Berkshire. Abandoning my walk I got a lift to nearby Lamborn that I'd always understood to be in Wiltshire. Arriving in the village a bit damp and on a budget, I negotiated with one of the pubs to sleep in their stable in return for buying a meal. The food was great and the stable was full of fresh straw and, I imagined, spiders but I don't remember seeing any.

Sitting in Newbury with newly cut hair I discovered that there was a campsite in Lambourn and that Lambourn was in fact in Berkshire! What with the stable episode some 25 years before, Lambourn had meaning for me so I grabbed it.

* * *

Lambourn was sort of in the wrong direction but I couldn't resist it. On the way it became apparent why the west of Berkshire is known for its woodland. As I drove I passed through long stretches of woodland, often on both sides of the road, then out into open fields but with woodland never more than a field or two away. The fields were not the massive prairies I'd seen elsewhere. Clearly someone was looking after Berkshire, which was after all historically the royal hunting ground, and I had a suspicion I knew who was doing the looking after.

The campsite at Lambourn was a delight. It was a paddock on a farm a little way outside of the village. They had no spare electrical hook-ups for me and the field was on a considerable slope, probably the worst slope I'd camped on, but I didn't care. The slope was the price I paid for a view across a small valley with a patchwork of fields on the other side, all intersecting angles, lines of hedgerows, bucolic charm and the typical image of the English Countryside. Had I discovered typical England? Is there a typical England with all the places I'd seen? If this was typical England, is that why it is so beloved of the establishment who like to hunt here?

As usual the campsite that described itself as being in Lambourn was actually a mile or two away and, not having been into the village proper on the way, I decided to drive down to the chip shop to save on cooking.

Lambourn was nothing like I remembered it. I couldn't find the pub where I'd slept in the stable, or the café where I got talking to one of the locals when I arrived all those years before, or the village green, or the bus stop where back then there was only one bus a day, or any of the other features I'd remembered. That's what a third of a lifetime can do to your memories.

Stopping for directions, a kid on his bike directed me right and then right but no chip shop. He hadn't seemed very confident. The second guy had no idea but I got the impression he was from out of town. The third guy told me to turn around, go left then right, or something like that and I couldn't miss it. The fourth actually got me there. I learned one thing: Lambourn was a lot bigger and more complicated than I remember it in 1986. Was it even the same village? Is this another example of implanted memories and the fact that I'm really a replicant?

Back at my tent, on the hillside, I discovered that I really shouldn't order large cod and chips. Was the cod and chips I'd had in Dorset overly large or are all such portions just beyond my expectations? Are portions of fish and chips getting larger as is everything else? (The portions of chips in Devon seemed to be getting smaller.) I settled down to an evening of drinking tea with wine chasers (being inventive trying to establish a flat space to stand a drink on the slope). Practicing the ukulele I gazed out at the view while attempting to stay stable on the incline. Eventually I'd had enough and retired to my sleeping bag thinking of stables from twenty five years before, as I tried not to slide downhill.

Day 33 - Berkshire to Hampshire

Sunday June 2nd

Miles on Truck: 2629

I woke up in a heap.

The thing about the inside of a tent is that it's all about layers. Some layers keep you warm, some keep you dry, and some keep you clean, just like clothing really. I always use a groundsheet under my tent despite the Khyam having an integral groundsheet. An extra groundsheet serves as a base layer and it protects the integral groundsheet, which is really the bottom of the inner tent, which is less durable and more difficult to repair. It also keeps it all clean. On top of the integral groundsheet you have all the things you put in your tent. I use a sleeping mat and cover that with a blanket which sort of serves as a rug, the surfaces of the mat and the groundsheet not being as pleasant as sitting on a nice woollen blanket. On the blanket goes the sleeping bag and inside that goes me.

All of these layers, independent of each other, had all moved in the night. Each layer had moved downhill but by differing amounts. I'd managed to set myself at an angle on the slope with my head upwards. (I find I can detect even the tiniest slope and can't abide sleeping head down so I'd be rubbish as an astronaut.) Sleeping across the slope wasn't an option as that would have resulted in me waking up sort of crescent shaped. Overnight the topography of the inside of the tent had changed and there was a scrunched-up pile of blanket, sleeping mat and me, inside my sleeping bag, on the downhill side of the tent. Somehow also, the base groundsheet had moved under the tent apparently independently of the tent itself.

After extricating myself from this mess I breakfasted on the usual bread and cheese, showered and packed away in glorious sunshine. I'd heard on the radio of the new Mary Rose museum that had just opened in Portsmouth. This was Hampshire day so I didn't have any trouble knowing what to do.

Everything was in the Truck and I fired it up. It ran lumpy for a few seconds and died. Over the last couple of days it seemed to have returned to this behaviour but otherwise it had been running perfectly over the last few weeks. I couldn't remember when I last had to be careful starting it, probably not since the Midlands at least. The day before, in Wiltshire, it had died after a few seconds of lumpy running but on the second attempt it had started, much to my shame in a cloud of smoke almost choking a passer-by. Still, it had been fine during the day and I'd relaxed enough to have forgotten about it. This time it died after about three seconds.

I turned it over again and it wouldn't go. I kept trying and very quickly the battery was dead. There was a Land Rover on the field but the owner had just hitched it up to his caravan and was about to set off so he was unable to help. In the end, after knocking on the farmhouse door, the farmer brought his gleaming white truck down and jump started it.

Thanking the farmer profusely, I headed off, planning not to let the engine stop unless I had to. Therefore, unable to switch off in a petrol station, coffee would have to wait until Portsmouth. I'd had two suggestions of causes for the fault, injector seals or the fuel system more generally. Fuel was the first thing the farmer had said and the Frontera guys had removed part of the fuel system when they'd cleaned out the inlet manifold in the weeks before I left. Let me make it clear that they did an excellent job and all in return for a few beers. (Is there such a thing as the beer economy, a subset of the various arrangements in the informal economy that is largely invisible?) The result of their efforts was that I'd seen something like a 25% improvement in fuel efficiency but had they disturbed something in the process? Could it be that the fuel drains back over-night (slowly syphoning perhaps) and that's why I was having this problem? Was it made worse by parking facing up a steep slope? I headed off to Portsmouth and vowed to park on the flat if I could.

Kathy took me back down the country roads from Lambourn in a south-easterly direction. Passing by Newbury, she put me on the closest thing to a motorway that I'd encountered so far. However, just like my rule about taking the shortest route, the anti-motorway rule was becoming something I couldn't afford. I needed to keep the Truck on the road and doing a nice long steady run, charging the battery and filling the alarmingly low tank were the main priorities.

Of course stopping for fuel would mean stopping the engine so I skipped a couple of petrol stations, making a judgement that there was enough in the tank to get me to the next one. Around Winchester Kathy took me off the main road and quickly onto country roads, then tiny country lanes. Clearly there wouldn't be any petrol stations on these roads but I could only hope that she had a cunning plan to get me to the next main road where there would be petrol stations aplenty.

Kathy tended not to let me in on her plans. Of course I could interrogate her maps to see where her route would take me but that was always too clumsy to be convenient. Is this going to be the future as we hand over more decisions to AI, not knowing how they have arrived at the decisions they have made with little opportunity for us to interrogate their reasoning? That's surely the definition of a trust relationship.

Clearly, today, she was being good to me as there followed an hour or so of driving through deep woodlands but no petrol stations whatsoever. I found myself crossing the Western Weald, the western end of the South Downs National Park, with striking landscapes of deciduous forest interspersed with small areas of pasture. The woodlands almost defined the meaning of dappled and I really felt I should have abandoned my plans to reach Portsmouth and investigated the landscape further. However, that would have inevitably resulted in me driving around in circles while trying to find a nice place to stop, having passed twenty perfectly nice places before but continuing on to find somewhere where the grass is greener or the dapples more dappler, but I'm sure you get my meaning. I would have ended up reversing into a field entrance where I couldn't really see anything other than the occasional car going past and wishing I had picked that spot earlier where the woodland floor was as dappled as dappled can be, but my ambition for greater dappling led me on a foolhardy chase that could never be satisfied.

Baba Ram Das urges us to 'Be here now.' Struggling to find the perfect spot to admire the view, lusting for better, might not have been the answer. If where we are is on a journey, moving, rather than being in one place, then perhaps to *be here* is actually to continue moving until the circumstances change around us or we come to a natural pause.

However, no matter how confusing unplanned motoring trips to forests might be, it was wonderful just to drive through and I was glad to do so. Country lanes can be an entertainment in themselves and with English forests what's not to like? So it really was a case of trusting Kathy until, eventually, with the fuel warning light flickering on, I arrived in Portsmouth at 3:00.

I'd done many miles in the last month and that morning's experience had brought the condition of the Truck, and the whole precarious nature of the trip, into sharp focus. If I had to call out the RAC because of an intermittent fault they wouldn't give me a second chance. I'd have to abandon the whole trip and head home as they wouldn't make a second visit to a fault I'd reported before.

Half an hour in a petrol station gave me a chance to give the Truck a birthday, top up all its fluids, have a sandwich and a coffee myself and look at the internet in that surreptitious way that you do when you are not supposed to use a mobile phone in a petrol station. Let's face it, a mobile phone isn't going to cause a spark. Cars have alternators that are small electrical generators, many of them with brushes running against coils. Those of you in the know, and you know who you are, will understand that this is how you generate electricity, spinning magnets and opposing electromagnetic fields notwithstanding. The point is that those alternators get hot so they are cooled by dragging air through them right across where the brushes are running against the spinning components. If anything is going to create sparks then this is, albeit very tiny sparks. If petrol stations were so full of petrol vapour in quantities that might ignite, then the places would be going bang every day.

Anyway, by the time I'd had my sandwich and checked the Internet it was getting on for late afternoon so there was no prospect of seeing the Mary Rose, which was a shame as I've heard it's very good (add it to the list). The Isle of Wight was an alternative but phoning to find the price of a last-minute ferry crossing, with a return the next day, I learned what people mean when they say that, mile for mile, it's the most expensive ferry in the world.

I needed a plan C and it turned out to be another castle. Beeston Castle had been good but Tintagel had been better. A few days before a friend had suggested I check out Portchester Castle and at this stage it was very appealing. I found it in the English Heritage book and asked Kathy, who reported that it was just ten minutes away.

* * *

Approaching the castle it struck me that my English Heritage card still showed the wrong year. This would be the first time I'd used the card since Tintagel and I was hoping that it wouldn't be a problem to get in. Still this time I was armed with my receipt so I was confident that it would be okay.

Portchester Castle was a lot quieter than Tintagel and it had a nice little shop with all the customary merchandise that I'd become used to. There was just myself and the two English Heritage staff in the dark green T-shirts there as I handed my card across the counter surrounded by guidebooks and pencil sharpeners in the shape of medieval catapults.

'Err, it looks as though my card's out of date but the girl at Whitby Abbey made a mistake and put the wrong year down,' I continued to explain, hoping to establish that I wasn't a fraudster before she could form any opinions about me. 'I've been touring the country since I joined and I've only got the temporary card as I've not been home since the first of May.'

'Oh that's okay, I can correct that for you,' responded one of the staff. Oh brilliant, I thought. Getting a new temporary card would mean I could relax and visit as many English Heritage sites as I wanted in the last few days of the trip. A new card at Tintagel would have been much better but at least she was going to sort it out now.

Picking up a pen she took my card and, while I watched with some surprise and not a little astonishment, she proceeded to overwrite 2012 with the correct year 2013. Actually she didn't do that, she just changed the 2 to a 3. It wasn't even the same colour ink.

'There you are, all done.' She handed the card back to me.

Err, I could have done that myself, I thought to myself quietly, not wanting to rock the boat. Now it looks as though I've tried to forge the date!

'So have you visited a lot of English Heritage sites?'

'A few,' I responded. 'I've done Whitby Abbey and Beeston Castle, a few weeks ago. I was at Donnington Castle yesterday and Tintagel a few days ago. Tintagel was particularly amazing with all those steps and that difficult location.'

'Oh yes, I like Tintagel, and Beeston Castle is very impressive on that rock outcrop.'

Clearly she shared my passion for ancient monuments and I was beginning to think she might be my kind of girl. It was at this point that her colleague found something to do in the next room and I wondered if she didn't want to be the gooseberry.

So we chatted for a few minutes and discovered a shared interest in Richard II (who'd had Portchester Castle built within an existing Roman fort) while I tried to think about how to get her phone number and whether it would be in any way inappropriate. I didn't and it probably was.

***

Portchester Castle is a delight. I know I said that about Donnington Castle but Portchester is pretty much a complete castle. It stands with an intact curtain wall built by the Romans and developed right up to the Napoleonic era, being used by the Normans, the Edwards, one of the Richards and the mad George when it was used as a prison during the Napoleonic wars. (Okay so every castle I've looked at has been described as impressive but each one has surpassed the previous, surely Portchester has to be about as good as they get.)

I spent a great couple of hours exploring the castle, listening to the excellent audio tour and generally having a good time. The castle itself is impressive with the usual skeletal stone ruins for most of it, but the keep is largely intact and actually has floors. If you want to know what a medieval hall would have looked like, check out Portchester. The floors might be modern restorations but I imagine they're a pretty good indication of the genuine article, if only smoother.

Day 34 - Hampshire to Sussex

Monday June 3rd

Miles on Truck: 2763

I spent the night on a campsite within 100 yards of the sea although I didn't see the sea, having chosen the site for the fact that it had a laundry rather than the proximity to the beach. There's not much I can say about Southsea, though I don't know what I was expecting, Spanish gold and investors in South American trade perhaps.

I started the Truck with some trepidation. After fuelling and oiling it the previous afternoon I'd become more relaxed about it again. However, after an overnight stop I was concerned not to repeat the issue I'd had in Lambourn. I turned the key and it fired up. I managed to rev the engine quickly enough to ensure it ran, but I was conscious of not wanting to appear like the guy on the motorbike on the campsite in Dorset. After a moment I let the revs drop back, held them there for a second or two before taking my foot off the accelerator. It didn't cut out.

Setting off, I asked Kathy to take me to Hastings, again avoiding motorways. Unfortunately her definition of a motorway seems to be a bit more flexible than I remember, as a four-lane highway with a hard shoulder looks more like a motorway than the A road it claimed to be. Even if Kathy can be trusted the road network cannot.

I'd had a vision of winding along the south coast towards Hastings on a small coast road, up along windswept cliff tops, down steep descents towards sandy beaches, only to be swept inland or through tiny villages with frequent views of the sea or pastoral landscapes with villagers going about their agrarian lives... Oh hang on; I seem to have inadvertently wandered into the 18th century. Instead I found myself on an A road that could have been anywhere in the country. The next road sign said Chichester. I knew Chichester had a cathedral, which was better than the south coast motorway of deceit, so I pulled into the town.

Chichester was originally a Roman town which is quite apparent by the grid layout. I can't say I noticed a lot of arrow-straight roads on the way in or out but you can't have everything. Having dismissed Kathy, who was still intent on taking me to Hastings, an ambitious journey by my standards so far, I found myself driving around the city looking for somewhere to park.

I can't say I've spent a lot of time thinking about the definition of car parks but, in this instance, I had a choice of long stay or short stay and struggled to understand the difference. What constitutes long and short stay? presumably a long stop in a short stay car park would be expensive but if you want to stop for a couple of hours, long enough to look around a cathedral, buy a guidebook and some shortbread, and perhaps a hotdog on the way back to the Truck, then does that count as a long stop or a short stop? Is a long stay car park in the south of England the same as a long stay car park in the north? I suppose I should know by now but I can't honestly say I've been taking a lot of notice. Shouldn't these things be defined somewhere and if they are where are they written down?

Deciding that I was becoming far too concerned about this sort of thing to be healthy for a boy of my age, I parked the Truck and got on with my life, allowing myself two hours to see the cathedral, which was surprisingly small therefore suiting my parking arrangements.

On arrival I was greeted by a representative of the Church who seemed to be asking about my visit. For a moment I felt a little unsure about how to respond. In Worcester the meet and greet guy was interested to hear about my trip and commented that he would be interested to read the book that came from the adventure. I didn't tell him about it, he just seemed to figure it out. Perhaps God told him. Anyway he was a very nice man so I shook his hand and continued with my visit making a note to buy some shortbread or a bookmark or something.

However I was a bit freaked by the Chichester meet and greeter; I might have been thrown by his costume, or his uniform or vestments or whatever they are called. More likely it was his asking why I had come to church that day and as a result I found myself unable to say, sort of like a rabbit caught in the headlights of impending religious doom or something. Anyway, I made my excuses and moved inside, feeling very slightly like an impostor. Note to self, buy extra shortbread to make up for guilt.

What is interesting about Chichester Cathedral is that it has a separate bell tower, built after one of the towers fell down. Interestingly there is a history of falling towers at Chichester and it seems this sort of thing isn't as rare as we might imagine. Apparently, as I had thought in Worcester, medieval engineers didn't have the benefit of the calculations that we are able to make today and sometimes they did get it wrong. I've argued elsewhere that engineering is ultimately based on faith. That was somewhat tongue in cheek but with medieval cathedrals it really is the case.

* * *

I've wondered, over the years, about the natural state of humans. Are we a rational species looking for a logical reasoned understanding of the universe, using patterns and coincidences as an indication of the underlying structure of things; or are we, ultimately, a sentiment-based irrational species relying on gut feel and intuition with no care for causal connections?

Clearly people in what we describe as primitive cultures hold fallacious beliefs based on all sorts of things: the apparent motion of the planets, the nature of the weather and seasons, success or failure of crops, chance events, etc. These are really logical misunderstandings that would be dispelled by greater, evidence based, understanding of the environment.

It could be argued that even the most apparently irrational individuals who hold beliefs in what some would think of as the strangest of ideas, such as telepathy or divination, are still seeing the world in a mechanistic and causal way. (I've deliberately chosen telepathy and divination as examples of phenomena that are unsupported by the laws of physics as science knows them.) It is often said by supporters of such ideas that, with apparently supernatural phenomena, there are mechanisms that allow these supernatural events to take place but science has yet to understand what those mechanisms are. Science would counter with the suggestion that the phenomena are outside of the laws of physics; this would be countered with the idea that perhaps the laws of physics don't describe all phenomena, science counters with more technical explanations such as Newton's laws of motion, various laws of thermodynamics or even the four forces of the standard model and that there simply isn't space within physics for such unexplained phenomena; this is countered by arguments about ever-changing scientific paradigms and, in the end, everyone would have been better off going down the pub where they might have got along swimmingly if these issues had never been brought up.

The point is that both camps are really ensconced in the mechanistic perspective, just one is in the established scientific perspective, the second is in some hypothetical extension of that scientific perspective. Supernatural then becomes a supposed extension of the natural (an extension of that which is scientifically explained), not outside of the natural, for whatever happens within the universe can only ever be subject to the universe and its laws (there can be no outside, for the universe *is* everything). It's just that the hippies (for want of a better term) think there are more phenomena, undiscovered laws, within nature that science will not admit to. Whatever the case, each is describing an ultimately mechanistic universe.

The scientific perspective argues that the hippies are fooling themselves, that their thinking is flawed, that their collection of evidence is selective and all that jazz. But when it comes to selective evidence we begin to drift into the realms of perception and social science. Of course social scientists, such as psychologists, will swear that the rigour of their discipline is equally as meticulous as any other science. However, put a physicist and a psychologist in the same room to discuss their scientific credentials and I imagine the physicist might have something to say about the existence of psychological grey areas that they would have no truck with. Put a physicist in the same room as a sociologist and you could end up with a fist fight. Of course, social scientists are more rigorous in their thinking than many popular non-rational movements but who decides where you draw the line and for what purpose the line is drawn?

Another perspective is that of the people who built Chichester Cathedral, who believed in a creator god. That god was capable of creating the universe or rather creating the world. If God created the universe then he must exist outside of that universe. So biblical writers, and believers, aren't the same as people who think their divinatory or telepathic powers are yet to be explained by science, for their god created the laws of nature that science describes.

However, the application of logical, reasoned thinking is something that takes place in the conscious mind. The unconscious mind, on the other hand, is awash with all sorts of other concepts, symbolism, apparently forgotten episodes, weird associations from deeply held cultural or formative experiences and all manner of illogical stuff.

Were we purely creatures of conscious understanding, then we might say we are naturally rational, just waiting until our social development has reached a point where we have a sophisticated enough understanding of the universe and its laws? But the unconscious mind throws an illogical spanner in the logical works and, because it's unconscious, we can't even see the spanner. It's probably a spoon! So this begs the question, can humans ever be objective? Can we claim to be objective when there's all these spoons and spanners messing up who we are?

Statistics is the backbone of the scientific method. Only by the application of statistical analysis of experimental results can we say that a hypothesis is valid or at least a null hypothesis is disproved. Statisticians will rightly tell us that divination is a case of selective interpretation of the turn of a card or the throw of a bone. Statistics will happily point out that the occurrence of an event is purely chance and not an indication of that portentous event. However, statisticians are often the first to point out that people don't behave rationally especially when we get together with other people. Large groups of people such as markets are often described as behaving in ways that are driven by emotion rather than logic, often described as something like group think or crowd behaviour. Do we, therefore, become more irrational when we are influenced by other people? Economies, the understanding of which are dependent on statistical analysis, are riddled with such behaviours. Can we ever claim to be naturally rational?

After an hour or so in the cathedral, buying a guidebook, a fridge magnet and some shortbread, I set off back for the Truck. However, I was distracted by a burger and hotdog seller next to the town cross like the one where I sat with the Forrest Gump of Princes Risborough. (Remember him? that was weeks ago, I wonder how he's doing. I hope he's okay and still enjoying his lunch.) What attracted me was that his hotdogs weren't the usual-pink-boiled-in-water-that-have-probably-never-seen-real-meat-in-their-lives type hotdogs. (Okay hotdogs don't have lives but you know what I mean.) These were real sausages, like you buy when you want some really posh sausages for your BBQ but you also buy some other ones but make sure you keep some of the good ones back for yourself. (Other people do that don't they? Please tell me other people do that.) Well they were those sort of sausages, all interesting coloured too, speckled with what must be herbs and spices and twice as long as normal sausages. Anyway, I was walking off down the road after seeing these and thinking that I'd chosen not to have a snack in the cathedral café as I had done in Worcester because I didn't want to be eating as I walked down the street. So I was walking away but the sight of them stuck in my mind such that I couldn't help myself so I went back. And for three quid I had what might have been the best hotdog I've had in my whole life. I say this in case you are ever passing by Chichester on the motorway that pretends to be an A road. If you drop into the city, a short stay car park should suffice, nip down to the town cross like where Forrest Gump sits and get yourself a hotdog. It was wonderful and I didn't feel at all self-conscious walking down the road eating it as I might have done with a Chichester Cathedral sandwich.

I don't know why I told you that but I felt I wanted to share.

* * *

Leaving Chichester it had turned into another proper summer's day, little fluffy clouds in a blue sky with a bit of a breeze and lots of people wearing shorts, or at least those long trousers that aren't quite shorts, as is the fashion.

I decided that I really wanted to drive along the coast. I knew Kathy would resist and take me by the inland main roads so I decided to navigate manually for the first time in nearly six weeks. I knew I could trust her to get me to my destination but I also knew she wouldn't share my desires for sea views and photo opportunities.

The next hour saw me navigating through Bognor Regis toward Littlehampton, diverting down roads that looked as though they might take me to the sea but took me to streets full of bungalows and houses that tantalisingly hid the sea from view. At the end of the road would be a private estate that I just knew hid access to the sea for those of us that can't afford to live in these places and so, access to the sea becomes privately owned and, thus, I envy their bungalow sea-view heaven.

Not that I would want to live in these places but this is just what this sort of thing does to me. I have this idea that there is a coast road that runs around the country and if it were only accessible to all of us we could drive around looking out at the view, only occasionally colliding with other vehicles because we aren't looking where we are going.

Anyway, after some faffing around I decided that Kathy probably knew best after all. The day was glorious, I was on the coast, the best thing to do was to go and sit on the beach.

Kathy had a feature called points of interest but I'd always assumed they would only work in America because of the sorts of things listed, such as mountain passes and camp grounds that you imagine have bears. However I knew it listed beaches so I thought what the hell. My eyes were immediately opened as it suggested beaches in Littlehampton and Worthing or further afield. Enthusiastically I asked her for Worthing and asked for the shortest route; half an hour later I was parked on the seafront in free parking and getting ready to leave the Truck. Perhaps we should abandon all personal abilities and trust in technology after all.

If I was going to sit on the beach rather than find something else to do, something I've resisted in each of the 33 counties that have preceded Sussex, then, perhaps, I should have a plan. I could take my kindle and read a book or better still I could take my ukulele and sit somewhere out of earshot of other people and have a practice, facing romantically out to sea, gazing wistfully at the horizon as I strummed away. So with my ukulele in its gig bag slung over my shoulder, my computer and a few things in my small canvas satchel, I stepped out of the Truck and along the promenade. Admittedly it was breezy, in fact on Worthing beach it was blowing a veritable gale. Still, if I could find a bit of shelter I could retrieve my kindle, or my uke, and live out my fantasy.

Walking down the prom I passed a row of beach huts that could do with a lick of paint and a man painting the shelter where you sit to get out of the breeze. They seemed to be doing quite a bit of work on the sea front which I thought was encouraging, as English resorts deserve to take advantage of people holidaying at home in these straitened times. Perhaps they'll be getting to the beach huts later. There was another shelter that didn't involve wet paint but the wind was blowing onshore and I was too shy to sit on the leeward side where that would put me facing away from the sea and towards the passers-by like some incompetent busker.

So I walked down the prom, up the pier and back again. My uke never came out of its bag. I sort of felt like a teenager who carries a guitar around for pose value. I really did intend to have a practice had I found some isolation; I just didn't find any. That's my story anyway.

So after a brief stroll in the bracing sea air I was back in the Truck after an hour and heading off to a campsite at Lancing between Worthing and Shoreham. Ironically Kathy took me along the very coast road with the very sea views that I'd been searching for all day, but I suppose what you get in life is dependent on where you start from.

Day 35 - Sussex to Kent

Tuesday June 4th

Miles on Truck: 2852

I was becoming used to the experience of waking up in the sunshine and Sussex continued the trend. The campsite was windy, as you might expect within a mile of the sea, but I was ready for the wind with the Truck strategically placed across the entrance of the Khyam. It meant the view from my tent in the morning didn't match that of, say, Berkshire or Norfolk but needs must and, as in Cumberland, I was more interested in the practicalities of keeping a burner alight for a cup of coffee than I was, enjoying a view across the campsite to the new toilet and shower block. Of which the campsite owner was very proud. This time I knew exactly where I was going in Kent so I asked Kathy to take me to Bodiam and set off.

* * *

Driving across Sussex to Bodiam I considered my conclusions from the day before. If the unconscious mind is a haven for the non-rational—all symbolism and associations where concepts might be connected by virtue of their likeness (colour, smell, emotional impact, or whatever) rather than normal causal connections—and if the conscious mind is a place for the rational—seeking mechanistic or causal explanations of our environment no matter how mistaken due to lack of proper scientific discipline such as in pre-enlightenment cultures—if that is the case (and it's a big if), could it be the case that we are hard-wired to be irrational? Are we hard-wired to make these errors of mistaken causality? Are we therefore hard-wired for what many scientific thinkers would call superstition? Is it the natural state of humans to hold non-rational beliefs?

If we are hard-wired, if irrationality is in our blood, or rather in our brains, is it really right to fight against anything that's not rational as defined by members of the scientific establishment? Is meaning a simple stimulus-response association with something that previously had impact?

* * *

I'd known about Bodiam Castle for some years as the classic castle of its age. If I said that about Portchester Castle then I say it again about Bodiam. Portchester is older and larger and has a keep, whereas Bodiam was built in the late 14th century as a quadrangular castle with the buildings built along the defensive walls. Portchester continued to be used, latterly as a prison right up to the 19th century whereas Bodiam fell into disuse sometime after the Wars of the Roses, though it may have been occupied into the 17th century. If Portchester was continually developed over hundreds of years, Bodiam is a snapshot of the ideal of a castle of the late medieval period. This is the time when the grail romances were being read by knights in shining armour with an interest in poetry and romance. Apparently knights really would wear the favour of a lady, being granted some small item of clothing to wear as a good luck token.

So Bodiam finally is the archetypal medieval castle of children's stories. It's square, has a round tower at each corner and sits in the middle of a wide moat surrounding it on all sides. The castle isn't really defensive as it has one or two silly features such as a large chapel window in the outer wall, which would be a massive weakness. But it comes from a time when the aristocracy wanted more comfortable living but still needed defensive structures before moving into the out-and-out country houses in the centuries that followed. It's also in that period before the regular use of cannon so styles of warfare hadn't really changed since the earlier medieval age.

One of the great attractions of Bodiam, that it also has in common with Portchester, is that many of its towers have floors. So many remaining castles are nothing but empty shells, the floors having rotted away centuries ago. Bodiam, as is the case with parts of the keep at Portchester, has had considerable restoration. Repairs were carried out by Lord Curzon in the 20th century and latterly by the National Trust. (Sadly my newfound English Heritage membership would be worth nothing here.) Some of the towers have even been re-roofed and had floors restored so, as with Portchester, it's possible to climb the scarily steep spiral staircases, step out into the rooms and get a real feel for the way people— high status people mind you—lived. I spent two or three hours exploring the castle and I recommend it to anybody who is a fan of medieval history. If you are not, and you just want to understand how hard it would have been to build these things, it's still worth a look just for the sense of wonder.

After a few hours it was only when I was talking to the local National Trust people that I discovered that Bodiam Castle is actually in Sussex. I could have sworn I'd looked on the map and seen Bodiam in Kent but somehow, it doesn't matter how, I was mistaken. This gave me a dilemma. Granted I could drive across the border, a matter of a mile or so but I had effectively given two days to Sussex and nothing to Kent. There had been the days at the beginning of the trip that I'd managed to do nothing more than drive from one camp to another but that was down to inexperience; by this point there was no real excuse and I'd spent so long at Bodiam that I felt I'd been profligate with my time in Sussex. There was nothing for it: I had to visit Kent in some significant way.

For some time I'd been fascinated by the idea of Dungeness. It's infamous for the fact that it is the location of one of Britain's nuclear power stations but, despite my interest in engineering and technology, that was not my reason to visit. A friend of mine, Jeff, whom I call the Fred Dibnah of Buckinghamshire, an engineer who can work in any material, brick, wood, metal or icing sugar, and who has all the best tools when you are short of a sash clamp or three, once told me that he'd visited Dungeness and discovered that it is the only part of the British Isles officially designated as a desert. What I didn't understand was that deserts do not have to be hot; they merely have to be dry. Dungeness is said to be classified as a desert because of the low rainfall although I've heard others dispute this. The other connection was that Athlete recorded a rather mournful song titled *Dungeness* that sometimes stuck in my head so I thought it worth a visit. It's not a bad song but not a particularly great one either, but it does capture the spirit of the place. I'd also heard that you could get a pretty decent portion of fish and chips in a pub in Dungeness at the point where you can't drive any further without provoking the attention of the nuclear power station people who, one might imagine, would be watching from secret cameras and ready to pop out of disguised, but occasionally flooded, foxholes all over the show.

In the car park at Bodiam it was just coming up to 5:00 and Kathy suggested that Dungeness was just over an hour away. If I left straight away I could eat in the pub there and take pot luck on finding a campsite.

Driving away from Bodiam the roads were all wooded, passing through the rolling countryside you might expect from the Garden of England. Quite why Kent gets to be the Garden of England I don't know, because just about all of England that I'd seen was beautiful, each county in different ways. As far as I'm concerned any county could lay that claim; well, perhaps not Lincolnshire, much of which is bleak and unforgiving what with the flatness and the total lack of any features such as hedgerows because the industrialised farmers have grubbed them all up.

Strangely, there was a sudden point passing through the wonderfully named parish of Playden and then Rye, on the Sussex-Kent border, that I was reminded of Lincolnshire. Turning left I found myself on a straight flat road clearly passing across reclaimed land as in those eastern counties or the Somerset levels. This turned out to be Romney Marshes, the beginning of the flat lands of which Dungeness is the headland on the southern edge. Despite Romney Marshes having these distinctive level views to the horizon, the place didn't seem as characteristically bleak and monocultural as Lincolnshire, or had I just become used to such landscapes having discovered them around the fringes of England over the previous five weeks?

An hour or so after leaving Bodiam in its rolling countryside, I was motoring across the flats of the Dungeness peninsula. Spotting a convenient campsite completely at random, I pulled in, paid up, erected my trusty Khyam in the shelter of an embankment and continued my journey to the only desert in England.

* * *

Dungeness is strange and fascinating. I'd lived in Kent for a year or so before I went to Dungeness and I'd expressed an interest in visiting after work on a long summer evening. However I'd been discouraged when I'd been told that there's 'nothing there.' Now, having visited, that statement sort of reminds me of that scene in The Matrix where Neo and Morpheus are in the training zone, all white space and no walls; but that's the point of Dungeness, to me at least, because it is actually a bit like that.

There's no getting away from the nuclear power station, a collection of great square buildings on the horizon visible from some miles away. You approach across this flat, would-be bleak, landscape surrounded on all sides by boundless sky. You really don't have to go to Montana to see big skies: Cambridgeshire, Norfolk, Lincolnshire or Somerset will all give you big skies and wide horizons and they all have their own character. Somerset is beautiful and, perhaps, the least spoiled, although the Yorkshire coastal lands north of the Humber Estuary seemed to have preserved themselves similarly from the ravages of industrial agribusiness. Lincolnshire seems to have surrendered, as I'm so fond of going on about. Cambridgeshire and Norfolk are partway between the two. All offer big skies though. Whether or not the landscape works seems to depend on leaving some landscape features in place. A few hedges and trees go a long way towards making somewhere hospitable and in a storm you can pitch your tent in the lee of a good hedge. But the Dungeness peninsula does it in a wild, wind-bleached manner, with mossy short grasses and a preponderance of telegraph poles. Having said that, the Dungeness peninsula doesn't really have any trees either, but it probably never had any. The fact that the landscape is in its original state is what seems to matter. That's as original as an English landscape can be with 5000 years of agricultural land management. All landscapes are developed over time and the English countryside, the lowland landscape at least, has developed into the patchwork of fields and hedgerows that it's famous for. Scotland has its mountains and lochs. Wales has its mountains, lakes and valleys. England has its patchwork of fields.

As you approach Dungeness there is a turnoff from the main road that indicates that this is a private estate. Unsure if it was okay to continue, always feeling put off by signs of private ownership, I decided it's better to ask forgiveness than permission; besides there was nobody to ask so I drove on down the only road, which became ever more lumpy, ever more patched, feeling ever more as though I shouldn't be there, ever more grateful for the suspension on the Truck. Having left the more substantial buildings behind, low-lying brick built houses and bungalows, I passed over the narrow gauge tracks of the Romney Hythe and Dymchurch Railway, at 15 inches wide seeming hardly sufficient to carry anything other than a toy train. I continued on along an ever more patched road into a wilderness, increasing expanses of shingle as the vegetation struggled to keep a hold of the landscape. The grass that had been long and tussocky further inland was, here, shorter and stunted, giving way to open shingle with just a few plants clinging on in clusters. The modern world has little place here other than when a huge industrial effort is taken, such as to build a nuclear power station, and even then it seems to sit temporarily, incongruously, *on* the landscape rather than being embedded in it as so much of human influence is.

The place is as windswept as expected but what Dungeness lacks in trees it seems to make up for with telegraph poles. I don't know if reclaimed marsh or shingle is unsuitable for burying cables or if someone generally thought that telegraph poles set off the big sky, but wherever you look across

Dun geness you seem to see telegraph poles. Somehow, though, they don't spoil the view; they just seem to add to the bleakness of the place, skeletal poles with threadlike tendrils spreading out across the blue.

However, for all its apparent lack of hospitability, Dungeness is not deserted. Right out on the headland there are small buildings everywhere, single story shacks (presumably the shifting shingle does not support foundations well) all bleached to grey by the incessant wind and sun. The road stretches ahead, patched and tattered, disappearing over the horizon which seems strangely close. But the land drops away into the shingle and, beyond that, into the sea so the road has that infinite *into the distance* impression that you might only expect to see in the deserts of the American Southwest. Still, this is Britain's only desert so perhaps it has something of the desolation of New Mexico.

All around are cabins and huts that look as though you might live in them if you were determined but you probably wouldn't want to spend the winter here. Returning in the spring you'd not know what to expect. Some of the cabins are converted railway trucks, quite substantial and, you might expect, able to resist the most extreme of maritime conditions. Alongside many of the huts are all manner of boats, some of considerable size, equally weathered with much of their colour bleached out to look like that great black and white picture you always knew you could one day capture if you could just get the detail of the wood grain and a moody sky behind. Some of the boats look as though you'd be taking your life in your hands if you went to sea in them; some may have been beached for years. Apparently, though, there is a small fishing community here so I wonder how many of these craft go to sea more often than you might imagine. How do people make a living from catching a few fish? I suppose their needs are minimal. Others visit Dungeness at weekends and for holidays so, apparently, some of the cabins have become quite sought after and prices can be high, especially considering the famous cottage owned by Derek Jarman, though I wasn't told about it until I returned home. Considering such economic pressures I find myself wondering how long the community can survive.

Eventually there is the massive hulking presence of the power station that utterly dominates the landscape and gives the impression that you can go no further. I'm sure if I'd taken the time to explore, and didn't have to return to see if my tent had blown away (which of course it never would as I'd learned being a Khyam they simply don't do that but, hey, tent anxiety is irrational), I would have found a path around the perimeter, but it being a nuclear power station, I felt that I was being watched by unseen people from a room filled with banks of screens that scour every inch of the windswept landscape.

Just as you arrive at the power station (though you might be half a mile away such is its size) is a scattered cluster of buildings and two lighthouses, one built at the turn of the 20th century but made obsolete when someone realised that the new power station blocked the view of its light. I don't know if that's actually true but it's a nice idea. Somehow stories of incompetence seem to make the world a more meaningful place.

* * *

It strikes me that humans need to have their cake and eat it, in a sort of contradictory two-worlds sort of way. We seem naturally driven by the oblivious structure of associations that populate our unconscious mind and cause us to mess up our golf swing; meanwhile we attempt to create an understanding of the world with causality and rationalism that just doesn't fit with our unconscious mind. The alternative is to live in a world of bleak technology that sucks the joy out of life, destroys the flavour that comes from all of the mistaken interpretations of human history, the myths and legends of our ancestors, the very things that fill our unconscious. The result of trying to live in both the realms of non-rationality and the rational is the sort of incongruity that seems to parallel Dungeness Power Station plonked on the natural shingle peninsula. Trying to live a life where there is room for non-rational beliefs yet remaining rational to the point that the laws of physics still prevail means that you have to ignore one or the other. But walking around Dungeness, it's almost possible to not notice the massive power station, it's ever present but if you can do the trick in your head it disappears from your attention and the headland becomes once more bleak, desolate and beautiful. Of course it doesn't really disappear but you sort of only notice the stuff between you and it, unless you choose to focus on it but that's a choice you make in Dungeness.

* * *

Then there is the pub. Just about as far as you can go, confirming that it is indeed okay to drive across the private estate otherwise the pub would have no customers, there is the Britannia that boasts fish and chips and other home-cooked food. To be honest the place seemed a bit of a let-down, looking as though it hadn't seen a redecoration for some time. It was big enough to mean that the few customers it had made it look empty by comparison, but it was early in the evening and later on it might have been full of salty sea dogs and nuclear power workers in the sort of odd mix of patrons that can make a place thrive. Later in the season it might even have been full of actual tourists. The much vaunted fish and chips, that I was determined to have having missed my chance in Whitby, was just a bit disappointing. It could have come from any cafeteria in any part of the country and despite being described as local, I had my suspicions that it was from some wholesaler with a refrigeration lorry. Still, times is hard and everyone's got to make a living and it sort of fitted with the whole, slightly melancholy, Dungeness experience.

Day 36 - Kent to Surrey

Wednesday June 5th

Miles on Truck: 2956

I'd imagined that camping on the Dungeness peninsula could have been challenging, or at least as challenging as a hilltop in Cumberland or anywhere else down the road from the beach. However, the good people of Romney Farm Campsite had gone to the trouble of building embankments around the field, and by tucking myself into the corner and using the Truck as a shield on the other side, I had quite a pleasant night.

Leaving the peninsula in blazing sunshine, the weather looked as though it would be better than the previous few days. The fast straight roads across the flat landscape were marked with reminders in three languages to drive on the left for the benefit of people having disembarked from the continent, though I still can't think of any ferry terminals in the area. The road to Tenterden flaunted great swathes of hawthorn and cow parsley, making the hedgerows so abundant with white flowers that they obscured the leaves.

With no idea where I was heading, I just knew it was a long way to Surrey and, like the return trip from Land's End, I was aware that the journey could eat the day, especially with frequent stops to make notes or take pictures to jog my memory. Of course in everyday terms the journey from Kent to Surrey is insignificant, but I'd pretty much lost all sense of what an everyday journey was, or an everyday anything else for that matter.

These flat lands, Romney Marshes, Norfolk, Lincolnshire, etc., are all peppered with level crossings. Being from the hilly country of the Chilterns (admittedly not as hilly as the Mountains of Malvern) I'm not used to level crossings. I can only assume that an undulating landscape gives natural opportunities for bridges over or under railway lines. However, whenever I've visited East Anglia, and now Dungeness, I'm forced to encounter level crossings. Frankly they give me the willies. I'm always tempted to inch my way across because you can never see left or right on the damn things until you are in the death zone. As I've been driving around I've been nipping over them as quickly as possible, convinced that death was imminent, caused by a faulty warning light or a defective gate somewhere. Some of them aren't even that level. There was one in Norfolk that I nipped across quickly only to discover that the two sets of rails were on different elevations and I needed the suspension of the Truck to absorb the shock; definitely not a level crossing. So when, driving back across Romney Marsh, I came across a closed level crossing, it was both a bit of a relief and an entertainment to sit for a moment and watch a train go by. Rather disappointingly it was only a tiny thing with hardly any carriages so my break from driving was brief, but it was a change all the same.

* * *

English Heritage say of Surrey that Fareham Castle Keep and Waverley Abbey were my options, but I didn't want to look at any more ruins and I wasn't sure my social networks would stand it either, having Tweeted and Facebooked the previous day until I was told to stop. This lack of anywhere interesting to visit, for an outsider at least, might be a feature of the Home Counties. At the start of the trip I couldn't wait to get away from the South East and I was much happier once I was in a different landscape. Finding things to do in other parts of the country seemed easier somehow. Is it the lack of familiarity with other regions or just that the Home Counties are so overcrowded that there's no space for anything other than a few castles and ruins that have been in existence since the year dot? Kew Gardens would have been a great idea but I wouldn't have made it in time. Heading off, I decided to let things happen on their own.

As I said before, I've never really understood why Kent is known as the Garden of England, or at least not until now. I've only ever seen North Kent and I now understand that's not the best aspect of the county. The Thames estuary is highly industrialised in many places, and elsewhere North Kent is blighted by the motorways and other main roads that give access to the Kent channel ports. When you think that a significant proportion of the traffic between Britain and Europe passes through this area, it's easy to see why. However, descending from the picturesque village of Goudhurst I could see how I'd been labouring under a misapprehension that North Kent was typical of the county. This really was a patchwork of small fields, as far as the eye could see. The fields were tiny and apparently random, divided by not so much hedgerows as strands of trees that clumped together to form small copses and dense woodlands. Agribusiness hadn't managed to gain a grasp here, and I imagined that property prices in Goudhurst, where I felt very scruffy when I stepped out to take a picture, ensured that things continued that way. There was not a grubbed-up hedgerow anywhere in sight. Clearly this is my kind of place and I have delusions of grandeur.

I had an idea to head for the Devil's Punch Bowl, more because it was somewhere I'd heard of than any other reason. I dreamed of sitting on a hill-top at a beauty spot watching the world go by as the afternoon sun drifted towards early evening, before I turned around to find a convenient campsite right behind me where I'd not noticed it before. But my experience said it would probably be impossible to park, or there wouldn't be a view, or some-one would have fenced it off with massive signs saying keep out unless you are a resident, or somesuch. Instead, a search of the Internet spoke of a ca-nal-side café and boathouse which seemed a perfect alternative. Making the decision, I headed off.

* * *

So forgetting about the Devil's Punch Bowl, let's take the perspective of the Devil's Advocate.

What is the danger if some people see the world in a non-rational way? It's often argued that people who hold non-rational perspectives (I'm delib-erately avoiding the word belief) are fooling themselves or that they've been indoctrinated or worse, even brainwashed. But what's more important, hav-ing an accurate view of reality or having a good life?

People who live in so-called primitive cultures, or even pre-European enlightenment cultures, have beliefs about their world that are not entirely accurate but they might be functional. A belief that the sun goes around the earth, traveling from east to west, is perfectly adequate if all you want to do is remember that home is towards the setting sun. That heuristic might be less reliable at certain times of year, but so long as it gets you to familiar ter-ritory then it's good enough. I have beliefs about how my phone works based on repeated experience but I don't know about the details of the op-erating system; those beliefs are still useful to a degree. What is more impor-tant then, to understand the truth of reality or to have a good life so long as all things are equal otherwise?

Non-rational or inaccurate perspectives are sometimes, often even, compared with madness. People get locked up when it's discovered they are living in a delusional world. Clearly I'm not a clinician, but I wonder what percentage of the population would be locked up if we examined everyone under clinical conditions. Of course that's not to say that people who are a danger to themselves, or others, shouldn't be cared for and that they might need to be detained in some circumstances. But even in this severe situation, the judgement is that the individual should be able to function in society. If they are able to function then we don't interfere. What's wrong with an individual having a worldview that doesn't match the scientific establishment? Or are we going to lock up the Archbishop of Canterbury, and if we were to do so who will speak for the poor?

Of course, there are positions that are unacceptable. The fervent belief that you can cure someone of their ills when you have nothing but belief takes advantage of, and does nothing to help, desperate people. I've been saved by doctors more than once in my life and I know which I'd prefer. Medicine is just one example where the scientific perspective wins out in the greatest majority of cases. Double glazing might be another, for it took technology to make our homes warm and efficient.

If we start judging people according to their worldview (or even our perception of their worldview if we don't spend time developing an understanding of their worldview) then that way lies the thought police.

* * *

To get to Farncombe Boathouse, I found myself battling through the worst maze of congested dual-carriageways and would-be motorways, England had thrown at me in my whole six-week journey. Having spent most of my time in less congested parts of the country this was my first encounter with the 21st century South East England. Having grown up in the South East I'd sort of forgotten about it and acclimatised to less frenetic conditions. The journey down from Lancashire to Cheshire, passing between Manchester and Liverpool, had been similarly congested; however, the drivers I encountered in the South East seemed more aggressive somehow. Of course there are much more pleasant locations in Surrey, but without local knowledge I didn't stand a chance. It sort of makes me wonder about the experience of tourists entering Britain through this corner of England.

In the boathouse café I managed to get a cup of tea and a rock cake, which was nice, but to be honest it wasn't really worth the effort to get there. I'd imagined sitting by the water with an idyllic view of a boathouse with fascinating boats out of the water in various states of repair, having their bottoms blacked and other enthralling scenarios. Instead I found myself sitting in an admittedly nice café but unable to see the water, boats or anything else. Still, the tea and rock cake were genuinely second to none, and had I wanted to hire a narrow-boat for a holiday I'm sure it would have been the place to be. Soon I wandered off dejectedly, thinking it to be another lost day with nothing of interest, looking forward to an evening in my tent with nothing but my Facebook friends to entertain me. Then serendipity stepped in and proved how wrong I was.

∗ ∗ ∗

Sitting in the Truck contemplating how long I might be able to overstay my pay-and-display ticket at gone five in the afternoon, I consulted the Monster Monster Book of Campsites and soon found the Merchant Seamen's War Memorial Society Campsite. I was intrigued. There was a brief conversation with some guy who seemed to be in a call centre and nowhere near the site, during which he very nearly persuaded me that I couldn't camp there for some reason, but I stuck to my guns, proclaiming my Caravanning and Camping Club membership, and I was soon on my way.

The drive down from Farncombe to Alford was spectacular. Swathes of lush woodland swept past me, with windy lanes twisting back and forth, up and down undulations, past small fields and paddocks, forested hillsides and just so much beauty that I had to constantly reassess my conclusions about which parts of England were the most beautiful. In the end the list just got longer. The greens were lush and intense, like an over-saturated Photoshop image. Clearly I'd found the Surrey that I'd heard of and that I might have seen if I'd headed for the Devil's Punch Bowl.

Half an hour later I arrived at the Merchant Seaman's War Memorial Society at Springbok Farm and I heartily recommend it. On a gorgeous sunny evening the place was deserted, quiet and without a breath of wind. I was the only camper in the large paddock other than a lone camper van a couple of hundred yards away and four matching bell tents in the next paddock. It later turned out that the bell tents are a feature of the place during the summer and it's possible to hire them for your glamping holiday. Although I rely on my trusty Khyam Igloo for overnight camping I've also got a five-metre bell tent with rugs and a stove so I can recommend the full-on canvas experience.

After eating, during which I was visited by a team of inquisitive ducks (that's not the only collective noun for ducks but it's the most suitable I could find), I strolled across to the house to see what was going on.

This curiously named location is the site of a country house purchased with donations from the people of South Africa in gratitude for the merchant seamen keeping the shipping lanes open during World War II, and thus ensuring that South Africa stayed connected to the rest of the world. Springbok Farm provides various accommodations and care arrangements for retired seamen ranging from independent bungalows and apartments, sheltered housing and holiday accommodation for retired seafarers from the Merchant Navy, Royal Navy and fishermen.

An investment of a pound gave me membership of the club for the night which enabled me to drink in the bar where the beer was cheap and plentiful. Very soon I was chatting away to a group of retired salty sea dogs, jolly jack tars, ship mates, first mates and ship's cooks. The guy who worked in the kitchen of the Mission was a former ship's cook himself and, as well as the residents, there were visiting former mariners from as far afield as Liverpool some 250 miles away. I really would like to regale you with the shaggy dog stories that they told me but to be perfectly honest they are simply not the sort of thing I dare put into print, suffice to say the tales were bawdy, frequently indecent and occasionally downright vulgar. It was great, a true highlight of the six week tour!

Having spent the evening in the company of serendipity's seafarers, I ended up talking to one retired old salt called Pete, learning how shipping had changed over the years, with British hands being largely replaced by those from the developing world who will work for less money and don't insist on the same employment rights. It was an unfortunate tale but one that is repeated across many industries and comes as no surprise in a globalised world. However, things took a turn for the unexpected when, over the final pint of the evening, my companion asked where I was from. Telling him where in Hertfordshire I lived, he described the local community centre hall at the neighbourhood shops no more than five minutes' walk from my home. I had travelled through nearly every county in England and he had sailed every sea on the planet only for the two of us to meet on this particular night so that he might describe how, more than fifty years before, he used to drive up the A41 (for the motorways hadn't been built by then) to see the popular bands of the day. I have to admit that, having downed a considerable quantity of reasonably priced bitter, I didn't make a note of the famous names that he described but people such as Gerry and the Pacemakers come to mind and others that predate my birth. Furthermore, as we explored these connections we discussed the legendary Busy Bee transport café on the A41 near Watford where they used to stop on the way home. Swapping stories, we discussed how café racers used to hang out at the Busy Bee, their daring antics including racing down to the next roundabout and attempting to return before the end of the record on the juke box. Some didn't make it back alive.

Such stories, while originating from before my time, I've heard from various friends who used to ride old British bikes in the sixties, and it's long been my intention to write them into the third Hidden Masters novel if I can ever get the second one finished, which will only happen if I can ever get this travelogue finished.

It was a very weird, unexpected and strangely meaningful experience. Is it the case that two people with completely different lives and histories crossed paths for a moment in their lives and discovered a connection? It meant something to me, though I don't know about him, but shared experiences may well have something to do with the nature of meaning. Of course such connections go unnoticed all the time if we don't speak to strangers-so is our increasing isolation sucking potential meaningful experiences out of life? Does closed-mindedness and judgemental disrespect for the people whom we don't know increase that situation?

Getting back to my tent I checked my messages and there was an email. It simply said, *'Re second hand books. Hi. Suggest you find an alternative supplier, as quite honestly I can't cope with compulsive talkers. Life is too short. Malcolm.'* And thus a thirty-year friendship came to a rather abrupt, completely unexpected and somewhat painful end. In the months that followed I made the odd attempt to say hello, such as by liking or commenting on Facebook posts of his favourite guitars in his increasingly renowned collection, but all clicks and likes failed to bring any response and, at the time of editing, that remains the case to this day. (Hashtag sad face.)

Day 37 - Surrey to Middlesex

Thursday June 6th

Miles on Truck: 3015

The next morning I had a call from Graham. He'd had further news but it wasn't a sudden or miraculous turnaround. He was due further tests which meant he was going into hospital which sort of seemed hopeful but it didn't mean he was due a reprieve. I suppose it just shows that, no matter what people say, even if there's nothing they can do for you in the long term, the NHS still won't abandon you.

After hearing his news, I told him about Malcolm's message. His conclusion was that Malcolm can be a bit intolerant at times, especially of people who don't hold his rational perspective, and he was becoming more so as he got older. Even so, Graham suggested that I didn't deserve such treatment. Still, the sun was shining on a glorious June morning and I was unexpectedly in a beautiful part of Surrey with paddocks and woodlands stretching into the distance, I was just a few days away from finishing what was, for me at least, a significant journey and all I had to do was to get on with it.

Before he rung off the phone, Graham suggested that I could have some books from his library as he, after all, wasn't going to need them where he was going. So it was agreed, I would pay another visit to Blackpool to collect them, hopefully before he fell off the perch.

* * *

I really had no idea what would happen with my day in Middlesex. It's one of those counties that no longer exists, having been swallowed by Greater London so it has that in common with Rutland and Westmorland. Not that they have been swallowed by Greater London, that would, indeed, be a desperate world of urban sprawl. However, as with Westmorland and Rutland, it wasn't going to be easy to identify when I was within the old county boundaries. I also had no idea if there would be such a thing as a campsite in London. After all, who would want to camp there?

With that in mind, I decided that the best thing was so forget any ambitions of finding something to do during the day and I didn't fancy finding parking if I did think of anywhere to go, so I concentrated on finding somewhere to sleep. If I found a site early enough and there was any time left, then I might be able to think of something to do, but the vagaries of poor internet access, London traffic and the actual existence of London campsites meant that camping had to be my top priority.

Is it the case that the necessities of finding accommodation and other mundane daily activities push out meaningful experiences which in the case of this trip were the things I planned to do each day? Do we find little of meaning in our lives if we are constantly struggling to keep everything else together? Is this what Abraham Maslow was on about?

I'd got a rough idea that Middlesex was largely that area north of the River Thames with Surrey having once extended as far north as the southern bank of the Thames, as it is often referred to during the Oxford and Cambridge Boat Race. The tablet was doing its favourite trick of freezing while downloading web pages, so I couldn't even get to Wikipedia. However, a few days earlier a friend had told me that she knew, presumably from rugby match tickets, that Twickenham Stadium was in Middlesex so I thought I'd head there. Despite the fact that Middlesex hadn't existed officially for nearly fifty years, people were still in the habit of using Middlesex on their addresses; plus organisations such as the Middlesex County Cricket Club ensure that the tradition continues. (I later discovered that Twickenham Stadium is the home of the Middlesex Sevens, a rugby union sevens tournament held at the stadium each year.) Clearly the ancient name of Middlesex has a significance, or perhaps meaning, despite the county having disappeared all those years ago.

The drive to Twickenham was, yet again, more glorious than the day before. with a cloudless sky for most of the day. Otherwise Middlesex seemed a wasteland of housing and high streets, unwelcoming to an explorer without local knowledge of parking or destination. Serendipity seems not to be facilitated in densely built environments. Handing the decision making over to Kathy, I had time to think about all this non-rational and rational stuff.

✱ ✱ ✱

I've come to the conclusion that I'm torn between the certainty that rationalism gives me, with its perfect fit over the world of internal combustion engines and our ability to send robots to Mars (which is all very cool and interesting), and the emotional fulfilment that I get from non-rational behaviours such as meditating in a cathedral, despite the fact that I'm not sure I'm doing it right; torn between the non-rational ideas that I cherish and not wishing to be seen a fool by rationalists whose thinking I respect. Would Malcolm respect me more if my thinking were more strictly rational? Would I have become a friend had he been a hard-core rationalist right from the start? Do we pick our friends according to how their thinking is similar to ours and if we do, do we ever have an understanding of people whose thinking is in any way different to us? Is each of us living in a philosophical cul-de-sac?

I appreciate folklore and the flavour it brings, be it poetry, re-enactment or something more spiritual. What I don't like about fundamentalist rationalism, despite my fascination for cars, computers and space craft is that rationalism often seems to suck the joy out of life.

Working late in the office alone, you hear a creak and know intellectually that it's just expansion, or a draft or whatever, but it would once have been interpreted as a ghost and I'm sure that's where all the ghost stories came from, but have we lost something with that cleaning up of our understanding? Antiques dealers talk about patina on wonderful collectibles, the dirt and grime of ages, hundreds of years of polishing that comes from generations of handling. Are we wiping away the patina of life to a point where everything will be new and clean?

While I was writing this I came across a story of a guy whose blog makes great claims for the fact that he can now use his phone to fact-check everything he hears in conversations with other people. Personally I'd find it irresistible not to punch him after five minutes. I imagine he writes a blog because he doesn't have any friends left, but then I feel bad that such a thing might actually be true, and if so rationalism has caused him a great disservice. Whatever the case, if you were stuck in a lift and had to choose between two fictional companions would you choose Sheldon Cooper or Adam Smallbone?

Of course not all perspectives are equally valid, as moral relativism shows us. Would we say the ideology of a Nazi is as valid as that of a Buddhist? Can we identify similar contrasts between rationalism and non-rational perspectives? Not all non-rational ideas are equal. Practitioners of alternative therapies often make great claims, but where their practices are nothing more than placebo, contrasted to what are now described as evidence-based treatments, then they might be doing actual harm, fluffy treatments for cancer being a case in point. And I'm reminded of that great

Facebook meme from the United Church of Bacon that says Bacon is our God, because bacon is real.

I draw a line beyond which I won't accept non-rational ideas. Beyond that line, for me personally, lies an independently existing sentient god and also magic bread. This side of the line lies bacon and Mars rovers. Of course there is a place for scepticism, but surely we have to be careful not to throw out the baby with the bathwater? Hopefully the water would soak the fact-checking git and brick his smartphone.

Okay so that's a bit harsh, to say that bacon exists, thereby implying that God doesn't. For me, personally, there's a line, albeit a fuzzy one, beyond which non-rational ideas are beyond credibility. But we must be careful to resist the temptation to be abusive of another's beliefs. We each decide where we draw the line. People of faith have a completely different line and we each own our own line.

To balance this, there is the story of the people living in isolation on a South Pacific island. (You may want to turn away if you are having your lunch at this point.) Their culture involved ancestor worship, which is not uncommon in parts of the world where modern religion has not reached and overwritten millennia of indigenous culture. These ancestor worshippers were different, in that they believed that by eating the brains of their deceased relatives, they would thereby gain the wisdom of their ancestors, and, presumably, that of previous generations as they too had previous done the same back into the annals of time. So this is all very well, if slightly unpleasant to modern tastes, up until the point that the population somehow contracted CJD, the forerunner of mad cow disease. I'm not entirely down with the science but I understand that CJD can occur naturally in individuals, probably at old age. This is okay, if unfortunate, because it's not contagious and extremely rare, perhaps one in a million. If you are in the habit of eating the brains of your parents (just put that sandwich down for a few minutes longer) you're okay as it's a million-to-one chance that they have the infectious agent. If you are part of an island population with a few thousand individuals, then you might go on like this for generations but, eventually, people are going to get ill. Not all non-rational practices are harmless, even if they seem so at first.

∗ ∗ ∗

While thinking about this I came across a story of a mother whose son died on a frosty winter evening. Parents outliving their children is something that we are not used to in the modern world but just a few generations ago it was all too common. I don't know the details but the mother tells a story that a butterfly flew into the room somehow. I don't know if the window was open in the winter or what, but the mother explains that this was her solace in a moment of unbearable grief. I don't care where the butterfly came from, what the logical explanation was, how it had survived the low temperature, or any of the details of the story. Where the butterfly came from is irrelevant, the point is her reaction was a perfectly natural, and reasonable, response, to draw a non-rational association between her son who had died moments before and the apparent creature of fluttery spirit that seemed to appear in the room with no obvious explanation.

* * *

Kathy delivered me to a non-descript road junction that I presume must be the centre of Twickenham, so I drove on until I could find a side street to pull into in the hope that the tablet would be more obliging.

During the drive it occurred to me to search for the term 'North London campsite'. Hoping for more cooperative technology, I managed to load up Google and entered my search. Miraculously the tablet was in a good mood and, lo and behold, Google recognised my search term indicating that lots of other people had searched on North London campsite before. Who would have thought it?

I selected one of the options and quickly found a campsite with a TW post code, phoned up and established that they were indeed in Middlesex, though I wonder what they thought of my need to establish that. The site was in West London, right on the Thames, but still in Middlesex.

* * *

The site was okay but they placed me right next to another tent, already erected with the residents nowhere to be seen. Over the weeks I'd become a bit conscious of not intruding into other peoples' space. Being told by the fairly prescriptive site manager that I had to camp right next to this unoccupied tent, when there was space elsewhere, made me feel somewhat awkward.

Otherwise the site was a considerable complex with serried ranks of large, identical frame tents, faded by the sun, most of them apparently unoccupied. There were a few campers or caravanners dotted around which looked like people touring. Using a camper for cheap accommodation in London seemed to be the thing to do, which, when you think about it, makes a lot of sense.

After setting up and nipping out for shopping, I dozed in the tent until the neighbours returned. Unlike at other sites they didn't say hello when I appeared in my doorway. It turned out that they were builders taking advantage of the cheap accommodation and not holiday campers, which might have explained things. This made me wonder just how much of this sort of thing goes on. Are there loads of office workers living in tents during the week, dotted across the country with all of the facilities of domestic life, or is this sort of behaviour restricted to tradesmen and people travelling the country researching the 39 Historic Counties of England like the bloke on the noisy motorbike in Dorset?

Day 38 - Middlesex to Essex

Friday June 7th

Miles on Truck: 3083

Disappointed with the lack of anything obviously interesting happening in Middlesex, or at least easy to find, and the need to get away from the city, I decided to try a different approach on my last full day. (Surely there were hundreds of interesting things in north London, had I really become that cut off from the modern world in just six weeks?) Not being able to rely on the Internet, I drove to Essex with the intention of following the first brown tourist information sign I saw. Of course I'd need to know when I reached Essex but I could judge that. There had been rain in the night so, after packing and waiting for the tent to dry, I set off at the crack of 10.45.

Deciding on Chelmsford as an initial destination, that would at least get me into Essex, I was sorely tempted to take the motorway but I simply couldn't bring myself to. I'd pretty much decided that I would go home on Saturday night instead of camping in my home county; that seemed enough like giving up; to take the M25 to Essex would have seemed a double defeat. How is it that it can be so hard travelling around my own back yard? In my case that's the South East of England, particularly that bit north of London. Is it the case that you take away the motorway network and you find yourself living in a different country?

Driving around London is as much an act of faith, trusting in Kathy, as it is to drive in the most hidden areas of the countryside. If you don't know London it all looks the same, and you can have as little idea where you are as if you are deep in the countryside. It took getting on for three hours to get from the campsite on the Thames into Essex without using motorways, emerging through Epping Forest, which is as beautiful as anywhere else I've seen.

***

Along the way, battling through the urban sprawl, encountering areas of London that I'd heard of but never passed through despite growing up just a few miles away, I couldn't help but wonder at the diversity around me. Of course this is apparent for all of us to see every day. You only have to drive through a town you've never visited and look at each house and wonder at the fact that in each one, amongst the tens of thousands of homes, reside people that you will never know, yet their lives are as detailed and significant as yours, as full of personal experiences, tragedies and triumphs, relationships and personal fascinations. Of course this is obvious but it seemed more significant after driving 3000 miles and six weeks of encountering strangers with their own unknowable experiences; the retired couple outside Whitby apparently railroaded by the council, two blokes on the River Severn with their speedboat, the Forrest Gump of Princes Risborough perhaps still eating his lunch with determination (or was he just someone who didn't want to make conversation). Amid all this diversity is it any wonder that we can hold differing worldviews? I wonder if what rationalists are objecting to is simply a lack of critical thinking, but we can't understand each other's thinking if we shout at each other from either side, refusing to understand the other's perspective, or worse still, ridicule the other side with clever jokes. Life would be so much friendlier if we could have a discussion about our perspectives without prejudice and without proselytising.

We once lived in a world where everything came from on high. God told us how things were, or at least the priesthood did, probably quoting from some weird bloke who wandered into the wilderness to live in a cave with an orangutan. At the end of the age of meaning derived from religion, we gained freedom from the shackles of doctrinal belief, only to be confined and ultimately dissatisfied by the equally doctrinal shackles of reason, still spoken from on high, for who today can understand particle physics? There had been a brief age, during the enlightenment, when normal people could make discoveries for themselves, but most people were too busy struggling to survive, so most progress was made by the aristocracy and the growing wealthy business class.

Today the hippies are making their own meaning, building pseudo-religious practice that has different origin and meaning for each of them. There's an inclusiveness in their practice that allows for something like a compartmentalisation of worldviews. Surely it can't be belief if they are able to hold differing and conflicting worldviews depending on whether they are paying homage to the seasons or trying to start a car that has a flat battery. These people don't necessarily believe in faeries, but they may be experimenting with non-rational ideas for entertainment or just to give their lives more colour (magic bread notwithstanding). What would it be like to believe in faeries? You'll never know what the hippies' perspective is until you get close to them; just don't think you know their minds from a distance lest you think you've got telepathic powers yourself, and then can't claim to be a rationalist.

As I edit this there's a note on my desk that says, 'top-down structures are being unravelled.' I have no idea of the context of where I heard the phrase but it was probably on Radio 4. It could just as easily have been on a programme about business and entrepreneurs, a programme about software developers building apps, politics or any other subject. I simply don't know what this related to but that's the point. This seems to be the nature of the age in which we live. There seems to be a shift from top-down religion to bottom-up spirituality, whatever spirituality is. Having driven 3000 miles I still have no idea, but that's probably my rational counterbalance to my non-rational tendencies.

Granted, the level of philosophical exploration of a plumber from Plumstead or a solicitor from Solihull might not be world-shattering but we can't all be Bertrand Russell. If all we can manage is cod philosophy, should we not explore beliefs or ideas at all? (I should have waited to get a degree in philosophy before writing this but I simply didn't have time. Besides I had a story to tell, even if it's just a story of two drunk blokes and a speedboat.) Experiment from an experiential perspective may be the only method that suits many of us. Otherwise we end up with the world as described by Huxley in *Brave New World*, where everyone knows their place and those without education should shut up, and presumably stick to TV soaps and manufactured pop stars. Surely those with the greatest education shouldn't be the only ones allowed to explore and express something meaningful – of course that's not to allow magic bread – critical thinking is important but not to the point of painting the whole world grey. Even magic bread may be representative of something that isn't immediately apparent. The highly educated, behaving like priests, dictating the thinking of the rest, pointing and laughing in the mass media, is a tyranny akin to fundamentalism. An ironic outcome of encouraging people to explore their beliefs might actually be less magic bread rather than more. The process of shaking off the shackles of received wisdom, thinking for ourselves, given a properly supporting environment rather than abusive ridicule, might actually result in more rationality rather than less. People are adding colour to their lives and discovering meaning where they find it in shared pseudo-religious experience (but without God from on high), personal development and perhaps more.

This is philosophy from the bottom up, from the grass roots, often literally. An electrician from Edgware might never have had the time to stand on the grass in his bare feet and consider the sensations it brings. That simple act might be the catalyst for a chain of exploration that takes him away from the world of current and voltage into something much less clearly defined, something less objective, more subjective, but ultimately personally meaningful where he learns something about himself, the universe or his relationship with it.

***

Following the directions for Chelmsford, I passed through Epping and then Ongar and was beginning to think the brown signs strategy wouldn't lead to anything. There was the occasional brown sign for a golf club, which might have been an interesting experience, but I imagined being turned away for not having a blazer or wearing the wrong shoes or something. If this isn't the case and my perceptions of golf clubs is stuck in the sixties, then perhaps golf clubs need to consider their reputations. Or perhaps they like it that way?

Suddenly, approaching a roundabout, the prospect of finding nothing more than a golf club or a church melted away with the most unexpected brown sign that I'd seen in the whole country. The sign indicated the usual collection of destinations both mundane and exotic. This part of Essex boasts delightful locations such as Chipping Ongar and Stanford Rivers but, amid the varied list of villages and towns, all strange and exceptional to a visitor from another county, was the most astonishing statement. Picked out on a brown background against the larger white panel where the local destinations were displayed were the words 'Secret Nuclear Bunker'. Clearly someone in Essex had a great sense of irony and I just had to investigate.

A couple of miles further on, through Chipping Ongar and Marden Ash, down a windy road and over a narrow bridge, along a country way through the marvellous rolling Essex countryside with high hedges and trees arching over the road, I eventually came to the curiously named Kelvedon Hatch, which seems like the right place to put an underground bunker if you were ever going to have one.

Suddenly, emerging through the trees, there was a sign by the side of the road reading, 'Visit the vast ex-government secret nuclear bunker'. Opposite was one of those entrances to a track along the side of a field, the sort of entrance that you look at and wonder if it's a private drive or just an untarmacked road, or could I camp down there for the night and nobody notice?

The landscape of this part of Essex was undulating with slopes and rises that you couldn't really call hills except that it wasn't in any way flat. Through the entrance there followed about half a mile of twisty gravel road around the edge of fields and up and down slopes until I found myself in a large unsurfaced car park on a steep slope near the top of a small hill. A tall radio mast stood on top of the hill and the sounds of people shouting and generally having fun could be heard in the woods below. It turned out that the site was also used by some sort of adventure playground offering all those things that you wish were available years ago when you were a kid such as aerial rope walks and slides, paintball, archery and all sorts of things that would have your mother worried saying, 'you could take someone's eye out with that.'

Leaving the sunshine behind and a little disappointed that I wouldn't be able to explore the adventure playground (add it to the list), I followed the signs for the Secret Nuclear Bunker down to a house hidden in the woods.

Anything you read about the Secret Nuclear Bunker at Kelvedon Hatch, and there seems to be plenty written about it, describes the house as a cottage hidden in the woods, apparently an innocuous cottage just like any other you might find. The 'cottage' is actually the guardroom for the entrance to the bunker and having seen quite a few military buildings over the years, it really looks no different. If they wanted to make it look like a cottage, they should have given it a garden instead of a car park, and the sort of windows you might expect of a cottage instead of the standard fifties Ministry of Defence look that it had. Still I suppose, when it was in use, it probably had a permanent guard stopping you getting closer than the field entrance. In times of war it might have been different, with the occupants withdrawing inside to rely on the stealth properties of the building to protect them from mobs of roving, cancerous morlocks, unless, of course the whole building had been destroyed by the 15 megaton blast that would no doubt have been let off overhead as soon as the balloon went up. It might be secret but not so secret that the bad guys didn't know where it was...

The concrete steps led up to a porch with an open door into something definitely other than a normal house. You might have imagined the first room to look more like a reception than the entrance hall of a normal house. There wasn't a soul to be seen but various instructions said where to walk, where not to walk, not to take photos and how much to pay if you did take photos (I didn't so I'm relying on memory), and to pick up a wand for the audio tour.

Taking a wand and obeying the instructions to listen at the earpiece, pressing the buttons at the right time, I stepped through the next door into a different world.

Beyond the door was a long corridor sloping down into the distance. When I say corridor I mean tunnel, and at 100 yards long it's quite a sight. The audio tour, which is rather good and one of the best features of the place, explained how the long tunnel, with a right angle at each end, was designed to minimise the effects of any blast that might take place outside. However, the narrator, who had a wonderfully plummy English voice, went on to explain that the long straight corridor was also designed as a good defensive feature. A couple of soldiers placed at the far end would be able to pick off any remaining cancerous morlocks who had managed to survive the various blasts to see through the stealth properties of the cottage above (assuming it was still standing, which seems unlikely). These bunkers were intended as a seat of regional government, but the audio tour leaves you in no doubt about the separation between those inside and out and the lengths to which those inside would be prepared to go to maintain the situation. The old adage of who would be left to govern comes to mind.

The tunnel emerged into the lowest floor of the three-storied bunker and the tour explained the various rooms equipped with tele-printer machines and the like, including a broadcast studio that featured a fairly good waxwork of Margaret Thatcher. It seems this regional government centre would have likely been used by some of the Westminster government. Beyond that there were the sort of rooms you might expect to see in a government bunker complete with giant maps and computer terminals, massive generators and air recycling systems.

On the whole the place is interesting if a little shabby. Clearly the people running it don't have much money to spend on the place so, instead of nice waxworks of military personnel, they have shop window dummies dressed in military uniforms. (One or two of the dummies had limbs that have fallen on the floor or were missing altogether). It's possible to see how the rooms full of computer terminals were cobbled together from whatever they could get hold of, with a varied selection of original artefacts and the sort of relics you could collect from business bankruptcy sales. Never-the-less, it is a wonderful place to explore and it does give you an impression of what it would once have been like in the days when the rest of us only heard rumours of the existence of such places. What I will say is that the toilets were clean, functional and, I imagine, authentic so I guess I can say that I've taken a whiz in a bunker, just as the Prime Minster would have done in a national emergency.

Day 39 - Essex to Hertfordshire

Saturday June 8th

Miles on Truck: 3128

Saturday morning I was faced with a dilemma. I'd decided I wasn't going to camp in my home county, so that would free up the day without even the background anxiety of working out where to sleep. But should I head straight home or try to find something to do? I decided I'd use a combination of the first idea I'd started out with six weeks ago—taking the shortest route—and my strategy of brown-sign-spotting the previous day.

Heading out from the campsite at Kelvedon Hatch, not far from the Secret Nuclear Bunker, Kathy loyally took me back through Epping Forest and onto Waltham Abbey and Cheshunt. Entering Hertfordshire I passed through Cuffley, the location of the scout camp my older brothers went to when I was too young to join them but a place that held a (personally) legendary status on the other side of the county which was a world away to a sixties eight-year-old in a family without a car.

There wasn't a brown sign to be seen as I avoided the M25, trundling through Potters Bar and South Mimms. The weather was bright and sunny again and I fought my way through traffic wondering if I'd ever find anything of interest.

The road from South Mimms to St Albans brought me into the lee of the M25 proving that, no matter how hard you try, you can't avoid motorways. Suddenly, on my left there was a brown sign but I'd driven past it before I had a chance to see what it said. Making an awkward U-turn at the next mini-roundabout I headed back to discover the de Havilland Aircraft Museum. Being on my doorstep and having worked in the Hertfordshire aircraft industry on and off during my career as a technical writer, I'd been vaguely aware of the place for years; however, I'd never been able to find it. Being a bit of a childhood aviation enthusiast, and desperate to find something on my last day, I turned into the drive, glad to have found something that wasn't another castle.

* * *

To be honest I'm not entirely sure where the rational and the non-rational begin and end, or is there a blend point that fundamentalists from each camp refuse to see? Language, which pervades our thinking and therefore our perception, is a symbolic thing. Could it be argued that our perception of the universe is influenced by the way it is described to us during socialisation, based on symbolism embedded in language? Is this where rationality and non-rationality cross over? We can't talk about rational ideas and concepts other than through a system of symbolic ideas all, apparently, overlaid on our naturally irrational unconscious mind.

There's a situation that's described in theatre where the audience *know* that something is false and at the same time *believe* it's true. Of course, we become absorbed by drama be it film or theatre and that's not difficult to imagine; we quickly develop emotional attachments to characters and they become real to us as we become involved in their situations. But the paradox is more profound when you think of puppetry. With productions such as *Warhorse* or *A Midsummer Night's Dream*, we've seen how audiences almost make deeper emotional connections to things that they cognitively know are engineering constructions. Puppeteers suggest that this is because the audience has to partially create the character themselves; after all, the puppet isn't alive, so they try harder without even being aware that's what they are doing, creating the character in their own head, or perhaps heart.

It's almost as though what's needed is a compartmentalisation of worldviews. We know that the earth goes around the sun and that the sun isn't a fiery god in a chariot chasing a silver ball that only dares to emerge at night; but if you can suspend that disbelief it's almost as though we seem to gain access to a new level of experience. The trick is knowing, or feeling, when it might be worth suspending disbelief. After all, you wouldn't want to be in a non-rational mind-set when dealing with the brakes on your car. Conversely, perhaps those that don't make this judgement, those who never apply critical thinking, end up trying to bake magic bread.

Who is to say that mystical experiences are in our imaginations and how do we tell? If they are in our imaginations is that a problem? Where lies the experience of listening to a great piece of music or falling in love? Are these experience devalued if they are intangible? Graham once suggested that a mystic is someone who has seen more than they have language to communicate.

There's also the question of playfulness. People blow on dice when they want a double six in Monopoly when, clearly, they know it won't make a difference. My dad once swore he'd lost his pyjamas and suggested they'd been abducted by aliens. When he later found them neatly folded under his bed, where he'd looked, he suggested the aliens had put them there. I bet people didn't know aliens interfere with people's pyjamas.

* * *

The de Havilland Aircraft Company didn't deal in pyjamas, though I'm sure Geoffrey de Havilland wore them. His company built aircraft around South Hertfordshire during the mid-20th century until it was swallowed up by the many mergers that led to the diminishing of the British aircraft industry to its current sorry condition. They'd had factories at Leavesden and Hatfield where significant aircraft had been developed, including the legendary Mosquito and the Comet, which was the world's first commercial jetliner. Today the industry is all gone, the Hatfield aerodrome was developed for housing and offices in the 1990s and Leavesden became the Warner Brothers film studio that now houses the Harry Potter Experience. Had I been travelling on the M25, the first brown sign I'd seen might well have been for the Harry Potter museum instead of the de Havilland museum and this book might have finished somewhat differently though, I suspect, making the same general point.

With the rich aviation history that South Hertfordshire has, there are still many aviation support industries that remain in the area, not least documentation services, some of which I've worked for myself. Because of that heritage there are also a great many retired aircraft engineers and mechanics, designers and fitters along with all the other people that gave significant parts of their lives to the endeavour of building aircraft through the 20th century.

Today the de Havilland museum at Salisbury Hall (which is the actual site where the famous Mosquito was developed, in secret, away from the main Hatfield aerodrome) houses a considerable collection of aircraft. Many of the exhibits feature the distinctive de Havilland engine cowl with the offset air intake that made their aircraft so recognisable right back to the early Moth designs, through the Chipmunk (in which I first flew), until it all changed with the development of the jet engine. The museum has three Mosquitos along with various Vampires, Vixens, Venoms and the like. Unfortunately they don't have a full Comet, although they do have a fuselage and cockpit that you can climb into, albeit peering through an acrylic partition. To be honest the museum is too small to house a full Comet, and they have no runway so new acquisitions arrive in crates or on low loaders. In fact the place is so tiny that you have to wonder how they get so many aircraft in such a small area, but that's part of the charm of the place. While they clearly have some quite precious aircraft, others are wonderfully scruffy so that you can touch them, or climb up some steps at the side to peer into the cockpit.

Whatever your thoughts on the defence industry, when people spend significant parts of their lives designing and building such machines it's easy to see how their association with them can become very significant and, as I wandered around taking photos, I came across a number of overall-clad blokes with their heads and oily fingers inside some half-dismantled aircraft or part thereof.

***

There is a concept known as discovering one's true will. This is not to be confused with free will, which is something completely different. Discovering your true will is a bit like finding the thing in life that is the best fit for who you are. Someone brilliant at music might express their true will as a musician, someone brilliant at nurturing others might express their true will as a parent, someone brilliant at sport might express their true will playing sport or teaching sport. It's been said that this is a bit like discovering your destiny. It is said that those who discover their true will find that life is like riding along on the crest of a wave, or riding on a current. In the light of this concept, could it be the case that the men with oily fingers and their heads inside cowlings have continued to follow their true will even after retirement?

***

Walking around, I found myself looking at the Chipmunk, a fine Mk 10 example of the post war trainer in RAF markings. Having said that, I'm not enough of an enthusiast to know that's what I was looking at. As far as I was concerned it was just a Chipmunk.

'Morning,' said a bloke standing ten feet away. He was of that age that meant he probably grew up in a world where people would politely greet strangers in the mornings on the way to work. I remember that a little from when I was doing a paper round and the streets were almost empty at 6:00. Today children would be suspicious of a stranger greeting them.

'Morning' I replied as we both looked at the Chipmunk. I'm not sure it actually counted as morning but you don't say 'good lunchtime'. 'I took my first flight in one of these.'

'Oh, where was that?'

'RAF Catterick, on an Air Cadets summer camp in the seventies.'

'And did you go into the RAF?'

'No, I didn't think I would pass the medical. I suppose I might have tried but it never happened.' Briefly I found myself wondering at the things we avoid because they might not work out when the actual cost of failure is no different from not trying at all. 'I worked in aviation though.' I continued, attempting to bring back a positive slant.

'Was that around here?' he replied.

'Yes, I worked at Rolls Royce on the helicopter engines and a few other jobs over the years.'

'What did you do?'

'I was a technical writer. For a while I wrote the service bulletins for the Gem engine on the Lynx helicopter.'

'That would have been Leavesden then?' he guessed. 'I was at Hatfield until about the same time as Rolls Royce closed at Leavesden.' I nodded in response. 'And do you still work in aviation?' he asked.

'I do a bit of this and that. These days it's more often other technologies, photocopiers, medical equipment, scientific instruments, all sorts really. I like a bit of variety. Between jobs I try to do some creative writing.'

'Creative writing?' he enquired.

'I've written a bit of fiction in the past. At the moment I'm just getting home from a six-week trip around the country, writing a travelogue about visiting the Historic Counties of England.'

'Oh, what's a historic county?'

'It's one of the old counties that existed before all the modern boundary changes and reclassifications,' I replied. 'I didn't fancy camping in inner cities or whatever, and I fancied finding out about places that disappeared, like Rutland and Westmorland.'

'Camping, for six weeks? That must have been a challenge?'

'Well yes, but not as much as camping across the Great Rift Valley or somewhere,' I replied.

'So what did you find out about the Historic Counties, the ones that disappeared?'

'Well, Rutland was a bit crap, or at least I struggled to find anywhere to camp.' He nodded. I'm not sure if his acknowledgement was an agreement that Rutland is indeed a bit crap or just politeness. 'Actually it's not Rutland's fault that I couldn't find a campsite as I wasn't really planning ahead.'

'So that's a change from technical writing,' he responded.

'Yes I suppose it is,' I replied, 'but, ultimately, it's just a case of describing things; just you are describing events and experiences instead of how to remove an electric motor.'

'So how has it gone, overall?' he asked. 'You are just getting home?'

'Actually it's been a bit of a surprise. Not what I expected.' I found myself wondering how much to say.

'Oh?'

I felt his simple response gave me permission to continue but he might just as likely been thinking *I've got a right nutter here*. 'It's sort of turned into an examination of different ways of looking at the world.' I paused to give him a chance to ask a further question, or run away, but he let me continue. 'I've got a longstanding interest in belief systems; the way people look at the world and the way those perspectives relate to science or the reality of our existence.' He seemed to be listening interestedly. 'So the trip has led me to think about the difference between how people see things, where they find meaningful experiences rather than truth per se.'

'Okay,' he replied noncommittally.

I continued wondering if I should really be saying all this, considering I'd avoided it all the way around. 'Does a rational, or scientific, perspective have intrinsic benefit over a less dismissive view of the non-rational experiences of life?'

'Is a scientific perspective dismissive?' he asked, perhaps quite perceptively.

'Well that's what I've been struggling with,' I replied. 'I'm a fan of science but I also have an appreciation for the non-rational things we experience, things that we can't measure or describe in scientific terms, even some ideas that seem just plain erroneous, such as mythology.'

'And what is your conclusion?' he asked.

'Well actually that's my point,' I paused. 'In the end it doesn't matter what *I think*. It's not for me to say. Where anyone finds meaning is really up to them. Nobody can experience the perspective of another person, we all have to decide for ourselves, and that decision cannot be judged by anyone else because, ultimately, we cannot put ourselves into another person's shoes.'

'Okay, I suppose that's one way of seeing it,' he replied.

'Well yes, and it strikes me that it would be wrong of me to argue otherwise,' I concluded.

'Well I suppose I'd have to agree with you, but then again I would,' he paused, 'because I don't exist.'

'What?' I did a double take at his response. 'What do you mean?' I wondered if he was getting all philosophical on me or just plain taking the piss.

'Well you've made me up for the purposes of making your final point,' he explained.

'You can't say that!' I complained.

'I'm afraid I just did. There's nothing you can do about it.'

'Oh that's not fair, you're playing with me,' I complained.

'Well I am but you created me,' he challenged me. 'So you stop me.'

I didn't know how to respond.

'How many of the other conversations in this book were fictitious?' he asked.

'None of them!' I replied a little nonplussed, '…well, except one,' I added. 'And that one was transplanted from another time and place to protect the identity of someone who might be able to recognise themselves.'

'What if I identify myself?' he asked.

'What do you mean you identify yourself? You just said you don't exist!'

'Ah, so you admit it!'

'No, it's all true, it all happened,' I insisted.

Eventually we made polite noises and left the de Havilland Chipmunk to its own devices. I continued to explore the mixture of weathered hulks and priceless antiquities and tried to avoid bumping into him again in case it proved awkward.

✳ ✳ ✳

You might imagine that, as someone who has spent a large part of his life writing, writing would be where I find meaning. However, I remember once posting on Facebook that, on the whole, I'm never happier than when I'm standing outside my back door, in the sunshine, with a pile of tools and some wood, making a box or building a bird feeder. There is a certain getting lost in the moment when nothing else matters and happiness visits. For me it happens when I'm building something, but it can happen in all sorts of situations, not just riding the perfect wave or the deepest meditation. (Apparently Michael Gambon has a collection of lathes for just such experiences.) I find it can even happen to me when washing up, giving my attention to the task at hand, the water at the perfect comfortable temperature, brushing in perfect circles around the outer edge of the plate, the plate comes clean to glisten with a flawless whiteness, lost in the moment. Writing can do it but not every time, whereas a set of tools seems to work every time and a good washing up brush (never a sponge) *can* do the same. Long-term happiness, it seems, is about giving yourself the maximum number of opportunities for such visitations.

In the modern world people find meaning in all sorts of things, things which might have, in the past, been exclusively religious. Perhaps before formal religion that meaning came from things that today we, rather inexplicably, call spiritual, such as gazing into the sunset across the savannah wondering how the great ball of fire in the sky falls into the earth only to arise the next morning. Today scientists find meaning in the explanation that we know the great ball of fire doesn't disappear into the earth and that, instead, it is swallowed by the Flying Spaghetti Monster only to be regurgitated the next morning after the Noodly One has run around the other side while you weren't looking. Others find meaning in community, music, family, Slack, theatre, sport or, dare I say, getting their hands dirty at the weekend in old aeroplanes.

Whatever the case, wherever you find your meaning, you can be sure that others will find theirs in different practices. To others, meaning may be based on experience, imagination or many different things, some of which may make no sense to you at all and may appear from your perspective to be totally fallacious. Meaning is all about associations, that's where it comes from. But, like the bloke who plays his car stereo loud expecting everyone to think his music is cool, you can be sure that people won't necessarily see meaning in that which you find meaningful, and you may not find meaning in theirs; it doesn't indicate that meaning isn't real.

Afterword

I was listening to the famous *Elements* song by Tom Lehrer this morning just as I was due to send off the final text for In SatNav We Trust. I've always loved this song and it's probably led me, slowly, to develop a better understanding of the periodic table. For those that don't know the song it's sung to the tune of the *Major-General's Song* from The Pirates of Penzance. It's starts with the lines,

> *There's antimony, arsenic, aluminum, selenium,*
> *And hydrogen and oxygen and nitrogen and rhenium,*

It goes on through all the elements that were known in the sixties and is a considerable feat of memory.

In the particular YouTube video I was watching today, filmed in Copenhagen in 1967, after he's finished the main song Lehrer says that there is an earlier song attributed to Aristotle, that simply goes,

> *There's earth and air and fire and water.*

He ends with the comment that they were simpler times.

This got me to thinking about these models. The periodic table of elements was developed by Dmitri Mendeleev in the latter half of the 19th century although the knowledge on which it is based would have been researched over the preceding 200 years. It was this information that provided the structure of the table, rows and columns, defined horizontally by the number of protons in the nucleus and vertically by the number of populated electron shells.

The idea of indivisible chemical elements that form the basis of all matter might be seen as a model that served the understanding of our world at the time. For Aristotle the four elements were the basic building blocks of nature, those bodies into which other bodies can decompose but cannot decompose further. Those four elements were abandoned as the years passed and by the time Boyle, in the mid 17th century, started to talk about atoms as irreducible units of matter there were many more.

The age of enlightenment, from around the time of Boyle to the Victorian period, gave us enough understanding of the universe to enable the industrial revolution. The materials used in the Spinning Jenny, though, probably don't depend on much more than carpentry and blacksmithing which, might therefore, have been constructed in Aristotelian times. Decent steel might owe more to enlightenment chemistry.

The pre-enlightenment model of chemistry enabled the development of clothes, farming, cooking utensils and of course the stuff that is still visible, churches and castles. On the whole the Aristotelian model served to develop a fairly sophisticated culture. We consider belief in, or thinking in terms of, the four elements to be irrational. But Aristotle did think he was irrational? I've never met him so I don't know; I imagine he thought he was at the cutting edge.

The model of the periodic table still applies. Since the 20th century we've landed on the moon and developed the Large Hadron Collider, and so it goes on. But the enlightenment understanding, now more complete than ever is still useful (Mendeleev was aware of 56 elements whereas the current table stands at 118, or it did this morning). And, of course, to the rest of us it's fascinating.

So what of Aristotle's four elements? I tend not to get involved in materials science in my daily life and where I encounter it at work my understanding only needs to be of the level that I can do some quick research on the web. I'm thinking of building another shed. I enjoy a bit of woodwork and, of course, I'll use an electric drill (although a low tech hand drill is often less hassle for quick simple jobs). My drill depends on 20th century chemistry and physics, as does my saw, but that work has been done for me. If I need to service a tool I might learn more first but, day to day, the application of skill and effort would probably be understood by Aristotle. It's almost as though science has moved on but people haven't. If I'm doing woodwork I don't need to understand the periodic table to build a table.

Interestingly I have a friend who works at a physics research establishment. He likened the four elements of earth, water, air and fire to solid, liquid, gas and plasma. Given Aristotle's lack of measuring equipment he might have been spot on.

About Jack Barrow

Jack Barrow lives in Hertfordshire, England, where he earns a living writing about things in engineering. This usually means photocopiers and bits of aeroplanes. He'd like to stop doing this but, despite appeals to the Illuminati and the like, not enough people have heard of his work to be picked up by a larger audience. He's written a novel about master magicians who save the world at weekends. He'd like to find the time to write a second, or possibly even a third Hidden Masters novel, thus jumping on the serialisation bandwagon that seems to be so popular. However, needs must when the shed needs replacing so it's back to the copiers.

He shares his home with R2D2 and C3PO, occasionally mentioned in his blog posts. People used to say he should get out more. At the time of writing he is currently shielding from the apocalypse, having been of a sickly disposition as a child, and wondering if he will be able to go to a live music pub ever again.

jack-barrow.com

The Hidden Masters

and the

Unspeakable Evil

A Hard Drinking Occult Adventure

with Gambling...

and Frivolous Trousers

by Jack Barrow

Has a dark presence from the other side risen up to conquer Britain's northern holiday resorts? The Three Hidden Masters (two from Hemel Hempstead and one from Bricket Wood) need to find out before it's too late...

ISBN: 978-1-5272-6312-3

Lightning Source UK Ltd.
Milton Keynes UK
UKHW010631250920
370514UK00003B/619